The Paradox of Protection

African History and Culture

SERIES EDITOR

Peter Alegi, *Michigan State University*

African History and Culture is a book series that builds upon and expands Michigan State University's commitment to the study of Africa. The series features books on African history, anthropology, sociology, and political science, as well as interdisciplinary studies, works on the African diaspora, and digital scholarship.

The Paradox of Protection

THE MAKING OF INDIRECT RULE IN SOUTHERN SIERRA LEONE, 1850–1915

Trina Leah Hogg

Michigan State University Press | *East Lansing*

Michigan State University Press
East Lansing, Michigan 48823-5245

LIBRARY OF CONGRESS CATALOGING-IN-PUBLICATION DATA
Names: Hogg, Trina Leah, 1980– author
Title: The paradox of protection : the making of indirect rule in southern Sierra Leone, 1850–1915 / Trina Leah Hogg.
Other titles: African history and culture
Description: East Lansing : Michigan State University Press, 2025. |
Series: African history and culture | Includes bibliographical references and index.
Identifiers: LCCN 2024058959 | ISBN 9781611865486 cloth |
ISBN 9781611865479 paperback | ISBN 9781609177928 | ISBN 9781628955552
Subjects: LCSH: Internal security—Law and legislation—Sierra Leone |
Sierra Leone—Politics and government—1808–1896 |
Sierra Leone—Politics and government—1896–1961
Classification: LCC DT516.7 .H64 2025 | DDC 966.4/02—dc23/eng/20250319
LC record available at https://lccn.loc.gov/2024058959

Cover art credit: Group of Imperri Chiefs photographed at Gbangbaia, Imperri, Sherbro, 1898.
Reproduced by kind permission of the Syndics of Cambridge University Library.

Visit Michigan State University Press at *www.msupress.org*

Contents

Acknowledgments

THIS PROJECT HAS BEEN THE RESULT OF MANY ENCOUNTERS WITH PLACES AND people spanning almost two decades. First and foremost, I could not have written this book without the guidance and mentorship of Fred Cooper. Our conversations and your advice have shaped me as a person and writer in indelible ways. Second, a simple "thank you" is not enough to Lauren Benton who has been a constant supporter and unfailing mentor. Her generosity and work ethic has been a source of inspiration to me as both a scholar and a woman, and I pictured her cheering me on many times when writing this book. Greg Mann provided innumerable insight, advice, and feedback over the years that has carried into these pages. I am also grateful to Allen Howard's encouragement of me, this project, and his incredible insight into the history of Sierra Leone.

During graduate school, I was lucky to have strong support from my cohort, most especially my dear friend Reynolds Richter. I also want to thank Charlotte Legg, Erin Braatz, Ademide Adelusi-Adeluyi, Laura Ann Twagira, Jessica Pearson, Westenley Alcenat, Sam Fury Childs Daly, and all my other graduate school comrades who have stuck by me over the years. An extra special thanks to Larissa Kopytoff for our continued friendship after graduate school, monthly writing group meetings, and incredible generosity in reading this book at every stage.

So many wonderful scholars have lent insight into this project and assisted me along the way. Thanks to: Emily Burrill, Nathan Carpenter, Catherine Evans, Marcus Filippello, Emily Lynn Osborn, Binyamin Blum, Benjamin Lawrance, Henry Lovejoy, Michael Lobban, Kara Moskowitz, and Charlotte Walker-Said. Heartfelt thanks to Kate Luongo who I count as a dear friend and mentor for reading drafts of earlier chapters. As a writing partner, Jessica Reuther has been source of continuous support and insight in reading drafts of this book.

While researching and living in Sierra Leone—my thanks to Paul Glynn, Jakob Lund, Mark Fiorello, David Marchesseault for being such good company during my various stays in Freetown. To Sarah Delius and Katrina Keefer, our conversations inside and outside the Sierra Leone Public Archives (SLPA) have been a source of joy and insight. The works and feedback of other historians of Sierra Leone have also been especially insightful. I thank them all for our rich conversations over drinks and coffees over the years: Myles Ali, Bronwen Everill, Tim Soriano, Christine Whyte, Suzanne Schwartz, and Gibril Cole. I want to especially thank Lynda Day for her time and incredible insight into all things Mende related. Staff at the Sierra Leone Public Archives have always gone above and beyond. Thanks to Mr. Albert Moore, Mr. Fonah, and Mustapha Kallon for assisting me in the archives. Huge thanks to Abu Koroma, who has been at the SLPA since my first research trip to Freetown in 2007 and is now pursuing his own academic dreams.

Support for research and writing at New York University included time at the Global Research Initiatives Center and a Mellon Dissertation Fellowship. I received a Faculty Development Grant at Columbia College Chicago for travel, and subsequent travel funding from Oregon State University. From 2018–2019, I had the great fortune of being a Walter Johnson Fellow through the American Society for Legal History. During that year, I was fortunate to receive valuable feedback on this book from Reuel Schiller and Sally Barringer Gordon, as well as my “fellow fellows”—Kevin Arlyck, Amanda Hughett, Winston Bowman, and especially Wesley Chaney and Elizabeth Lhost who read earlier chapters of this book during our COVID writing group. That same year, this work was supported with a fellowship at the Oregon State University Center for the Humanities. Thanks to the director Christopher Nicols for his encouragement of my scholarship and facilitation of a public lecture during my time there.

Arriving at Oregon State University in 2016, my colleagues have provided a calm and collegial space to think and work. I want to especially thank Kelly Bosworth,

Marisa Chappell, Rena Lauer, Alicia Patterson, and Joel Zapata. Special thanks to Mina Carson for making me feel so welcome during my first years in Corvallis. Thanks to my "Tenured Ladies" for their consistent support through all our mothering, writing, and trying to stay afloat: Tekla Bude, Megan Ward, Lily Sheehan, Mila Zho, and especially Ana Milena Ribero, whose friendship and support has been invaluable in my life. Finally, to Nicole von Germeten for her mentorship, support and encouragement in helping me balance research, teaching, a pandemic, and becoming a new parent.

Thank you to Lisa Silverman for helping me make my way back to myself and this project.

I also want to thank my undergraduate and graduate students. Our conversations have helped me think clearly about how to write this book. Thanks especially to Shelby Bremigan, Elisabeth McCumber, Ismael Pardo, and Lihani du Plessis. I also could not have done this without my interns over the years—Olivia Loftin, Abby Nickerson, Justus Hollingshed, as well as Rachel Dressler for her amazing transcription and data compilation skills.

Thank you to the two anonymous readers of this book for their insightful feedback. Thanks to Peter Alegi at Michigan State University for believing in this project. Thanks to Judith Lakamper, Amanda Frost, and everyone on staff. Thanks to Allison Janicki for her copyedits.

Finally, my dearest friends have supported me through all the ups and downs of life, including researching and writing this book. To Chris Redman for your friendship and travelling with me to Sierra Leone for my very first time just to have an adventure. To Gregor Sokol for your constant support and listening ear. To Laura Neilson for your friendship and constant readiness with a salad and good conversation. To Adriana Kemp for coming into our household at exactly the right time and bringing so much love and care to everything you do. To Vasiliki Touhouliotis for being such an incredible pillar of support—especially in 2020 when we were both newly pregnant at the beginning of the pandemic. And to Houssam Abbas for our campus walks and trying to sort what being a person, parent, and academic all means. To Zoe Lepiano for our nearly daily phone messages and conversations about keeping it together amid constant chaos and change. To Erin Silver, for our growing friendship and intellectual connection—special thanks for your thoughts on drafts of this book at the very end stages. To my pal Matt Lemche. We have been friends for more than three decades, and I can't imagine not having you in my life.

The maps you created for this book are beautiful and so special to me. And finally, thanks to my dearest friend Christine Atkinson. What can I say? You have supported me in countless ways with words of encouragement and love.

Finally, this book is as much my parents as it is my own. Garry and Alina Hogg—you have always provided unlimited support and love. My career and this book would not have been possible without your unfailing encouragement to pursue my goals and never look back. To my partner, Isaac Sandlin. Words fail to convey how having you in my life was the essential ingredient of completing this book. These past few years have been such a learning curve for us on so many levels. You have never failed to step in and do whatever needed to be done or keep cheering me on during especially tough days.

Finally, to my daughter, Orla Wren. My life has been forever altered since your arrival, and I cannot wait to keep showing you all the world has to offer.

Introduction

Amidst the hundreds of dusty volumes in the Sierra Leone National Archives, there sits an ordinary cardboard box. Inside is a series of treaties signed between the colonial administration and local African leaders. Containing promises of peace and protection, these documents are a snapshot of a time when Africans met with Europeans as sovereigns of their own land.

Holding those frail treaties, one cannot help but be struck by the hundreds of names on these documents. Some are famous for their deeds and written about in history books or remain alive in the minds of their descendants—but most of their stories remain lost to time: the only archival remnant of their lives is an X at the bottom of a page. These African men and women signed their names to a wide range of agreements, the majority of which pledged to put an end to warfare, support imperial commerce, and protect British subjects. It was clear on my first research trip that the promises of protection embedded in these treaties were central to understanding the formation of a new legal landscape and a world that would ultimately be transformed forever by the imposition of indirect rule.

The aim of this book is to show how protection emerged as the central legal concept through which Africans and Britons negotiated shifting meanings of governance, law, and economy from informal to formal rule. Unlike other studies that often cite economics as the primary engine of change on imperial frontiers, this book offers a new conceptual lens to understand how law and politics were reordered through long-standing debates over protection—both within African communities and between themselves and Britons. Initially, treaties were regarded as reciprocal agreements between "friends" or two sovereign states. Soon, however, endemic warfare led to active British participation in African conflicts, reframing the frontier from an economic sphere to an active zone of interest that became subject to British tactics such as military campaigns in African territory, incarcerating and executing non-British subjects, or intervening in African courts and customs. These British protection schemes on the frontier established new and highly violent systems of policing and punishment that, I argue, significantly informed the legal institutions of indirect rule. Emboldened by the formal establishment of a Protectorate in 1896, colonial administrators and lawmakers mobilized the language of protection to enact a political and judicial framework that reformed or criminalized aspects of African legal and political systems they believed threatened British hegemony. Much to their astonishment, the "peace and security" that the British endeavored to impose in the Protectorate continued to produce the same unprecedented levels of political turbulence that it had on the frontier.

Across the long nineteenth century, protection shaped competing visions of the legal rights and responsibilities of people to land, resources, and the communities they ruled. Nineteenth-century British protection schemes—an assemblage of written and unwritten legal strategies that aimed to secure British subjects and trade interests—ironically forged an enduring foundation of *insecurity* in the Sierra Leone Protectorate. The impact of these protection schemes on the African populations who (either willingly or forcefully) engaged with them initiated a cyclical process that I refer to as the "paradox of protection": the more African leaders and their communities engaged with British protection schemes to secure their own personal or political protection, the more vulnerable they became to physical and juridical violence. When Indigenous protection strategies clashed with British interests, colonial policies utilized the language of protection to eliminate them through both extra-legal violence and formal criminalization, further exposing African communities to state-sanctioned violence. In tracing the long history of informal to formal rule, this book reveals how long-standing negotiations over physical and political protection on the frontier became a central and constitutive feature of indirect rule.

The idea of protection has long been at the core of British settlement in Sierra Leone. Established as the center of abolition and humanitarianism in the late eighteenth century, Freetown was founded as an abolitionist experiment to prove to naysayers in Britain that Africans (and, perhaps more specifically, formerly enslaved persons) could successfully participate in the development of "legitimate commerce" and become meaningful adherents to Christianity.[1] Initially settled by several free black communities from throughout the Black Atlantic, the Colony of Sierra Leone was additionally populated by tens of thousands of Africans "liberated" from slave ships along the West African coast. These men and women were subjugated to policies like indentureship, forced military service, and relocation to Christian villages that reflected the paternalist idea that African uplift required the firm tutelage of European hands. Particularly in the first half of the nineteenth century, British administrators in Freetown engaged in a style of rule that self-consciously saw their role as shielding vulnerable populations from the evils of slavery, the exploitation of less noble empires, and the "backwards" heathenism of the African populations from which many Liberated Africans had originated. At mid-century, Britons turned their attention to developing agricultural commerce in the rural spaces beyond Freetown. The language of protection was extended to secure British trade and traders operating in African territory. By the end of the century, protection was again reformulated to create a new form of colonial rule that aimed to "preserve" the African laws and customs that suited imperial interests and eliminate the ones that did not. For Britons, these multiple ways of "protecting" Africans were analogous to civilizing and Christianizing them, weaving together the concepts of humanitarianism and protection throughout the nineteenth century.[2] As historians Christina Twomey and Katherine Ellinghaus have noted, "the history of humanitarianism is indivisible from imperialism's self-justification as a project capable of bringing civilization to savages, and it has demonstrated the frequent (but never complete) association between protection and control, violence and dispossession."[3]

Of course, the situation on the ground was more complex than Britain imposing protection schemes on one side and Africans being forced to conform to them on the other. Amid the rapid social and economic change of the mid-nineteenth century, the need for protection made diplomacy a productive pursuit for African leaders in the southern coastal and riverine region.[4] Already enmeshed in their own world of political coalitions, African leaders engaged British administrators as they would any local power brokers during times of warfare or crisis. Established leaders who declared themselves to be the "rightful owners of the land" sought British protection as leverage to secure their sovereignty in the face of challenges from newcomers.

During the chaotic implementation of indirect rule, the formalization of Paramount Chieftaincy and chiefdoms exacerbated these long-standing disputes over land and legitimacy. New forums like chieftaincy elections and courts—distinct features of Protectorate rule—became spaces for Africans to negotiate enduring grievances between coalitions and communities, autochthons and strangers that stretched back decades. Like British protection schemes on the frontier, Africans attempted to use the institutions of indirect rule as new resources to secure personal and political protection for themselves and their communities. These "bargains of collaboration" required African intermediaries to be continually dexterous in their response to the ever-evolving "rule of law" and its enforcement.[5]

Like many imperial subjects across the globe, African communities in southern Sierra Leone engaged meaningfully with colonial legality. What makes this study rare is its attention to how Africans engaged and shaped British law and legal institutions in the decades prior to formal rule. For example, I show various leaders' paths to Paramount Chief, one of the most identified features of indirect rule in British Africa. The focal region of this study, the southern riverine and coastal region, contained communities with divergent histories and connections to the land. Tracing individuals and families in the archive from the period of informal rule onwards allows us to discern how and why various groups engaged in British protection schemes. Within this book, these leaders are referred to as "aligned": men and women who signed treaties with the British in the hopes of forming a military alliance against an enemy or acquire wealth by tapping into European trade networks. To solidify these ties, aligned African leaders engaged in correspondence, protected British subjects, and garrisoned colonial police as a way of securing alliances and claiming protection from the British crown. Of course, these processes meant that African leaders and other people who were decidedly non-aligned increasingly found themselves on the "wrong side of the law" and were subject to violence and dispossession. As historian Richard Waller reminds us, during colonial rule, "power always had two sides: to bless or to blast."[6] Ultimately, British law and legal institutions were both a tool and an impediment to obtaining or maintaining power and wealth.

This book also contributes to long-standing debates regarding the impact of the shift from slavery-based to capitalist economies among nineteenth-century West African populations.[7] Scholarly works on early imperialism have typically led to the conclusion that the imposition and legal structure of indirect rule was the logical outcome of economic interests. This study challenges these assumptions by placing conflicts over legal and political authority at the heart of nineteenth-century commercial change. Throughout the nineteenth century, larger regional conflicts over land and labor forged collaborative participation in British protection schemes. When British and colonial administrators attempted to circumvent Indigenous networks that regulated commerce and crime, Africans vigorously sought to protect these sovereign rights. For over four decades, these actions produced serious contestation over the meaning of patronage, subjecthood, and jurisdiction. African leaders' early attempts to engage the British in coalitions through treaty making exacerbated, rather than quelled, existent local conflicts over geographic and political jurisdiction. These early negotiations on the frontier, I argue, were central in establishing the legal framework of indirect rule.

British and African Concepts of Protection

As Lauren Benton and Adam Clulow have written, the idea of protection has a "long and strange history."[8] For Europeans, protection was a legal concept that allowed empires and states to project their authority, extend their influence, and incorporate both weak and strong polities.[9] For most readers in the West, this idea of protection in relation to governance likely seems relatively simple: the state protects its population and their property from harm and, in turn, the people support the state so long as they continue to feel reasonably secure. Laws bind the state and its subjects to these protection arrangements, either by explicitly or implicitly delineating the rights and responsibilities between them, as well as laying out the consequences when security is perceived to be compromised. With the addition of policing or military force, the politics of protection authorizes violence when disorder is perceived as too destabilizing. The limits of state force rely on a complex set of factors that includes the severity of the threat to order, who is being threatened, and whether the threat is internal or external to the state.

On imperial frontiers, and later in colonial protectorates, this process was not so straightforward. Imperial ambitions and the designation of African states as "uncivilized" legitimated the imposition of British law and authorized extra-legal violence in the name of protection without claiming formal jurisdiction over the land.[10] Treaties and protectorate laws bestowed the advantages of extraterritoriality and the protection of the Crown to British subjects without having to grant the Indigenous population the rights of British subjecthood. This flexibility was central to protection's utility, making the concept ideal in frontier zones and borderland regions where the question of "who was protecting whom or what was the exact nature of the relationship between the protector and the protected" was blurred.[11] In Sierra Leone, this ambiguity is precisely why the paradox of protection became so pervasive: over time, the colonial state controlled the means and conditions of protection to such an extent that its African allies became wholly dependent on the colonial state for their security, lest they be subject to the violence of the state themselves.

For the purposes of this study, how Europeans defined and utilized the idea of protection for their own purposes is only half the story. In southern Sierra Leone, constant warfare and raiding that escalated with the introduction of the slave trade necessitated numerous overlapping strategies for securing one's physical security. By the eighteenth century, the permeant settlement of slave depots on the Sherbro coast resulted in "unprecedented" levels of violence.[12] Anthropologist Rosalind Shaw has written extensively on how the transatlantic slave trade fostered a space of violence and terror that reshaped the political and physical landscape which, she argues, reverberated well into the twentieth century. Slaves became a "currency" of "universal value" and were exchanged on the coast for salt, metalware, and European firearms.[13] Raids for slaves created a perpetual state of insecurity in the region, making "Sierra Leone's river highways and its roads . . . dangerous channels for predation that ordinary people sought to avoid."[14] As Sean Kelley writes, the political geography of the region amplified the violence between its peoples: dispersed communities meant that leaders were less able to deter kidnappings and other illegal slave transactions like a centralized state may have.[15] The only way to guarantee ones security was to form coalitions that were inclusive enough to accommodate difference, but durable enough to provide meaningful protection.

Thus, while Europeans tended to see protection as a top-down process administered by the empire—or even by a corporation, as in the case of the British East India Company—protection in southern Sierra Leone was fundamentally incorporative.[16] Local and regional coalitions created a political and social web of alliances between community leaders and power brokers they perceived as beneficial. In times of warfare or social crisis like in the late nineteenth century, coalition members assisted each other in providing warriors, labor, spies, or military intelligence. Successful leaders projected power using kinship and economic networks that formed durable coalitions with extended family members, fellow elites in nearby communities, and other important clients.[17] One might think of this as amassing a diverse protection portfolio that could include neighboring leaders, war captains, shamans, Muslim spiritual practitioners (known locally as *morimen*), medicine societies, and traders. While some of these alliances were temporary in times of crisis, others were long-standing and ensured mutual aid in times of war for generations. Thus, while these communities operated as small independent political units that consisted of a central town and surrounding villages, high-ranking leaders from these places formed dynamic political confederacies that were cemented through shared spiritual and legal institutions.

This complicated nexus of people and places in rural Sierra Leone constituted what historian Allen Howard has called a "functional region": a legible and interconnected space where commodities and ideas flowed in established networks.[18] Coalitions structured how space in the Sherbro was understood, and leaders' reputations came to be associated with places those leaders came from. The relationships between places and people were understood regionally through kinship bonds, ancestral ties, religious sites, agricultural resources, and commercial relations. While networks between common people were fairly localized, those among elites could be quite far-reaching.[19] Trade and travel routes from the interior to the coast structured the social and political dynamics between people who lived along them. Though reciprocity was central to network building, conflict frequently occurred over the political and commercial nodes that lay along prominent transportation routes.

On the littoral, the close proximity of villages necessitated a cultural and political framework that emphasized "cultural convergence" where communities were, in the words of anthropologist Paul Richards, "compelled to draw upon reserves of world wisdom to merge differences and resolve disputes *in situ*."[20] Low density populations and high labor demands in this dense and swampy rainforest belt elevated the importance of layered patronage, creating a political system where neighboring leaders continually collaborated and competed for knowledge, people, and resources. Leaders who demonstrated the ability to effectively protect their clients and dependents gained strong reputations that allowed them to project power outwards from their central town, sometimes extending to form territorial states or regions. Understanding how these community leaders operated within this complex political and legal system allows us to reevaluate what we think we know about "decentralized" or "stateless societies" and how they worked.[21] This not only adds to our knowledge about such societies in the precolonial era, but also provides us with a nuanced understanding of how they were impacted by the imposition of indirect rule and beyond.[22]

With the escalation of warfare in the mid-nineteenth century, community leaders needed to incorporate specialized war captains into their protection portfolio. This high demand for mercenaries facilitated the rise of a distinct "warrior class." These men not only brought "warboys" to wage raids, but were often highly regarded for their abilities to make powerful charms and medicines. Over time, the political and social status of these hired men sometimes exceeded the leaders who had originally hired them as mercenaries in the first place. Projecting power by amassing people and goods through raids gradually shifted the meaning of wealth, especially as it now included acquiring capital in the form of manufactured goods, agricultural produce, and cash.

The increased construction of "war towns" throughout nineteenth-century Sierra Leone reflects this emergent world of war. These walled or fortified towns, some containing upwards of one thousand residents, were made up of several "concentric hardwood stockades interspersed by stake filled ditches."[23] Beyond these towering walls, towns were additionally protected by circles of trees, extending by a quarter of a mile beyond the manmade structure. Scholarship indicates this type of fortification arrived around the fifteenth century with the migration of the Mane people, but by the early nineteenth century could be found throughout southern Sierra Leone. The long history of these fortified war towns makes clear that while the wars of the late nineteenth century that this book focuses on were fought for different reasons and resources than the conflicts of previous centuries, populations drew from earlier strategies to secure safe living conditions amidst violence and instability.

While African protection strategies like mercenaries or fortified towns were comprehensible (and threatening) to British administrators, those related to the supernatural world were less legible. Religion and warfare were highly entangled. Items that ensured one's personal protection were obtained by brokering protection arrangements with spiritual practitioners skilled in the production of amulets and other powerful medicines.[24] They were worn around one's body, usually attached to a leather rope or string (Figure 1), smeared on the body as an ointment, or sewn into an article of clothing as supernatural shields. They were worn during warfare to

FIGURE 1. A Mende hunter with protective charms, amulets, and weapons.

SOURCE: KENNETH JAMES BEATTY, *HUMAN LEOPARDS. AN ACCOUNT OF THE TRIALS OF HUMAN LEOPARDS BEFORE THE SPECIAL COMMISSION COURT* (H. REES, 1915).

improve chances for success or to make oneself impervious to injury or death, but could also be used in peace times by hunters to ensure their safety.[25] The creation of these medicines were mediated by elders who had the authority to make them, as they often contained components like human body parts or substances that were regulated.[26] Obtaining or using them for malevolent purposes was viewed as tantamount to witchcraft or other forms of supernatural deviancy.

These objects were essential components of any leader's supernatural arsenal when waging war. As one African missionary explained, during a war campaign, a Muslim "priest must be employed to 'cook the war,' that is, to ensure the safety and success of the warriors [as well as] cause confusion in the ranks and councils of the enemy by sending a curse upon them. . . . If their lives were lost in battle, they either must have done contrary to the orders given with their charms, or their time for death had come."[27] Specialists who could manufacture these charms were considered particularly superior mercenaries because of their ability to bring a wider and more powerful range of physical and supernatural resources to the battlefield.[28]

As warfare subsided in the last decades of the nineteenth century, the diminishing need for physical protection was replaced by a need for new sources of power that bolstered one's political and economic capacity. In the mid-1880s, a new sodality known as the Human Leopard Society emerged that was purported to manage a powerful object that could bestow economic and political success for those who possessed it. At first, it appears that the Human Leopard Society was a tool used by wealthy traders and ambitious Big Men to challenge the authority of more established autochthon leaders. In response to this use of illicit and socially destructive medicines, leaders responded by hiring specialized diviners called the Tongo to seek out the human leopards to execute them. In the Protectorate, evidence suggests leadership of the human leopards shifted to aspiring and appointed Paramount Chiefs. Rendered politically weak by the structures of indirect rule and chronic competition from their peers, protective medicines became central tools for leaders to counter extreme political and social instability. Human Leopard Society murder cases became an extension of precolonial debates over what constituted legitimate and moral authority over people and resources.

Religious associations that utilized these ritual objects or powerful medicines were seen by the British as a threat to social and economic stability.[29] The supposed presence of uncivilized practices where human fat was used to "feed a fetish," or blood oaths were made to organize region-wide raids along rivers, compelled British administrators to double down on their role as "civilized protectors" and criminalize these "secret societies." When community leaders used their own legal procedures to regulate or punish the actions of their people, British administrators regularly justified their interference in African law for Africans *own* protection. As the British state began to annex territory on the coast, imperial lawmakers used the establishment of formal rule as an opportunity to remedy what they saw as the jurisdictional messiness of the frontier by reordering the perceived "disorder" of African law. This "rage for order" compelled colonial lawmakers to displace the Indigenous legal institutions, customs, and practitioners that posed a significant challenge to British visions of justice and rights.[30]

People and Places in the Sherbro Hinterland

The events chronicled in this book primarily take place along the Sherbro coast and riverine region, a landscape that has long been an integral part of the African

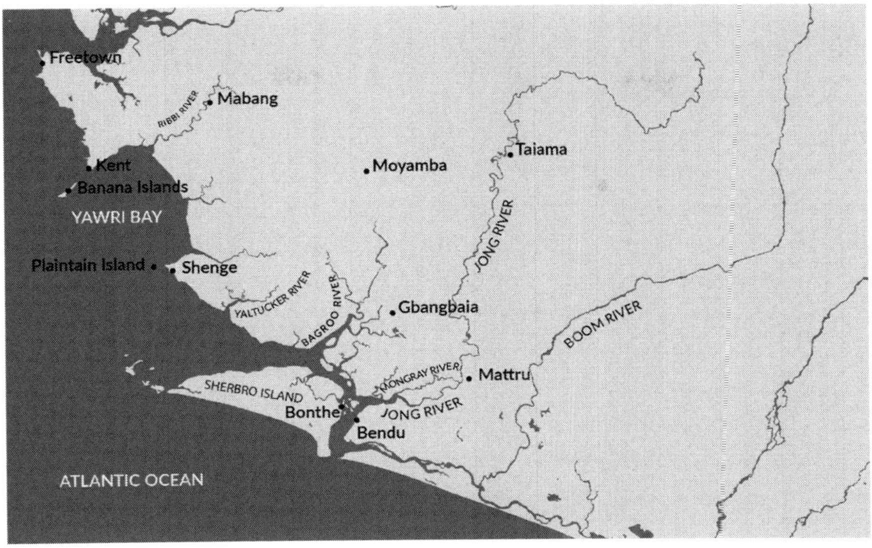

FIGURE 2. Map of Sherbro hinterland with major towns and rivers, circa 1880.

and Atlantic world. The Sherbro region is a forested and swampy place containing numerous broad and brackish rivers. People traditionally survived for centuries through shallow-water fishing, the cultivation of rice, and the production of salt and palm oil. The most established group in the region were the Bullom or Sherbro people, for whom the region is named.[31] Beginning in the mid-1500s, the Sherbro people encountered several new groups of strangers. The first were European traders, who settled along the coast to trade in slaves and other interior goods. In the 1700s, Muslim merchants and travelling holy men arrived in the region, followed by communities of Mende people. Over time, these groups founded important towns and lineages throughout the Sherbro region. On the coast, several Anglo-Sherbro families emerged bearing the names Caulker, Domingo, Tucker, and Cleveland.

In the mid-1780s, the former slave-trader-turned-abolitionist John Newton described the Sherbro Coast as politically distinct from other regions on the Windward Coast, stating that while people lived "much in the patriarchal way" there were "no men of great power or property among them."[32] In each town, he explained, resided an old man whose power "depends more on his authority than his possessions." Although he is called "King," this elder man was not "easily distinguished by state or wealth, from the rest."[33] What Newton described was a common feature of what scholars of precolonial African societies refer to as "wealth in people," meaning that authority was not derived from the accumulation of cash or precious objects, but from the demonstrated capacity to support dependents who provided both productive and reproductive labor.[34] As the Sherbro proverb goes, "You cannot sit alone and be a chief."[35] Legitimate leadership was based on a person's ability to demonstrate connections to a founding ancestor, as well as a combination of other factors such as the number of clients and dependents, marriage alliances, the ability to ethically obtain and redistribute resources, and the physical protection of one's extended household in times of crisis.[36] Society was built on uneven relationships that stressed reciprocity and protection between people of different statuses: leaders and their community, parents and children, men and women, owners and slaves, landlords and strangers, the living and the dead.[37]

The authority of community leaders was especially bolstered by the incorporation of newcomers. Strangers brought new kinds of knowledge, access to resources, or labor. The relationship between newcomers and community leaders was regulated by landlord-stranger laws that articulated access to resources like land and labor. Expectations of reciprocity and protection between patrons and newcomer-clients created social cohesion and delineated the boundaries of the political community. Seen as minors and dependents, strangers were bound by a mutually understood code of ongoing gratitude, obedience, and deference that included political loyalty and symbolic payments and gifts.[38] The cultural and legal distinctions between newcomers and patrons stressed how one's ancestral lineage bestowed legitimate access to the land.

With the arrival of such a diverse group of outsiders, how was social and political cohesion achieved? The binding force of these people and places was a centuries-old transregional institution called the Poro. Often referred to as a "secret society" by outsiders, the Poro was certainly not "secret" in one sense: men from all backgrounds—from slaves to Kings—were initiated into its ranks at puberty in the dry season. Along with Sande, the primary all-female sodality, Poro's primary role was regulating "the social behavior and mediat[ing] the crises of daily life for the average person."[39] Membership in Poro created a multicultural citizenry for all men, regardless of ethnicity or social rank, and equipped every man for the "part he is to play in community life" by acting as the "general government of the country."[40] The Poro was, however, not a democratic institution. The highest echelon of the Poro consisted of elders who had lineage-based connections to the founders of their towns. High-raking Poro used this supernatural authority to enforce a long-standing and flexible oral constitution that was binding to all lower-level Poro members. These hierarchies were further solidified through oaths and medicines, placing all members of the Poro in an arrangement of debt and obligation cemented by supernatural consequences.

Poro was not just a cultural institution, but a political and legal one as well.[41] The "King" that Newton described seeing in each town on the Sherbro Coast in the mid-1700s was likely a high-ranking Poro elder called a "Tasso," a figure who was said to possess the "hereditary right to perform key ancestor-oriented rituals and activities."[42] As both the elder of his lineage and the head of the Poro, the Tasso was the ultimate protector of the people and places in his jurisdiction. He could declare war and mobilize the services of all Poro junior members as "warboys" using shared signals, sounds, and symbols.[43] He also acted as a "judge in council" and ruled on matters under Poro jurisdiction. Smaller community disputes were decided on by councils of elders within that community.[44]

At some point, however, the position of Tasso was phased out and leadership of the Poro and the community diverged. This bifurcation can likely be attributed to the increasing numbers of non-Sherbro strangers who arrived in the region with their own families, clients, and dependents in tow. When these newcomers established their own towns among the Sherbro people, they eventually formed their own Poro chapters. While community rule continued to be based on one's membership in a hereditary descent group, the system evolved to include new "owners of the land" from the wide variety of ethnic groups who had established their own communities. This divergence may explain why some newcomers to the land (and their descendants) were able to establish a recognized ancestral lineage (or "founding family"), despite their initial status as "strangers."[45] Conversely, Poro membership as a pathway to belonging explains why groups who did not join, like Muslims, were perpetually seen as strangers after their descendants' initial settlement.

Evidence suggests that the political and familial networks between prominent rulers led to the formation of polities referred to in this study as "titular provinces": named and loosely territorially bordered regions that made up the Sherbro state or "Kingdom" itself.[46] By the early nineteenth century, the governance of these provinces, like Imperri or Bagru, were highly developed, including elaborate ceremonies of investiture.[47] I have used the name "titular provinces' as each ruler relinquished their birth name at their coronation and was invested with a unique title. Positions like the Sei Kama of Jong, Sokong of Imperri, and So Lɔkko of Bagru

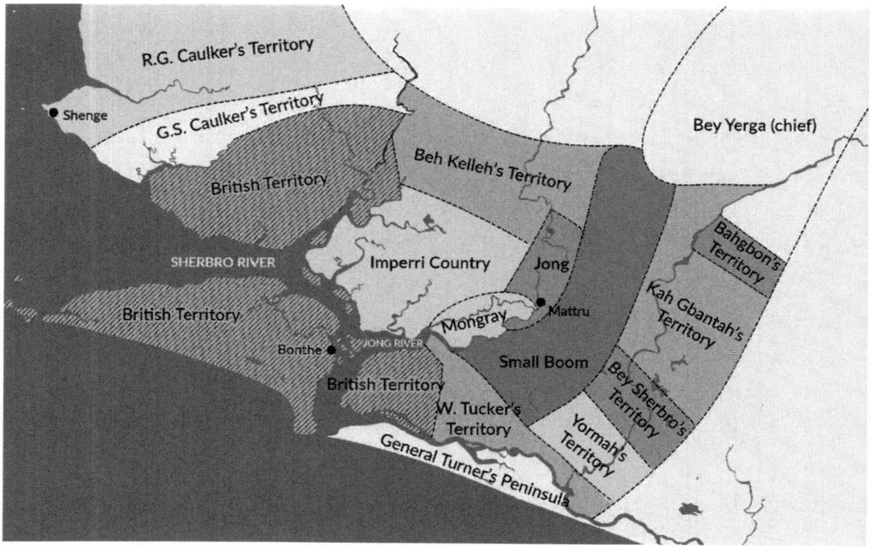

FIGURE 3. Tentative reconstruction of Sherbro state and its "titular" provinces, circa 1870s.

appear to be a likely evolution of the original Tasso system. These titular leaders were selected by a group of regional elders and were often referred to as "Kings" over the entire territorial state.[48] In Imperri, the coronation of the Sokong was later overseen by the "Tasso Men"—ritual figures that carried the bones of their predecessors and legitimated the election. Titular leaders were always high-ranking Poro elders. This likely provided an additional layer of political cohesion when resolving regional disputes and imposing law. This evolved into a political landscape one anthropologist likened to the medieval church and state: "secular" community leaders were responsible for the physical protection of their townspeople and land (including settling disputes in local courts), while titular leaders and other Poro elders utilized the authority from their ancestors ensure the land was spiritually secure by preventing regional conflict or the misappropriation of resources.

It is unclear why and when this political transformation took place, but it likely had something to do with the elevated precarity resulting from the slave trade. Political centralization may have been a strategy of uniting fractured or scattered communities in these unsettled times. By at least the end of the eighteenth century, European accounts describe all the titular leaders of Sherbro's provinces as collectively subject to the suzerainty of the King of the Sherbro, who held the title of "Beh Sherbro." The election of one Beh Sherbro was described in 1796 by a slave trader named Dalton, who stated that "each town or district sends delegates to a congress who elects a king, who has to do their will."[49] One hundred years later, a colonial official described a similar event, stating that the Beh Sherbro was elected through a council of twelve elders called the "Feffeh," each one of which was described as having a "distinctive office and title."[50] Described collectively as the "Komra Bais," it is unclear exactly who made up the council, but it appears to have consisted of a number of prominent titular leaders from throughout the region. The selection of the Beh Sherbro, as with the titled rulers of the provinces, required complete consensus to occur. Without this, the position of the Beh Sherbro (as with other titular leaders of Sherbro's provinces) would leave the community in a protracted state of interregnum until a unanimous decision could be made.

The existence of this political hierarchy complicates the commonly held image of Sherbro as a "stateless" society. While the region did contain many aspects of a typical decentralized state, one might imagine the political structure of the Sherbro region as a set of lungs that could contract or expand depending on political or economic conditions. In their smallest form, individual towns operated as a single political unit, possessing their own internal executive and judicial framework within a set of checks and balances by the leaders and Poro (and perhaps Sande) elders. Seen alone, the appearance of political isolation of these places often marks the regions as an acephalous state. However, when examining descriptions of these titular leaders in the archives, one can see that the physical and familial networks that connected these elites constituted a hidden state structure that had the capacity to unite a large population through mutual protection and consensus.[51] Community leaders and the Poro reinforced each other's political and legal power, together serving to reinforce shared social and political behaviors for the benefit of regional political stability.[52]

By the mid-nineteenth century when this narrative begins, a new group of African strangers migrated to the Sherbro coast from Freetown that transformed these established understandings of reciprocity and security. Now an established Colony for more than fifty years, Freetown's diverse urban African community totaled about sixty thousand people, and was made up of descendants of Black settlers from Jamaica and Canada, tens of thousands of slaves liberated from captured slave ships, and other imperial sojourners.[53] By 1850, the children and grandchildren of Liberated Africans and Black settlers referred to themselves as "Sierra Leonean," "creole," or even "Black Englishmen." Despite their heterogenous backgrounds and religious beliefs, these African British subjects largely came to embrace the British Empire's notions of civilization and commerce through missionary education and colonial proximity.[54] Though far from culturally cohesive, Freetown's African residents did possess many common characteristics due to their shared political and legal relationship to the colonial state.[55] At present, this collective group of the descendants of Liberated Africans and Black settlers refers to themselves as the "Krio," a designation that, while debated, will be used in this book to refer to Freetown's African community. Throughout this study, the question pursued is not whether this population was a "cohesive" one, but an exploration of how Krios used their collective identity to claim a series of rights and protections from the British colonial state.

Beginning in the 1830s, Krios migrated from their homes in the formal Colony and established trading "factories" along the southern coast and riverine regions.[56] These men and women were more than just a group of ambitious traders; most travelled to the interior believing themselves to be harbingers of progress. They believed their dual identity as Africans and British subjects gave them a unique destiny in the civilization of Africa and the development of the British Empire. In the 1850s, many formed the multiracial Sierra Leone Mercantile Association, cultivating close ties with British and other European firms.[57] In 1853, an Imperial Act formally designated all Africans born in the formal Colony, whether the descendants of Liberated Africans or of Black settlers, to be British subjects. Both their history and their subject status armed them with a particular definition of protection and their rights in relation to the colonial state when living outside of the formal Colony.

Many historians of Sierra Leone have asserted that the strict boundaries drawn between the formal Colony and the Protectorate created a bitter animosity between urban Krios and people who lived "upcountry."[58] This book complicates that picture by uncovering the ways that Krios participated in debates over protection on the frontier and in the period of formal rule. Treaties and subsequent ordinances attempted to ensure the protection of British subjects by allowing them to bypass African laws and legal forums. In doing so, their presence and engagement with local people in the interior assisted in establishing a new language of protection and rights that would be called into question in the decades that followed. Even after many Krio traders were killed in the "Hut Tax War" of 1898, they continued to integrate themselves into a system of indirect rule that was purposefully designed to shut them out. Krios continued to travel and reside in the Protectorate as colonial officials, railway workers, missionaries, and merchants. While perhaps not always altruistic, many also advocated for better conditions and more respect for their "native" counterparts. As we will see, Krio barristers and journalists successfully pushed the colonial Government to reform the legal system, both for their own benefit and within their broader commitment to imperial justice and the British rule of law.

Sources and Methodologies

This study benefits from extremely rich archival sources that rarely exist for studies of nineteenth-century Africa. Even rarer throughout much of Africa in this period is the high literacy rate of Krios who produced hundreds of petitions, newspaper articles, reports, court depositions, and letters in their own hand. Krios also acted as clerks to many Indigenous leaders, allowing those who were illiterate or semiliterate to correspond frequently with the colonial state. Though sparser, several African leaders discussed throughout this study were literate themselves, allowing us a direct glimpse into their thoughts and ideas. The language of protection permeates these precious documents in multiple and contradictory ways.

For the period before the establishment of the Protectorate in 1896, I utilize a number of different sources. Among these are dispatches to and from the Colonial Office (British National Archives) as well as those between local African leaders and Krio traders, located in the Sierra Leone Public Archives. Treaties also form a central part of my source materials. Using these and colonial sketch maps, I created a database of signatories, their territories, and towns to chart the uneven application of British diplomacy in the region. This allowed for a deeper understanding of the divergent ways leaders utilized British diplomatic agreements. Through this process, distinct political and geographic patterns emerged that I was later able to map onto the period of formal rule. I follow these threads to evaluate how these political spaces and their leaders fared in the period of indirect rule. Drawing these connections allows me to demonstrate how political and jurisdictional crises in the Protectorate were not simply the result of the imposition of "colonial rule." Instead, I show how conflict in the Protectorate was an extension of decades of conversations and conflicts between African and Britons, and between African themselves, over what constituted legitimate patronage and protection.

After 1896, the bureaucratic institutions of the Protectorate produced new kinds of records that both amplify and silence different kinds of African voices. For example, correspondence written by District Commissioners allows us to see how Britons understood Paramount Chiefs' role in the new Protectorate but often fails to capture how these African leaders felt about their role in the implementation of indirect rule. One remarkable source that provides a window in the transition from informal to formal rule is the Royal Commission on the "Hut Tax War," a six-hundred-page report written and compiled by Sir David Chalmers that includes hundreds of depositions from African, Krio, and European residents that never would have existed if not requested by Parliament. After 1898, the shuttering of the Department of Native Affairs and the "on-the-spot" methods of District Commissioners significantly diminish letters written directly from African leaders to the Governor. Instead, I piece together fragments of petitions, correspondence, newspapers, and published reports to find patterns in how leaders and their communities navigated the creation of Paramount Chiefs and chiefdoms in indirect rule. Transcripts from criminal court records from the Sierra Leone Public Archives also provide both compelling and highly detailed qualitative and quantitative data. Using a self-created database of three hundred criminal cases from the Moyamba Circuit Courts allowed me to identify a series of human leopard murder trials from 1904 to 1913. Transcripts or accounts of these new courts show how African litigants used them to challenge Paramount Chiefs' and other leaders' claims to political authority. An exploration of these transcripts reveals how the criminalization and litigation of human leopards served to depose Paramount Chiefs and other important men from their position.

While the voices of African lawyers, clerks, Queens, or war captains often speak loudly from the archives, the silences therein are equally as deafening. Reading against the grain, I use the imperfect and biased narratives of colonial officials, longtime European residents, missionaries, and traders to identify the varied ways the broader African population sought out or claimed protection based on their personal, ethnic, or regional position. These requests offer clues as to how protection was defined in broader cultural and legal contexts. These archival accounts are then augmented with more recent formal anthropological studies conducted from the 1920s onwards, as well as the distinguished work of historians of Sierra Leone who came before me. The result is a study that hopes to capture (albeit imperfectly) a conceptual history of what protection meant to a wide variety of historical actors and how its meaning changed over time and space.

Terminology

This study uses a number of terms to characterize people and places in southern Sierra Leone.

First, throughout this book, I frequently refer to the African population from the regions beyond the formal Colony as "Indigenous" at moments where it is necessary to distinguish them from Krios. For people in the twenty-first century, this may seem odd, as Krios are often regarded as just one of the many "tribes" within the present nation of Sierra Leone. However, during the period of this study, Krios constituted a visibly and legally distinct group of Africans from "native" Africans, a difference they often stressed as a means of obtaining particular rights from the British Crown.

Second, I signify leaders whose descendants founded important towns as "rightful owners of the land" to distinguish them from more recent "newcomers" or "strangers" who arrived in the nineteenth century. I also use "autochthon," though most often to describe the Sherbro people or other groups who have long-standing residential and cultural connections to the land. At times, this can seem confusing or contradictory, especially those well versed in contemporary Sierra Leone politics. This book serves as a reminder that these definitions had as much to do with colonial and African political strategies, as they did with actual dates and facts of arrival and settlement. Terms like "firstcomers" or "autochthons" are always contingent claims made within a particular political and social environment and not static categories.

Lastly, in terms of the landscape itself, I use the terms "hinterland," "Sherbro hinterland," or "southern coast and riverine region" to refer to the general land mass in the interior that extended from the coast to the headwater's region.[59] After the colonization of British Sherbro in 1861, I also refer to the land that extends from coast to the interior as the "frontier" as a way to indicate the physical and political space that broadly encompassed both African land and the margins of British territory.[60] The borders of the imperial "frontier" were both real and imagined, with ever-shifting boundaries to suit the claims for protection by Indigenous leaders, Krios, and Britons. The period of this study represents a time of considerable political flux where Africans and Britons engaged in geographic consolidation to lay claim to resources within particular borders. Throughout this book, I have created maps to visualize these spaces, using archival descriptions and historic sketch maps as source material, though it is important to remember that these are representative of the impressions of only a few colonial officials and African intermediaries. Maps from this period vary from somewhat inconsistent to wildly incorrect, and I have done my best to create approximate renderings of how specific actors understood where borders and places lay based on sketch maps and descriptions. In some cases, I have included images of the original map for the reader to better understand how these spaces were imagined. It is particularly important to remember that the gradual fixing of borders between African polities, most especially the boundaries of what would eventually become chiefdoms, was continually changing due to shifting local politics and do not necessarily resemble the borders that exist today.

CHAPTER ONE

Coalitions and Conflicts

Physical and Legal Jurisdiction on the Sherbro Coast, 1840–1870

For Freetown-born Thomas Ellis, the development of the timber trade south of the Sierra Leone Colony presented the perfect opportunity to make his fortune. As the ambitious son of parents who came to Freetown from Jamaica, Ellis was part of the first wave of Krio traders in the mid-nineteenth century who travelled from the formal Colony to establish trading posts in the southern coastal and riverine region.[1] Although African himself, he had likely heard many stories about the "heathen" African communities who lived outside of the formal Colony. What we know of his travels, however, indicates that he had an adventurous side and was open to engaging with the world beyond the bustling urban port town in which he was born.

Ellis' journey was situated in a time of great Krio migration out of Sierra Leone. Men and women took advantage of the establishment of new shipping routes and left Freetown to form communities in other West African or Atlantic port towns.[2] Thomas Ellis, however, decided to try his luck at trading closer to home. Perhaps hiring a boat from the busy docks on Water Street, he set sail for the Sherbro coast sometime in the 1840s. As he travelled down the coast, Ellis would have gazed at what seemed like an endless stretch of sand beaches, possessing a brightness made even more luminous by the green mountain ridge that formed the middle of the peninsula. He would have passed groups of fishermen working together to haul in their days catch, while women, knee deep in the surf, haggled over the cost of that night's supper. Even more familiar to him would have been the outlines of wooden homes and tiny churches of the "parish villages" built by the Church Missionary Society for the resettlement of Liberated Africans from throughout Atlantic Africa. As he passed the final Liberated Village of Kent on the southern tip of the peninsula, he would have said goodbye to the safety and security of British territory and entered a new world much different from the one he left.

Upon leaving the formal Colony, Krio traders like Ellis who went to the southern coastal and riverine region lived among another highly heterogenous population that was central to the Atlantic world since the fifteenth century. For hundreds of years, African migrant-strangers settled among established coastal communities using well-developed "landlord-stranger" agreements. This integrative process ensured that newcomers were protected and provided a pathway to eventual belonging in the community, while still maintaining the authority of those who claimed ancestral ties to the land. Over time, successful strangers elevated their status by demonstrating aptitude in war or trade, intermarrying into elite families, joining the ranks of Poro, and eventually founding their own towns. Through this and other processes, conflicts and coalition building between newcomer and established elites became a cornerstone of law and politics throughout the region.[3]

This chapter provides an introduction to how shifts in law and economy altered local patterns of political authority in mid-nineteenth century Sierra Leone. Local leaders increasingly sought to consolidate their rule by shoring up complex coalitions and territorial borders. The switch from the Atlantic slave trade to "legitimate commerce" in timber, palm produce, and other agricultural goods prompted attempts among African leaders to secure jurisdiction over riverine transportation routes from the interior to the coast. Local practices of coalition building during times of conflict prompted ambitious African leaders to integrate the British into wider African-based alliances through diplomacy and treaty making. While authority over the land and its resources was traditionally derived through ancestral lineage, this chapter shows how British imperialism created new opportunities for strangers and competitors of autochthon leaders to assert political and territorial control in new ways. I argue that these African leader's engagement with British diplomacy and treaty making transformed the nature of political and territorial jurisdiction in the region. These new alliances set in motion highly contested battles among autochthon elites and between themselves and strangers.

Conflicts over legal and political authority were at the heart of nineteenth century commercial change in West Africa. By the nineteenth century, the British Empire had a long history of making treaties with Indigenous people throughout the globe.[4] Regularly referred to as pacts, agreements, or conventions, treaties between Africans and Britons were frequently dismissed as illegitimate because of the unequal power dynamic between the two sides or because their terms did not confer a specific set of rights and obligations.[5] For Britons, treaties represented a more "civilized" (and cheaper) form of expansion than brute conquest, additionally allowing the assertion of moral supremacy over Africans, as well as other European Empires that did not widely use treaties to establish their empires.[6]

Early negotiations between British and African leaders in Sierra Leone laid the foundation for the paradox of protection. Mid-century British protection schemes that centered on securing British subjects and trade routes were understood by local leaders within the context of local coalition building that included mutual political and physical protection. Treaties forged a new imperial legal zone that justified the projection of British juridical and military power. British belief in their moral and racial supremacy systematically limited the security of African leaders by delivering false promises of reciprocal protection. The formal annexation of British Sherbro in 1861 gave new legitimacy to British projection of power of over African territory and its subjects, allowing for the imposition of both formal and informal laws. Unbeknownst to African leaders and their communities, participation in British protection schemes produced increasingly fraught spaces of confrontation and violence.

The Political and Legal Geography of the Sherbro Coast and Riverine Region

Thomas Ellis' route to the southern shores of Sierra Leone had been navigated by many a trader before him. In 1684, a young British sailor from Portsmouth named Thomas Corker arrived in Sierra Leone for the first time at age fifteen as an employee of the Royal African Company. Upon landing, Corker and his fellow shipmates "shook hands" with their new landlord, King Ya Cumba, who lived in the seaside town of Tasso. According to one oral account, King Ya Cumba's people were the original or autochthon people of the region. Their founding ancestor, a Kono, had been chasing an elephant, but unable to catch it, decided to rest on high ground between two streams. There he founded a permanent settlement called "Tasso," meaning "Let us rest here." He and his kinsmen intermarried with the local women, expanded the local village, and at some point, established a titled position named "Ya Cumba."[7]

Upon settling on the coast in 1684, the ruling King Ya Cumba and Thomas Corker likely negotiated a typical "landlord-stranger" tenancy agreement between them. This type of agreement, where the "stranger" would enter a contract "marked by a series of obligations [with] . . . a measure of deference and subordination" was typical throughout the Upper Guinea Coast.[8] In exchange for access to potential wealth or knowledge, these agreements ensured the stranger's legal and physical protection. As strangers were considered minors, it was the duty of the landlord to represent them in legal cases, defend them from attacks, and look after their interests.[9] Strangers often joined the Poro and other sodalities to gain access to high-ranking elites. As a European, and therefore high-ranking outsider, King Ya Cumba gave Corker his daughter Yema (known to Europeans as Senora Doll) as a wife, forging a kinship bond that bestowed Corker a place in the community and ensured peaceful relations.[10] According to the Caulker Family today, this marriage and progeny established the Cumba-Caulker House and Tasso became their capital.[11]

While a stranger would never be considered a full member of the community in their lifetime, the children of Thomas Corker and Yema had the possibility of fully "belonging" to the society in which they were born. This process was aided by the Sherbro people's cognatic descent system that allowed the children of strangers to inherit the social rights of their African mother. This allowed the children of lower-ranking fathers to assimilate into local communities using their mother's status and acquire authority over the land.[12] After Thomas Coker's death in 1700, Yema became the "Queen of Tasso," forging strong trading relations with Europeans and a legacy for her children.[13] After her death, her eldest son Stephen was crowned the "King of Kangbor," establishing the official formation of the Cumba-Caulker house.[14] Though other oral traditions place the center of Caulker rule on the Plantain Islands, eventually they established Shenge as their capital and made Tasso their official burial ground. In subsequent generations, Stephen Caulker's descendants forged strong partnerships with other elites throughout the coastal region by becoming high-ranking members of the Poro, marrying their children into other elite families, and establishing a successful mercantile trade in slaves and other goods from the interior. These actions made them particularly sought-after coalition members and allowed them to extend their authority beyond the coast.

These examples demonstrate that while distinction between strangers and "owners of the land" were central to political authority, there were pathways to belonging that allowed newcomers to integrate themselves and their descendants. Families who could claim a direct ancestral connection to a prominent town's founder formed a *ram* or elite "descent group" whose lineage distinguished them from other kinless residents like strangers or slaves.[15] Every important town contained one or several descent groups who claimed this type of birthright. Their familial connection to prominent ancestors gave them sole access to leadership positions, land and other resources.[16] Men and women who descended from these "founding families" often intermarried and formed regional networks based on kinship and historical connections that stressed reciprocity and mutual aid in times of warfare or crisis.

When Thomas Ellis arrived in Yawry Bay in the 1840s, his landlord was Thomas Corker's great-great-grandson Canreba Caulker. However, Ellis' arrival of one of the "Queen's Children," as Krios were commonly called by local people, signaled a distinctive shift since Thomas Corker's landing 150 years prior. The establishment of Freetown in 1787, and the abolition of the slave trade twenty years later, had dramatically shifted the fortunes of many coastal trading families across West Africa. For the Caulker family, Shenge's proximity to the undisputed center of abolitionism in the Atlantic Coast required them to switch gears into a new economic mode faster than other African slavers farther down the coast.[17]

The establishment of trade in timber and palm produce also transformed the lives of communities in the interior. As many of these goods were grown upcountry, new emphasis was placed on accessing the waterways that stretched from the coast to interior forests. Unlike slaves who had been predominantly transported to the coast on foot, heavy goods such as palm produce, rice, and timber required transportation in canoes along the major rivers.[18] Leaders sought to increasingly consolidate their power over riverine routes and the towns that lay along them. This meant not only seizing leadership roles over these communities but securing landlord-stranger agreements with Krio migrants who brought trade connections, wealth, and skills to their communities.

This shift in the political and economic landscape influenced and impacted the "Kagbor Kingdom" that Thomas Corker's son Stephen had established in the early eighteenth century. A century after its formation, the kingdom was divided by Canreba Caulker's father into two territories—the "Bompeh" and the "Plantain/ Shenge"—the latter of which he ruled.[19] As a small boy, Canreba was taken from the

Bompeh region and was raised by his enslaved mother in the town of Gbangbaia in the neighboring titular province of Imperri. Careyba's outcast status appears to have lit a fire that fueled his entire life. Ambitious and charismatic, as a young man he joined forces with his uncle Charles Caulker in an attempt to reunite the old Kagbor Kingdom and reclaim rule over Shenge from his uncle Thomas Stephen Caulker.[20] While some justification of this war was a return to traditional boundaries, there can be little doubt that access to Thomas Stephen's coastal frontage and islands were also high on the list of Canreba's priorities. Likewise, Canreba's timber-rich forests in the Bompeh likely appealed to Thomas Stephen whose control over Shenge gave him easy access to Freetown's mercantile community. As we will see later, the war over each other's territory, which became known as the Pemm Sabbah, would continue for multiple generations.[21]

Outside his own family, Canreba's claims over the Kagbor was challenged by another powerful coalition of leaders, the Kpaa-Mende. A unified coalition of fourteen states who were pushing westwards into Bompeh territory, the Kpaa-Mende constituted a culturally and linguistically distinct subgroup of the Mende.[22] The migration of the Mende people from the interior southwards towards the coast, sometimes referred to as the "Mendization" of the Sherbro, occurred through both migration, settlement, and direct warfare.[23] Aiding in the Mende's well-established abilities in warfare was the *Wunde*, a medicine society centered on training young men to be warriors and enforcing local law that was said to be more powerful than the Poro.[24] As the ethnically Sherbro people lacked a warrior tradition of their own, war captains from the Kpaa-Mende state had been hired by the Caulkers as early as the 1820s. Over time, these Mende migrants formed their own important towns in the Bompeh region and integrated themselves into elite Sherbro families by exchanging daughters in marriage.[25] Throughout the nineteenth century, the state steadily moved west and southwards, displacing other Mende, Sherbro, and Banta (a branch of the Temne-Yoni) peoples, and established their capital at Taiama on the Jong River.[26] As the century progressed, the Bompeh-Caulker leaders would increasingly find the settlement of the Kpaa-Mende a challenge to their sovereignty.[27]

Amid this political and economic turmoil, Canreba Caulker provides a fascinating example of how the need for protection was central to political authority and coalition building in mid-nineteenth-century Sherbro. His ability to marshal a wide variety of defensive forces ensured his reputation as a wealthy patron, warrior, and leader—qualities that strengthened his legitimacy to rule his subjects and build successful coalitions. He used his mother's ancestral home in Imperri to his advantage by shoring up military alliances with them and other neighboring states and then solidifying these bonds through marriage to their daughters, as he had with the Kpaa-Mende. He hired Muslim and Mende war captains and their men. It was even said he had built a "stronghold" deep in the woods that was "impervious" to outsiders that was guarded by these additional troops.[28]

Supernatural power was also of paramount importance. According to family stories, Canreba had the ability to wield supernatural powers, including one story where he sunk a boat with his mind.[29] It was well known he held a top-ranking position in the Poro, allowing him to declare war and compel lower-ranking members to fight on his behalf. Canreba's leadership role in this sodality allowed him to form binding alliances with other community and Poro leaders, especially those in the Ribbi region where the Poro was said to be "strong."[30] His role in Poro also allowed him to control the harvesting of agricultural products, the flow of trade along the rivers, and even the settlement of strangers.[31] This was essential, as the Bompeh region contained a great deal of palm and timber produce. To shore up the power bestowed on him from his ancestors, he hired various Islamic *morimen* to manufacture "greegrees" and other protective amulets.[32] These objects, often worn on the body, shielded the wearer from both physical and spiritual harm and were used during raids and in times of peace to protect a leader's rule.

The need to build an extensive protection portfolio also led Canreba to negotiate with the British Government. Since the establishment of the formal Colony in 1787, Indigenous leaders along the coastal and riverine region had signed various treaties and agreements with the British. Following in the footsteps of several Caulker family members before him, Canreba participated in numerous treaty signings with the British.[33] This diplomatic relationship was clearly conducted to strengthen his own rule and obtain wealth, not diminish his claims to political authority. In fact, it was rumored that if the Governor wished to communicate with Canreba he would be obliged to send for him or go to him directly as he "considered himself a greater man than the Governor," and had a "fear of trusting himself in the midst of men whose friendship he may be suspicious."[34] The first treaty he signed in 1849 alongside his rival Thomas Stephen Caulker sought to establish peace between them, though most agree that this conflict was not settled until another peace treaty was signed in June 1870.[35] This first treaty attempted to get the two leaders to agree on the border between their two territories, establishing the Yaltucker River as the division between their two lands. This was also the first treaty in Sierra Leone that explicitly promised to protect British subjects living within a leaders' territory.[36] Article VI stated that all "persons and property of the subjects of the Queen of England shall be inviolate, and they may freely carry-on trade in every part of the territories of the Chiefs, party hereto, and may have factories and houses therein" and that "no purrah" or "country law of any kind" is to be enforced against the subjects of the Queen.[37] Following these agreements, Canreba gave permission for the establishment of many trading factories and mission stations, and even engaged in the timber trade himself.[38] In 1853, he signed another treaty in Freetown that formally promised to hand over British offenders to colonial authorities. The 1853 agreement also marked the commencement of an annual stipend of £50 from the Governor, a considerable amount of money at mid-century. These early treaties can be seen as reciprocal as they and did not challenge or place explicit limits on Canreba's sovereignty. In fact, one could argue participation in British diplomacy in this early period cemented his family's legacy to rule the Bompeh region, as each leader of the Bompeh until the end of colonial rule would be his direct descendent.

Treaties signed between the Caulkers and the British administration signal a shift in the relationship between protection and jurisdiction in the Sherbro region. In their attempts to create peace and order, treaties defined new political and geographic spaces by explicitly linking specific rulers to bordered states. In this sense, treaties contributed to the centralization of Sherbro's political states well before Protectorate rule and became meaningful tools for African leaders to claim political authority over contested land. Like the 1853 agreement, treaties solidified new borders that aided in the production of colonial maps that were frequently consulted and reproduced. In this sense, while Britons viewed African cultural or legal practices as "uncivilized," the treaties signed between themselves and Africans at mid-century did take seriously African leaders' status as "equal" or "minor" sovereign states, frequently referring to them as "Kings."[39] In this way, there can be little doubt that treaties aided in shoring up the boundaries between African territories, borders that would prove meaningful and highly debated in the decades ahead.

Early treaties also redefined the meaning of subjecthood. When Krio traders moved further upriver, they brought their status as British subjects with them. The settlement of these sojourners complicated African tenancy laws that governed the arrival of newcomers. British treaty agreements that promised to protect British subjects altered the meaning of what it meant to be a stranger by denoting special status to Krios and Britons operating in the interior. Though less clearly understood in the records, it is probable that the reciprocal agreements that required Africans signatories to protect British subjects in exchange for British protection of their own people shifted the meaning of African leaders' rights over their own people.

The "Deplorable State of Affairs": Krio Traders and the Limits of Extraterritoriality

In 1857, Canreba Caulker joined the ancestors. His successor, Thomas Theophilus Caulker, was not as politically savvy as his brother before him.[40] His rule from 1857 to 1864 embodied the double-edged quality of coalition building. Without the authority and charisma of his brother, Thomas Theophilus was unable to hold the vast reach of alliances that Canreba had formed. Coalitions were most often broken when one member decided that their interests would be better served by another confederacy or patron. In Bompeh, a stranger-leader named Pa Keni declared the Ribbi, the central timber growing region within Bompeh, independent from Caulker rule.[41] Thomas Theophilus attempted to counter this act by using the Poro to cut off Pa Keni's source of wealth by declaring a *poro*, or ban, on the production of timber.[42] However, this strategy backfired when it not only stopped the flow of trade to Thomas Theophilus' Indigenous competitors, but also the British subjects trading there. Because of the treaties signed by his predecessor with the British, warfare between Thomas Theophilus and his competitors tested the limits of British intervention and protection in spaces they claimed to apply.

After serving for at least a decade as Canreba's translator and clerk, Thomas Ellis relocated twenty miles up the Ribbi River and established a trading factory in Mabang. Ellis settled there with his wife Burah, a local Temne woman, and their three children. A women named Nancy Nichols, who had come to the region as a child, also lived and traded in Mabang with her Freetown-born husband Joseph Dunn and their family.[43] Unfortunately for the Ellis and Dunn-Nichols families, their small town was located in territory that Pa Keni was seeking to cede from Thomas Theophilus Caulker. In September 1859, a group of warboys burst into Thomas Ellis' and Nancy Nichols' respective homes. As the two families were being seized by raiders, Thomas Ellis pleaded with the men asserting that "they were people from Sierra Leone and belong to the Queen."[44] Ignoring their appeal, the men tied up the heavily pregnant Nancy, her daughter, Thomas, Burah, and their three children. At some point on the march to enemy headquarters, Thomas Ellis, who was sick and elderly, was beheaded and left on the side of the road.

When details of raids like the one in Mabang reached the formal Colony of Sierra Leone, they generated outrage and extensive correspondence on the meaning of protection on the frontier. In August 1860, a large gathering of members of the Freetown community congregated at the Government School. Thomas Ellis' death had clearly shocked the community: his young son George was still missing and was presumed to have been made a slave. The news of this event was compounded by reports of the recent rape and enslavement of a missionary's wife in the Northern River region. Krio traders and their fellow countrymen were angry and afraid. And so, they gathered to engage in the great tradition of so many subjects of the British Empire: the presentation of a petition to the Governor to express their deep concerns.

The memorial was signed by over one hundred residents of the Colony of Sierra Leone. It outlined what the petitioners called the "deplorable state of affairs in the rivers and countries adjacent to this Colony."[45] Krios expressed that while the best "passport" they could have while trading in African territory a few years ago was "the distinction to call themselves British Subjects," lately only "insult and degradation with a relentless hand are heaped upon them." Now their property was burned and their "parents, friends, and children" were being "barbarously murdered or carried into a cruel and never ending bondage."[46] While the memorialists describe the hinterland as a generalized space of "moral and physical wilderness," the changes they were describing directly reflected the destabilizing impact of the death of Canreba and the escalating conflict between the Caulker family over the Kagbor that ensued. Krio petitioners insisted that their protection could only be secured through more "powerful measures," demanding that the coastal regions formally be ceded and brought within British jurisdiction, else the Colony and its surrounding areas be "plunged into . . . a state of anarchy and confusion."[47]

Krio demands for formal colonization reflect the complex legal status they held in the Sierra Leone Colony and the British Empire. As British subjects, their claims for protection when outside of formal colonial territory represented their substantial knowledge of the right of extraterritoriality when they travelled outside the jurisdictional limits of the British Empire.[48] Extraterritoriality promised protection from violence as well as having to engage in "barbaric" legal practices to settle their disputes upcountry. However, their status as "black Britishmen" markedly distinguished them from white British subjects. While Krios saw themselves as uniquely positioned to tame the "wilderness" of the hinterland through the introduction of commerce and Christianity, racist ideas held by the colonial administration clearly impacted the extent to which British officials intervened in cases like the raids on the Nichols and Ellis family in Mabang.[49] Instead, Krio traders were frequently told—in direct contrast to treaty stipulations—that if they insisted on trading outside the Colony, they were responsible for their own protection.

Colonial officials in London did embrace some aspects of extraterritoriality in Sierra Leone. British administrators took advantage of empire-wide legislation like the British Settlements Act that allowed for the "juridical simulation of conquest" to establish a consular headquarters and courts on Sherbro Island in the 1850s.[50] As a tool, extraterritoriality allowed colonial officials to justify incurring increased responsibilities and expenses despite protestations from the Colonial Office to refrain from doing so. Predictably, however, it did nothing to mitigate the warfare or protect trade relations beyond the extension of moral authority. Effective British protection schemes were only possible when local leaders independently chose to engage the British as leverage in their own disputes. On the tumultuous frontier, whoever obliged British inquiries for alliance building won favor with the colonial state.

British ambivalences over territorial jurisdiction and subjecthood is evident in the way the raid of Mabang was ultimately resolved. After sending a variety of letters to local leaders asking for redress, Governor Hill received word from Ellis' landlord Pa Keni that Thomas Theophilus had instructed his warboys that "whenever they have a dispute with a British Subject that they should kill him because if he were allowed to escape, he would complain to the Government and bring trouble upon him."[51] Ultimately, Pa Keni and another stranger Chief named Lahai Bundoo recovered most of the Nichols and Ellis family members. Even though neither had signed a treaty, the two leaders clearly used the raid as an opportunity to build an alliance with the British, despite the fact that their own people had been kidnapped in retaliation. After countering the attack, they asked that their actions not be perceived as "too warlike" in recovering them, clearly referencing their knowledge of the content of several treaties to not engage in warfare without the consent of the Governor. Their request for a ten shilling "present" is also reminiscent of a treaty stipend, or perhaps the recovery of ransom fees that they took the initiative of paying in advance. As paying ransoms and recovering one's stranger after their kidnapping was part of a landlord's role in local law, Pa Keni and Lahai Bundoo's actions signal a shift that reflected Krios' dual subjecthood in the British state and as strangers under African jurisdiction.[52] This seems especially true for leaders who were seeking to wrest power from more deeply established ruling families like the

Caulkers. Protecting Krios created potential opportunities for both autochthon and stranger leaders to leverage power amidst escalating struggles over land and resources.

The Shenge Caulkers and the Annexation of "British Sherbro"

The story of Canreba's long term rival, Thomas Stephen Caulker of Shenge, provides another window into how British treaty making and alliance building provided new pathways to protection. Thomas Stephen Caulker was himself a well-respected leader among his people. Although perhaps not as strong as his foe, Thomas Stephen amassed his own coalition of Caulker relatives and neighboring elites to protect his rule and his life.[53] Unfortunately for him, his stockaded town on the Plantain Islands was no match for Canreba's bombardments, forcing him to flee far down the coast to Bendu, a small town on the mainland across from Sherbro Island. There he built another walled stockade, forged a coalition of local alliances, and hired many war captains who came with their troops and war canoes.[54] To counter this, Canreba and his allies built four stockade villages encircling Thomas' own fortress. In their final and bloody battle, Thomas Stephen somehow successfully defended his new position despite heavy losses and the full force of Canreba's men. In his new home of Bendu, Thomas' power and reputation brought together a new confederacy of loyal alliances made up of Caulkers, local leaders, morimen, and former war captains—styling himself as "King of Bendoo."[55]

When comparing these two Caulker leaders, Thomas Stephen's political proximity to the coast compelled him to engage with British in diplomacy in a more nuanced way than his foe.[56] Unlike Canreba, he sought to enfold British political and Christian missionary alliances in his coalition. While in Bendu, he formed a relationship with the British "consul" Augustus Beale Hanson and the merchants living in foreign trading factories along the Sherbro coast. Unfortunately, these connections placed him under increased surveillance and scrutiny. Following the bombardment of his settlement in Bendu by French forces, Thomas Stephen was accused of being the cause of the disturbances and for trying to extort money from the King of the Sherbro to pay for damages incurred by the French attack. Leading traders, missionaries, and local leaders signed statements against him and, as a result, he was forcefully brought to Freetown and jailed.[57] His incarceration in 1859 perhaps represented the first treaty signatory to be arrested and held by the British, establishing another important precedent of incarcerating treaty signatories.

After six months, Thomas Stephen Caulker was released. On the way down the coast, he stopped to pay a visit the graves of his ancestors in Tasso and promised to end the war between himself and his family members. But no sooner did he do this did French traders again threatened his interests. With few powerful Indigenous allies to turn to, he offered to cede his highly contested coastal territory around Bendu to the British in exchange for protection. Despite a clear policy of non-interference, the Governor agreed. Thomas Stephen's political vulnerability had created an opening for the British to solve the persistent legal issue of placing police and customs houses in African territory.

Despite protestations from the Colonial Office to avoid annexation, Governor Hill presented a compelling case to London officials of why cession should occur. He recounted French imperial ambitions and recent problems with French traders (in reality, making a bit of a mountain out of a molehill), and argued that the formal acquisition of land would ensure a British future in the region and avoid complications or mixed loyalties on the part of local leaders.[58] He waxed lyrical about the economic potential of the region, the burgeoning timber trade (leaving out the kidnapping of traders at several timber trading posts!) and the accessibility of the rivers. Hill skillfully drew on the language of British protection, stressing that annexation would provide both British subjects and its Indigenous "inhabitants" with safety and security. He stressed that despite its proximity to the formal Colony and its abolitionist tradition, the region continued to be a hotbed of slavery and smuggling that needed to be suppressed to produce better economic conditions for imperial commerce. The treaty of annexation was approved, however unenthusiastically, with one colonial official scribbling "I see no help for it" in the margin of the dispatch.

The signing of the Treaty of 1861 was a well-attended affair and set the tone for diplomacy in future decades. Dressed in their finest, African leaders brought their wives, followers, slaves, and attendants to Bendu, the seat of Thomas Stephen's power. On the British side, officials dressed in their full regalia, incorporated military demonstrations of brass bands, military drills, and cannon and musket firing to local drumming. Krio traders from throughout the region came to witness the historic event. On the first day, Governor Hill read the terms of the treaty out loud through an interpreter, allowing the potential signatories to take a few days to "hang

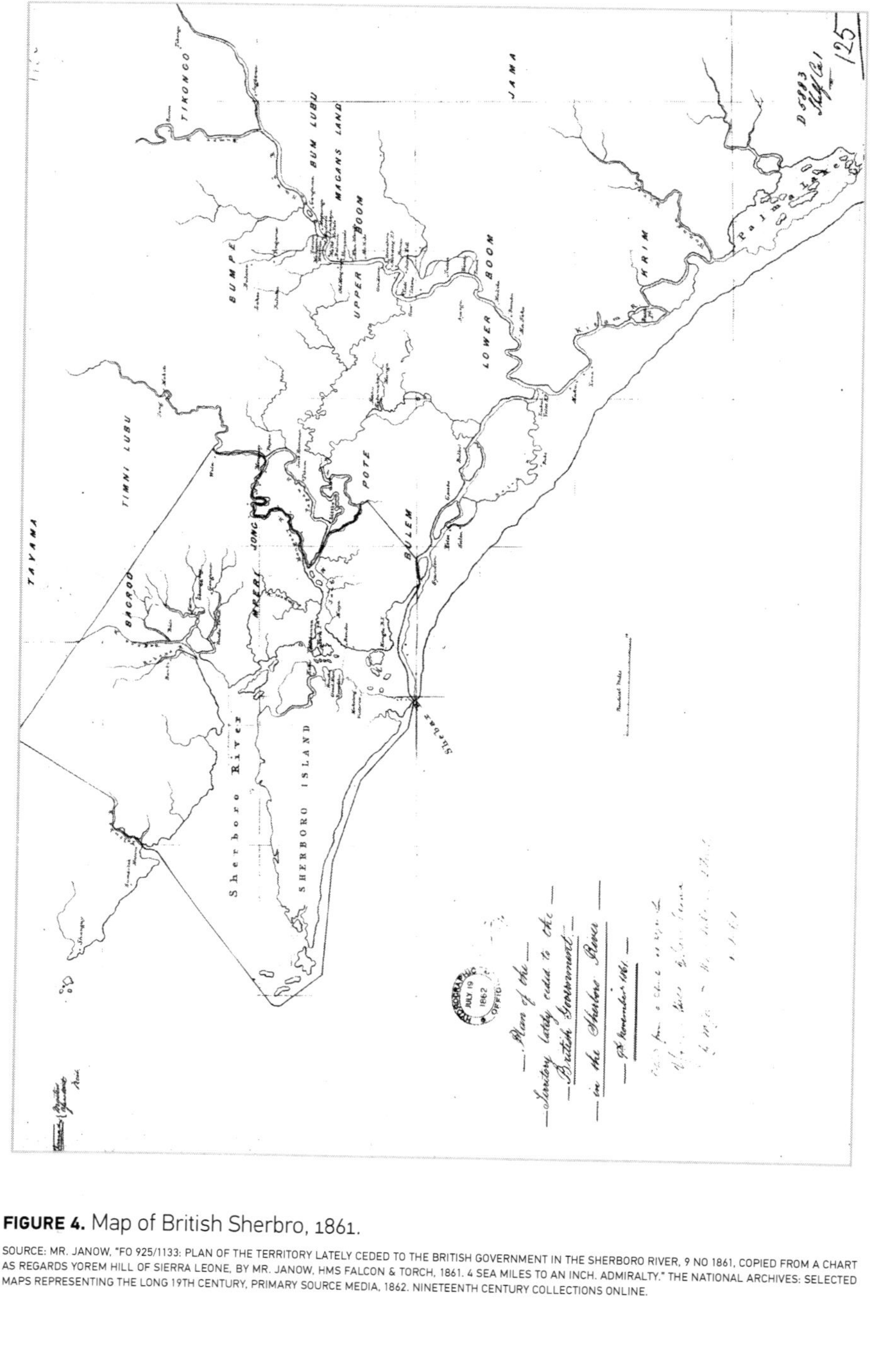

FIGURE 4. Map of British Sherbro, 1861.

SOURCE: MR. JANOW, "FO 925/1133: PLAN OF THE TERRITORY LATELY CEDED TO THE BRITISH GOVERNMENT IN THE SHERBORO RIVER, 9 NO 1861, COPIED FROM A CHART AS REGARDS YOREM HILL OF SIERRA LEONE, BY MR. JANOW, HMS FALCON & TORCH, 1861. 4 SEA MILES TO AN INCH. ADMIRALTY," THE NATIONAL ARCHIVES: SELECTED MAPS REPRESENTING THE LONG 19TH CENTURY, PRIMARY SOURCE MEDIA, 1862. NINETEENTH CENTURY COLLECTIONS ONLINE.

heads," which in local parlance meant to discuss and come to a consensus about the terms. In these intermediate days, much dancing and drumming occurred.[59] At the conclusion of those days, several surprising things happened. While Hill initially only received permission from London to annex land belonging to Thomas Stephen and other members of the Caulker family, the event unexpectedly led to the cession of much more territory. Hill stated that after the treaty signing with the Caulkers, the "Chiefs of the Bagroo [*sic*] came forward and begged their country might also be added to British territory, as it would prove the only means by which the peace and prosperity of the native inhabitants of the Bagroo could be secured."[60] It is unclear whether they did this on their own, or with the urging of Thomas Stephen with whom many were aligned. Indigenous coalition building practices likely led African leaders to believe that protection from the British and the retention of their sovereignty were not incompatible. On the final day of negotiations, three treaties, known collectively as the "Treaty of 1861," were signed by a total of forty-nine African leaders, and gifts were exchanged. Copies of the three treaties and a sketch map (Figure 2) were sent to the Colonial Office in London.

Treaties of annexation in Sierra Leone prior to 1861 were largely concentrated in coastal regions and islands, beginning with Temne land that would become Freetown and the peninsula.[61] South of the Colony, Thomas Stephen's uncle and Canreba's father "leased" the Banana Islands to the British in exchange for a yearly fee of two hundred bars in perpetuity, but was not understood as a relinquishment of African sovereignty over the land.[62] Five years later, the Caulkers signed a treaty alongside Banka the "King of the Sherbro," the Prince of Sherbro Kong Kuba, and several titular leaders: Queen Ya Cumba of Tasso, Ta Bompey of Bullom, and So Lokko of Bagru. This 1825 agreement, known henceforth as "Turner's Treaty" for the Governor who initiated it, was not ratified by Parliament, though later became a useful tool in claiming annexation over parts of the Sherbro state without the formal consent of its leaders.

When read alongside these older treaties, the Treaty of 1861 was anomalous in the massive landmass it encompassed and atypical in the way the British exercised dominion over it. Twelve years after the creation of "British Sherbro," the Government Interpreter Thomas George Lawson, himself present at the signing, recounted that after the treaty was signed, Governor Hill contradictorily proclaimed to the leaders present that "Sherbro was now the Queen's land, but that it was still their land, but the right of Sovereignty was the Queen's which their Country would be kept from being molested and the Government will consider what to do for them in the future." Hill's emphasis that leaders would "not being molested" suggests that African signatories were led to believe that Britain was acting as a protective ally, not as a territorial conqueror.[63]

Of course, not every African leader who signed the Treaty of 1861 had the same motivations for participating as Stephen Caulker. In signing the first treaty, he and other high-ranking leaders from along the coast and up the Jong River as far as Mattru represented one side of the larger confederacy in his war with Canreba.[64] Signatories of the second treaty, however, consisted of leaders from the titular province of Bagru—which was bordered by the two Caulker warring factions and the Bompeh's main allies, the Imperri. Bagru was also the site of several early timber mills operated by both European and American traders and missionaries. While the titular leader "Se Lokko, King of Bagroo [*sic*]" was at the top of the signatory list, the other signatories appear to be a mish-mash of "chiefs," "gentleman," "lady," "headman," and "war captains," suggesting they represented a coalition under Se Lokko or Thomas Stephen Caulker. For instance, while the borders of the new territory clearly encompassed the shoreline south of Yaltucker River, the important men who ruled towns there that were aligned with Canreba were notably absent from the signing. The third treaty, was signed by a variety of leaders from Sherbro Island, including a man who was listed as "Beah Boom, King of Sherbro."[65]

Identifying these signatories reveals that British annexation of Sherbro was sanctioned by the more vulnerable side within a broader regional dispute. The British Crown was clearly evaluated much like other potential African coalition members. African leaders viewed individual British officials, Governors, or even the "Queen of England" as powerful or resourceful patrons who they could obtain protection from. Their vulnerability cemented promises of protection that were full of unreconcilable contradictions that would reveal themselves in the decades ahead. Annexation in British Sherbro became a flexible tool that allowed colonial administrators to simultaneously promise and deny protection to Krio traders and Africans signatories depending on whether these demands furthered British interests.[66]

The annexation of British Sherbro set the framework for the use of imperial intermediaries. Despite technically being a formal Colony, British Sherbro was administered through African leaders through local laws and customs and not British common law. For example, one Governor told a leader whose territory lay within British Sherbro that he may "remain and exercise dominion." At the same time, the colonial Government placed a permanent police station on his land "to show the limit claimed for British protection, for though we *assert dominion* . . . it has not been included in British jurisdiction."[67] The legal murkiness between "exercising dominion" and "asserting dominion" typified the way territorial jurisdiction functioned in the decades after 1861 and set a precedent for the framework of indirect rule in 1896. Thus, while the treaty boldly declared the entire region a "dependency of this Colony [Sierra Leone]" in which Britain had "full, entire, free and unlimited right, possession, dominion and sovereignty," in reality, colonial rule continued to rely on the engagement of the African leaders whose position in local conflicts saw it necessary to enfold Britain into their own multi-regional coalitions.

Crying for the King: Jurisdiction Along the Border Between Imperri and British Sherbro

Like many places throughout the world, the borders between Sherbro's titular provinces were demarcated through a combination of natural features like rivers and hills, as well as man-made markers like towns or cairns. Unlike the Mende states in the north that were defined by the projection of power of a single leader, the borders of Sherbro's southern provinces appear to have become more fixed by the mid-nineteenth century. For instance, the states of Imperri (Mperi) and Jong are labelled on maps as early as the 1850s.[68] After the annexation of British Sherbro 1861, several maps clearly label the different provinces including Imperri, Jong and Bagru. Shoring up these borders likely became an increasingly advantageous strategy for African leaders to lay claim to the land and labor within.[69] In the process, however, the rivers and settlements that marked the jurisdictional limits of these polities increasingly became hotspots of colonial law and violent confrontation between and among Indigenous communities, Krios, and Europeans.

The annexation of British Sherbro in 1861 also created new jurisdictional patterns. Although blurry, the border between the "Queen's Land" and African territory was made meaningful through the settlement of strangers and Krio traders. As agricultural trade generated new kinds of wealth, more established leaders were compelled to shore up control over the rivers within their territory. African legal processes that were used to assert the dominion of Sherbro leaders were viewed as lawless and violent by British observers. When these disputes occurred on the fringes of British jurisdiction or impacted the lives of British subjects, they generated intense debates over the meaning of protection.

These changes were evident in the town of Gundema, located on the Mano-Bagru River on the border between British Sherbro and the Imperri province. Located on the British side, its leader, Bundooka, was listed in the Treaty of 1861 as a "war captain." In 1870, Bundooka was described by one colonial official as a "man of superior intelligence who has raised himself to independence by his own energy and industry but is not of 'Royal Blood.'"[70] Regionally, he belonged to the broader African coalition that included the Kpaa-Mende Chiefdom, Se Lokko of Bagru, and Shenge Caulkers—all of whom had signed the Treaty of 1861. As a stranger, he had likely arrived in the region as a war captain and had been given land by an employer after the war ended. Under his rule, Gundema had become a thriving trading post. with at least four Krio tenants—Patience Peters, Sarah Thomas, Edward Green Connolly, and Eliza Renner. Like Thomas Ellis, these four Krio traders would have been considered under the protection of the Colony. However, the location of Gundema placed them and Bundooka in considerable danger. Although clearly within British jurisdiction, its precarity was heightened by its close proximity to Imperri, a province made up of leaders who were frequently at odds with those in the Bagru.[71]

In 1870, the death of the Sokong, the titular leader of Imperri, prompted leaders from throughout the province to elect a new King.[72] The host of the meeting was a prominent Imperri leader named Beah Boom. His town of Gbangbaia was a major center of power, and was also, incidentally, the town where Canreba Caulker had been raised by his slave mother as a child. Though not the Sokong himself, Beah Boom's influence in the region was considerable, reflected by the diverse delegates who responded to his invitation to "cry" for the deceased Sokong. In addition to autochthon leaders from Imperri, attendees included various other "Big Men" like Tom Cabbie Smith, an Imperri slave turned trader who had established himself in Kambia on the Small Boom River. Others included a series of prominent Muslim leaders, including Ansummana Lolme, a Muslim-Temne war captain and trader originally from the Port Lokko area.[73] While Muslim leaders would not have been part of the official Poro that would have selected a new leader, their participation signals the diverse make up of precolonial leadership and confederacies.

While it is impossible to fully reconstruct the funeral cry, one man who claimed to be a farmer and aide to one of the delegates stated that at one point during the events, Beah Boom stood up and said, "my friends as the King is dead we must keep the burial by making war against the inhabitants of the Bagru Country and after we have conquered them and destroyed all their towns then we must come again to the Imperreh [*sic*] and cry for the King."[74] These declarations represent a common practice of reasserting the borders of titular provinces after the death of a leader. To get the job done, Ansummana Lolme contracted a number of additional war captains, including a man named Whobay.

When these hired mercenaries arrived in Gundema, Bundooka was nowhere to be found. Instead, they killed many people in Bundooka's family, including his brother, who was burned alive. The violence on the community was devastating and directed: male members of Bundooka's family were disemboweled, mutilated, or decapitated in ways that suggested their bodies were used to construct powerful protective medicines.[75] Bundooka's wives, female family members, and his four Krio tenants were kidnapped, along with fifty to sixty other captives.[76] The importance of the town's economy was also reflected in the raid: a large amount of palm oil and kernels were taken, and the Krio storehouses were raided. According to the Governor, what a "few days before had been a thriving town, I now found a blackened ruin, with piles of half burnt palm nuts, ground nuts and other produce lying about."[77] In a deposition after the raid, Bundooka attributed the attack to his connections with the British. He claimed that the men who did this "had been threatening him for some years with this attack as they alleged he sold the country to the English and was always friendly to them."[78]

This statement lends considerable insight into how the creation of British Sherbro was understood by Imperri's leaders. While several Imperri leaders had signed the Treaty of 1861 (likely Beah Boom among them[79]), the ones who organized the raid on Gundema clearly did not consider themselves under British jurisdiction, even though their land was technically situated within its borders in both the treaty and sketch map (Figure 2). The death of the Sokong authorized the raid on Bundooka as a reclamation of Imperri rule over his territory. The capture of goods and people restored political order by actively redistributing Bundooka's wealth to its "rightful owners."[80] This type of raiding was used throughout the region as a means of asserting the ownership of towns.[81] Unfortunately for Bundooka, his family, and his tenants, his connection to the British by signing the Treaty of 1861 complicated his ability to counter the attack with his own warboys. Instead, his military campaigns had the potential of being viewed as contrary to treaty stipulations, risking the promise of protection he tacitly held.

This was evident soon after the raid when the Commandant and colonial police launched an investigation into the murders. Colonial officials dismissed the conflict as the result of "the jealousy of outlying kings and chiefs."[82] This racial "explanation" would be recycled time and again by officials seeking to disassociate the impact of imperialism in the region. Following this logic, when Bundooka asked that the Commandant join him in pursuing Whobay's war party, Walshe declined, stating that legal measures would be taken to "punish the instigators and [their] ferocious attack" and that new laws would be "adopted to protect him for the future."[83] Likely unhappy with this reply, Bundooka chose to continue to encamp nearby with a strong body of armed followers. He reached out to other African leaders in his coalition and then proceeded north to meet with his Kpaa-Mende allies. Meanwhile, the Commandant called for the arrest of several men for the murder of one of the kidnapped Krio traders, including Ansumana Lolme and Beah Boom, the latter of whom he declared to be a "notoriously turbulent Chief."[84] However, due to a lack of evidence, only Whobay was found, arrested, and sent to Freetown.

The Sierra Leone Supreme Court trial *Regina v. Whobay* was the first criminal case to grapple with the definition and meaning of jurisdiction and subjecthood in British Sherbro. The details of the trial exposed, in the words of one Krio journalist, the "complications which have arisen out of the loose manner in which the annexation treaty was drawn up."[85] The case itself hinged on an intense debate in the courtroom as to whether one of Bundooka's Krio tenants named Patience Peters had been murdered in British Sherbro, or had been taken across the Mano-Bagru River to Imperri in a strategic move to avoid British legal jurisdiction, a tactic subsequent raiders would copy in the decades ahead.[86] Despite Commandant Walshe's testimony that there existed an "invisible line" that marked the western border of the "Queen's Territory . . . *about* 30 miles inland from Sherbro River," the jury was not convinced. Whobay was found not guilty due to the murder occurring outside British territory and his status as a non-British subject.[87]

After the verdict, colonial lawmakers and the Krio public wrestled with the implications of the ambiguity of the borders of British Sherbro.[88] Governor Kennedy himself stated that Whobay's case left little doubt that "any British Subject may be seized without form of law or pretext within British territory, carried over a Boundary . . . and there murdered with impunity." Acknowledging the purposeful way Whobay himself had evaded authorities by crossing the Mano-Bagru, he added that the lack of a firm border "will doubtless suggest to the native mind a very easy mode of either recovering or discharging debts or other obligations." The trial suggested that local populations well understood the borders between British and African jurisdiction and could use them to evade British law and policing.

Drawing from these personal convictions, the input of Krio colonial officials, and the public outcry, Kennedy drafted a new bill entitled "An Act for extending the Jurisdiction of the Courts of the West African Settlements to certain offenses committed out of her Majesty's Dominions," which extended the legal jurisdiction of the British a further 20 miles of the boundary indicated by the 1861 treaty of annexation. The bill stated that "persons not subjects of any civilized power" who are "known or suspected to have committed a crime or offense within . . . may be . . . kept in custody therein, in like manner as if the said crime or offense had been committed within such settlement."[89] The act was passed on March 1, 1871, in London.

Conclusion

The events surrounding the *Regina v. Whobay* trial were the first in a series of ongoing debates that reshaped the legal and physical parameters of British protection in the region. The case ignited a series of questions over the rights and responsibilities the British state owed to Krio traders and Indigenous populations living within British Sherbro. The final outcomes of the case demonstrated how the flexibility of British law could be manipulated to achieve almost any desired outcome when it came to the frontier. In an Executive Council meeting, Krio and British officials compensated Bundooka £100 for the destruction of his town and "the failure to bring the punishment of the man who had been tried by the Supreme Court for murder committed in the Sherbro."[90] Subsequently, Whobay was brought to court on a second murder charge of a six-year-old (local) African girl named Boye, presumably a member of Bundooka's household. Sarah Thomas, another of Bundooka's tenants who had testified in the first trial, again took the stand, stating that the murder *did* happen in the "Queen's land," that she now remembered they had not crossed a river on the way to the location where Peters was killed.[91] Jury members swiftly declared Whobay guilty. Less than a month later, he was hanged in the Freetown gallows. Even after his client was executed, his lawyer, William Rainy, continued to object, stating that the Government had no right to try and convict a non-British subject for acts committed in war.[92]

The arrival of Krio traders and British imperialism signaled a distinctive shift in the meaning of protection in relation to the British colonial state. Treaties facilitated debates about the limits of extraterritoriality and the rights of British subjects when living outside of the boundaries of British jurisdiction. By the late 1860s, conflicts between African leaders transformed into a regional-wide war expanding well beyond the Sherbro state. Within individual towns and titular provinces, autochthon leaders were compelled to form new and divisive coalitions that, at times, threatened their own authority. By the next decade, Mende and Muslim war captains from the interior quickly became an important component of coalition building through their skills as warriors, as well as their access to interior trade routes.[93] Hired as mercenaries to lead warfare and conduct raids, war captains quickly began to gain their own clients and dependents, sometimes allowing them to displace the authority of the leaders who had hired them in the first place.[94] In addition to this, formerly nominal leaders like Bundooka and Pa Keni who lived along the region's central rivers were able to generate new forms of wealth through their contact with imperial trade and Krio traders like Thomas Ellis and Patience Peters. In some cases, these new Big Men utilized their access to foreign goods, cash, and labor through raiding and trading to establish new centers of trade that attracted a wide range of clients and dependents.

Moving into the 1870s, treaty making with African leaders who lived outside of British territory emerged as the primary solution to securing protection for Krio traders and their property, resulting in an expansion of British ideas of crime and punishment. In exchange for protection, extra-legal strategies like deportation and deposing were embedded into treaty stipulations, forging an enduring set of precedents that would shape the legal framework of southern Sierra Leone both on the frontier and beyond.

CHAPTER TWO

Treaties and Tribulations

Policing and Punitive Measures on the Sierra Leone Frontier, 1870–1885

ON THE NIGHT OF JUNE 9, 1875, MRS. JANE TAYLOR, A KRIO TRADER WHO HAD BEEN operating in the Sherbro coast since 1862, awoke to the sound of men breaking into her home. Her town of Mamaiah, which lay on the border of British territory, had seen increased warfare in recent months, prompting the arrival of colonial police earlier that day. Coming out of her sleeping quarters, she came face-to-face with a man named Vangang, a well-known produce dealer and a war captain hired by a local leader named Lahai Serifoo. Vangang and his warboys were there for about three hours, during which they stripped her, tied her up, raided her storehouse, killed her cattle, and stole her canoes. Next door to her, a fellow Krio trader named Mrs. Parkinson was also being raided. Upon leaving, the men kidnapped Mrs. Parkinson and her three children. Although Jane Taylor was spared, six children (including her own adopted daughter Hannah) and the mother of one of those children from her household were kidnapped. In her report to the Commandant, Mrs. Taylor gave a detailed list of the kidnapped people, as well as her considerable monetary loss of around £1000, which included a wide variety of manufactured and country cloths, five hundred pounds of tobacco, rum and gin, ten kegs of gunpowder, rice, gold, silver, four cows, six hogs, and six canoes.[1]

The raid on Mrs. Taylor and Mrs. Parkinson was not an isolated event. Changes in regional economics through the increase in agricultural commerce further exacerbated competitions over the leadership of towns and regions that had begun at mid-century. By the beginning of the 1870s, these tensions culminated in region-wide warfare that engulfed the entire Sherbro state and beyond. Cyclical conflict elevated the importance of hiring mercenaries like Vangang to wage raids to reclaim debts, capture goods and people, or seek revenge. Securing a consistent source of income to do so became an essential component of exercising legitimate authority. This shift facilitated the rise of new power brokers like Big Men traders and war captains whose legitimacy was not necessarily based on ancestral lineage. This chapter illuminates how, in a bid to secure their political and physical protection, African leaders who claimed to be the "rightful owners of the land" sought British protection amidst this ever-evolving landscape of warfare and economic instability. While initially the colonial government sought to form alliances with any treaty signatory willing to work with them, by the mid 1880s, diplomatic initiatives and claims for protection by African leaders who claimed ancestral ties to the land altered how the British understood Sherbro's political landscape.

Treaties signed with African leaders on imperial frontiers constituted a significant part of the "explosion" in treaty making that occurred in the nineteenth century.[2] As historian Edward Keene has shown, treaty making in that century increased sevenfold from the previous one, largely due to developments in international law and the desire of European Empires to demonstrate more "legitimate" or lawful claims to their sphere of influence beyond military conquest.[3] The majority of studies on treaties signed between Europeans and Africans reflect Eurocentric concerns, resulting in a focus on territorial expansion or their role in the development of international law. This chapter reverses this approach by seeking to understand how treaty stipulations transformed African political and legal frameworks in the Sherbro region. Local institutions like palavers and poros rendered treaty signings mutually legible events, allowing African communities the ability to "cross cultural boundaries and enter into political and legal negotiations even if they did not always respect the terms of the agreement."[4]

Over five hundred African leaders in the Sherbro region alone signed treaties of "peace and commerce" with the British Government in the 1870s and 1880s. This remarkable assortment of leaders demonstrates one of the distinctive features of how decentralized societies navigated British imperialism in the late nineteenth century. Instead of a single central leader or King, British administrators had to negotiate with an extensive group of African leaders who arrived at the negotiating table with unique motivations. British engagement with this diverse array of leaders forged two enduring features of British protection schemes in southern Sierra Leone. The first was the establishment of a visible set of "aligned" leaders whose political and physical vulnerability was largely the result of shifts in the emergence of warfare and the agricultural economy. Second, within these alliances, leaders justified their authority and claims for protection based on their status as rightful owners of the land. These political claims on the imperial frontier established a precedent that would secure their status as a "Founding Family" after the establishment of Protectorate rule. In tracing the specifics of who and where African claims for political and personal protection from the British state emerged, this chapter reveals how the extension of the imperial frontier was not only delineated through economic expansion, but through African engagement in British law and diplomacy.

Treaties of peace and commerce extended the paradox of protection that developed on the coast in the previous decades. The articles contained in these agreements introduced new definitions of crime and punishment that limited African pathways to protection, retribution, or peace, leaving aligned leaders increasingly vulnerable. Ironically, African requests for protection from their enemies and competitors increased the use of violence by the colonial state. By the 1880s, the paradox of protection became a trap neither British nor African leaders could escape. While African leaders did not see their requests for protection as compromising their sovereignty, colonial administrators and lawmakers used their appeals to further extend their influence through extra-legal practices and the formal annexation of key riverine and coastal territories. Ultimately the extreme violence of military campaigns, followed by the incarceration, execution, and exiling of "political prisoners," forged a new set of legal precedents that became woven in to the legal framework of indirect rule.[5]

While these processes occurred throughout the Sherbro hinterland, this chapter focuses on the Jong, a province named for the Jong River that runs through its territory. Home to both stranger and autochthon leaders, the area became a hotspot of confrontation when the arrival of imperial commerce fragmented its political leadership. While only a few Jong leaders signed treaties in 1853 and 1861, the escalation of warfare in the 1870s prompted a wider range of community leaders to sign treaties and engage in British law and diplomacy as a way of preserving their political authority. While the colonial Government seems to have initially favored an alliance with a small group of Muslim Susu leaders, the legitimacy of these "strangers" were challenged by another set of leaders who claimed to be the rightful owners of the land. By 1882, intense competition between these two sides over the capital of the Jong province led to clashes with colonial forces. With the aim of preserving their political authority from competing interests, the more vulnerable Jong leaders formally placed themselves under the protection of the British state.

Warriors and Traders: The Struggle over the Jong in the 1870s

By the mid-1860s, palm products overtook the timber trade, with exports increasing an astounding 700 percent between 1851 and 1871.[6] Encouraged by what seemed like a flourishing and lucrative market, increasing numbers of Krio traders like Mrs. Parkinson and Mrs. Taylor began to "bestir themselves and go outside to seek fresh fields for commercial action" in the Sherbro region.[7] As Krio traders migrated further into the interior, the rivers became dotted with "trading factories." By 1870, large trading houses (both European and Krio) became increasingly challenged by smaller so-called "enterprising traders," described as continually "push[ing] up the rivers, contenting themselves with small profits and quick returns." These smaller-scale traders were "mostly Sierra Leone people . . . generally with little or no capital; but they worry the life out of the European merchants (like mosquitos at the barmouth) taking away sleep and giving no peace."[8] These Krio "petty traders" operated in direct competition with Indigenous middlemen. As one official commented, trade in the Sherbro region became a "regular fight all round for 'nuts,'" as local African and Krio traders clashed when trying to establish themselves along key trading nodes on the rivers. Competition over access to labor and commodities among and between Krios and local traders triggered increased conflict and raiding in the region.

To ensure their security, Sherbro leaders who did not have a warrior tradition of their own were compelled to assemble coalitions that contained members who could provide physical protection.[9] Mende and Muslim mercenaries like Vangang were hired for their skills as warriors and the makers of protective charms and amulets. Many scholars of Sierra Leone have observed that the elevated importance of these men signaled the emergence of "professional class of warriors" made up of war chiefs/captains (*ko-mahei*) and their "warboys" (*kobei*).[10] As warfare became endemic, vulnerable leaders required consistent access to cash to "buy war," meaning the ability to recruit and pay outsider war captains for military and supernatural protection and to wage raids on their behalf.[11] Undoubtedly, the elevated status of war captains can be attributed to the increased circulation of capital. With a landscape now dotted with trading factories, raiding became a surefire way for war captains and their employers to consistently obtain cash, valuable commodities, and captives for labor, sale, or ransom. As political leaders formed competing coalitions, raiding became cyclical as both sides engaged in counter raids to recover stolen people and property. In the Sherbro, some war captains usurped the authority of their autochthon employers and established or seized control of important centers of trade. This new pattern of migration and settlement further fragmented the politics of the region, as increasing numbers of powerful strangers ruled important economic nodes along the rivers.

The circulation of imperial capital also forged new relationships of debt. When local traders exchanged palm oil or kernels for acquired European manufactured goods, they then distributed those items to smaller petty traders on credit. Known regionally as Sama, this practice placed a limited time until the debtor had to "repay" the loan. If they failed to do so, it would be forcefully collected through panyarring: the lawful seizure of people (usually the individual's family or their landlord) and goods during a raid to secure a debt.[12] While panyarring had existed in the interior prior to "legitimate commerce," the increased circulation of European goods and need for labor for the manufacture and transportation of palm produce undoubtedly expanded the practice.

Identifying the pervasive use of panyarring also likely explains why British subjects were so frequently raided. The collection of their landlords' debts (usually a trader themselves) would have allowed for the legitimate raiding, kidnapping, and ransoming of their tenants. The targeted kidnapping of Krios also could have been due to their perceived high status or wealth as raiders often used ransoming, the "release of a captive prior to enslavement for payment or cash in kind," to procure capital. Thus, while kidnapping was violent in the sense that debtors or their families were forcefully taken, as seen later in the chapter in the Jong, local leaders would have the opportunity to negotiate with the captor and offer payment to help regain the freedom of the captured party. Failed ransom negotiations or other forms of illegitimate raiding could contribute to escalating violence, especially when local communities went on the offensive to free their kin or seek revenge.[13]

These patterns of trading and raiding occurred frequently in the second half of the nineteenth century along the Jong River. With its large mouth located directly across from the colonial headquarters on Sherbro Island, the navigable waters of the Jong River became one of the central transportation corridors for the movement of goods from the interior to the coast. The twists and turns in this broad, brackish river created natural landing sites for small boats laden with palm oil and kernels.

The Jong River also contained branches to important east-west tributaries that connected it to other important rivers like the Small Boom River. For centuries, its shores were home to a diverse population of people from the interior seeking access to trade in fish, salt, and slaves.

Like other rulers in the Sherbro region, many autochthon Jong leaders found their leadership challenged by African newcomers' abilities to utilize new forms of capital to attract a wide range of clients and dependents. One of these emergent "Big Men" was an ethnically Sherbro man from the Imperri state named Tom Cabbie Smith. Described as "ambitious and avaricious," Smith built a considerable reputation as a wealthy trader in the early 1870s. After first working as a laborer for the Mendi Mission in Komendi on the Small Boom River, he moved to the town of Kambia in 1868 where, as an outsider, he made a landlord-stranger agreement with local leaders to establish a trading post.[14] Over time, Smith amassed the resources to maintain a significant number of clients and dependents with a diverse set of local allies and a considerable number of wives, including the daughter of a wealthy Anglo-African coastal trader with deep ancestral ties to the land.[15] In addition to these connections, Smith belonged to the region-wide coalition that included the Imperri, the Bompeh-Caulkers, and other powerful leaders in the upper and lower Boom River. The wealth he amassed in the palm trade allowed him to ensure physical protection for members of his coalition and his growing dependents, which included a number of prominent Krio traders. While it is unclear if he was a former war captain himself, Smith was reported to be a "moneyed man" who used his wealth to "buy war" as well as to fortify his town of Kambia on the Small Boom River with large palisades. His rise to power peaked in 1872 when he was granted the "sovereignty of the country." On the day of his election, it was reported that the "chamberlain of the late King" and other elders of the community presented Smith with a horse tail, the "emblem of empire," and proclaimed him King.[16]

In the wake of his coronation, Tom Cabbie Smith had every reason to bulk up his security measures. His rise to power was not celebrated by all. His primary opponent was a man named Lahai Serifoo, the second or third descendent of Muslim Susu traders who had settled in the lower Jong River region earlier in the nineteenth century. Like other strangers, his forefathers would have initially negotiated landlord-stranger agreements, perhaps even intermarrying into local communities or rising to prominence as their landlord's Speaker or Sub-Chief.[17] In the 1850s, Serifoo's father "King" Kissicummah established connections with American Missionary Society missionaries who paid him an annual rent of $100.

He also signed two treaties at mid-century, including the Treaty of 1861 as part of Thomas Stephen Caulker's coalition in his war with Canreba.[18]

Over time, this community of Muslim and other leaders became known as the Mongray. Mongray leaders independently formed enduring coalitions with neighboring leaders, such as the Kpaa-Mende. These partnerships were likely lucrative due to the Mongray leaders' connections to extensive caravan routes that extended farther north to the Futa Jallon.[19] The capital amassed by these networks produced enough wealth to hire their own war captains, including Bundooka of Gundema (described in the previous chapter) and Vangang, the leader of the raid on Mamaiah that opened this chapter. However, despite their long-standing settlement in the region, the Mongray Chiefs' refusal to join Poro on account of retaining their Islamic faith and other cultural markers likely branded them as perpetual outsiders. These factors would have prevented them from transitioning from strangers to owners of the land in the same way that Mende and other non-Muslim strangers had access too.

In 1874, tensions between Tom Cabbie Smith and Lahai Serifoo came to a head when a member of Serifoo's coalition, Lahai Gorey, fell into dispute with one of Smith's tenants over the ownership of some palm trees. A series of raids commenced, spiraling outwards as both leaders "applied" to their long-standing regional coalitions as distant as the upper Boom River for assistance.[20] Cabbie Smith found a willing alliance with the Imperri leaders, not just because this was his homeland, but because of the encroachment that Mongray leaders had made into their land as well.[21] Thus, by 1874, there existed multiple intertwined conflicts in the region that threated to destabilize the already falteringly imperial economy. To secure traders and routes, the colonial Government drew on a new series of protection schemes that would forever change the legal landscape of the region.

Paper Imperialism: Treaties of Peace and Commerce in the Sherbro

Throughout much of West Africa in the 1870s and 1880s, treaties and diplomacy centered on establishing "peace and commerce" became the primary strategy of the British administration for ending warfare in imperial hinterlands. In the words of Government Interpreter Thomas George Lawson, British policy centered on using "friendly and moral persuasion to avoid outbreaks."[22] The content of these agreements was largely driven by European wants and ambitions: the desire to create favorable economic conditions for the expansion of imperial capitalism, the abolition of the slave trade, or the legitimization of territorial control within the context of the scramble for Africa. These goals informed treaties' aims to impose a new legal code that would compel local leaders to protect British trade interests and its subjects outside of the limits of the formal Colony (often in exchange for a stipend or other benefits). The terms of these treaties sought to institute a particular brand of imagined imperial order that stabilized the agricultural market by diminishing signatories' ability to engage in warfare, mediate their own conflicts, or engage in African laws and customs that were believed to promote instability. Instead, signatories promised to settle all disputes through a "British Agent" or the Governor whose "decision between the disputants must be considered as final." As they would with legislation during indirect rule, colonial powers used treaties to secure local intermediaries' assistance in extending British policies beyond formal territorial jurisdiction. This strategy allowed them to extend their influence without incurring the costs or responsibilities of formal rule.

While claiming a policy of noninterference on the surface, individual treaty articles gradually introduced British criminal law into African sovereign territory.[23] According to treaty stipulations, African subjects who committed a "crime or offence that were cognizable to the laws of England," and were to be "surrendered" and "punished and tried" in British courts. This extradition of criminals, however, was not reciprocal as British subjects were increasingly protected by extraterritoriality, while African subjects were not. Clauses like "No country law or custom shall be enforced against British subjects or their property" essentially gave British Subjects (including Krios) legal immunity from African courts and legal practices. It is likely these types of articles in Sierra Leone initially aimed to counteract the practice of panyarring, which frequently led to theft and/or kidnapping of British subjects.[24] Instead, treaties compelled Krios and Indigenous residents to settle disputes and debts with British subjects in colonial courts in Bonthe.

While West African communities may not have defined protection in the same way as European empires, it was clearly a concept that was legible to both sides. The wider Sherbro region was guided by an unwritten constitution that articulated laws of protection for different members of the community. Legal forums existed at both the community and regional level and were generally adjudicated by judges whose authority was derived from their political or religious position. Evidence suggests that it was the Poro who traditionally settled regional conflicts like wars, jurisdictional conflict over territorial borders or cases of supernatural deviancy that went beyond the confines of a single town.[25] This two-tier judicial system of local and regional courts/forums operated as an effective system of checks and balances wherein the participation of multiple leaders ensured the legal protection and rights of this heterogenous and decentralized population.

In the case of war, it was said that when a Poro messenger appeared on a battlefield, all hostilities immediately stopped and the settlement of the conflict began.[26] Hundreds of leaders might travel from significant distances to, in local parlance, "hang heads" and settle the conflict. No matter how ethnically or regionally diverse a palaver of this size might be, Poro members and other delegates adhered to a respected set of precedents required for the negotiation and resolution of disputes. The concluding decision of a meeting of Poro elders, known in English as a "one-word-poro," indicates that a high premium was placed on debating multiple sides of a question and concluding with a full consensus of all members. Poro messengers then disseminated the final resolution to people with remarkable speed, so that all levels of Poro ranks throughout the region could adhere to its outcome.[27]

Poro peace palavers likely provided the foundation for African understanding of diplomatic talks and treaty signings with the British. Warfare and other threats to regional security clearly brought African leaders to this new negotiating table in an effort to find effective strategies to secure themselves and their communities' safety. Undoubtedly, the figure of the British official replicated the local practice of utilizing prominent strangers to mediate and broker peace. Likewise, when both sides agreed to the terms, they would swear on various medicines and religious objects that ensured supernatural consequences for breaking their oaths.[28] Thus, while some of the specific articles in British treaties may not have had an equivalent in African law, the diplomatic process and rituals of cementing that pact was understood by African actors. It seems reasonable, by extension, to assume that its terms were seen as acceptable, or at the very least, a potential means of securing the protection of their own political position and the safety of their community.

Perhaps predictably, early treaties of peace and commerce failed to put an end to war in Sherbro region. As economic conditions declined, warfare escalated. Increased import duties in the Colony elevated the wholesale cost of these goods in Freetown and Sherbro ports, prompting Krios to charge higher amounts for them in the interior.[29] The global depression in 1873 decreased the market price of palm produce and significantly devalued the cost of palm oil.[30] This resulted in a drop in exports. As the cost of importing manufactured goods increased and the value of palm produce decreased, the profit margins for Krio petty traders lessoned, simultaneously increasing the debts of local traders operating on credit. In this same period, the import duties on tobacco and spirits (two prominent trade items in the interior) were increased, while the time to make the duty payment was reduced from six months to three months. This shift in customs policies resulted in increased smuggling along the parts of the southern Sherbro coast that had not yet been annexed to avoid paying duties. These complex economic transformations escalated inter-community tensions, as African elites scrambled to shore up access to labor and resources along major rivers and palm-growing regions.

By 1875, correspondence reporting warfare and raids from every corner of the Sherbro hinterland piled up on colonial desks. As one historian put it, by this point "trade and war" became "complementary rather than alternative routes to power and status."[31] Warriors burned and pillaged rice farms, razed villages, and carried off hundreds of captives. Rivers were reported to be "staked," meaning that logs were laid across narrow channels to prevent produce and people from coming farther downriver, making them easier to capture the boats laden with produce. People, especially women and children, were kidnapped and killed, storehouses were raided, and many residents fled downriver to British territory and police stations seeking the security of British protection. Warfare between community leaders extended all the way from the coast to the interior as long-standing coalitions rallied to provide mutual aid and assistance for each other. Here, the old adage "the enemy of my enemy is my friend" rang true throughout the land, creating in the minds of colonial officials the "dominant impression of the Sherbro as . . . one of near anarchy."[32] Older grievances between coalitions mixed with new rivalries that emerged in the wake of the new cash economy, destabilizing the nascent palm trade and threatening the lives of both Indigenous and Krio residents alike.

Krio traders found themselves swept up in these conflicts over control of the rivers. In addition to members of the Parkinson and Taylor households, over fifty British subjects were reported kidnapped, over £5000 of goods had been plundered, and over one hundred villages had been burned in 1875 alone.[33] War commenced throughout the entire southern coastal and riverine region. To the north of Imperri, the Caulker family returned to their in-fighting ways. A man named John Caulker resumed Canreba's attempts to reunite the Kagbor Kingdom by hiring a Mende war captain named Kinigbo to raid his uncle George Stephen Caulker in Shenge. These actions spiraled into a regional war that encompassed Shenge, Bompeh, Bagru, and Kpaa-Mende, and at times even dipped into British Sherbro. To the west, leaders along the Boom River armed themselves with war captains who commenced a series of raids along these waterways.

These wars sent the Krio community into a tailspin. Traders demanded the British Government do something to combat these "marauders" whose "sole aim is to plunder the traders, who are principally British subjects."[34] Without intervention, they insisted, their lives and the "revenue of the Sherbro" were in grave peril. Freetown newspapers began to publish scathing attacks on the ineffectiveness of the administration to protect British subjects from these "rogues," "robbers," and "marauding savages." One article urged the colonial state to give "the natives the treatment they deserve" and to "convince them of the utter insignificance of their power."[35] Editorialists dismissed treaties as a "solemn farce . . . which experience has shown is utterly worthless in the estimation of the native," and instead, pushed for immediate military intervention.[36] After a series of raids along the Boom River, Krio J. A. Williams begged the Governor to intervene for the sake of the "friendly chiefs" whom they resided with who "have all along depended for protection [*sic*] on our Government against other Chiefs who were antagonistic to them."[37] Another trader, Mr. Maurice, was more forceful in his requests, insisting that both Krio traders and African leaders had "every right to look for protection" given the treaty agreements that they had entered into with the British crown.[38] Supporting the demands of these letters and editorials, three hundred merchants, traders, shopkeepers, and skilled laborers joined forces and submitted a petition urging the Governor to annex the "entire seaboard and adjacent native countries."[39]

In the midst of Krio demands for protection, some African signatories tried to use their treaty connections with the colonial Government as leverage in these conflicts.[40] Returning to the raid on Mamaiah in June 1875, we can see how the two sides of the Tom Cabbie Smith and Lahai Serifoo conflict varied in their utilization of the treaty agreements they made in 1874. While twenty-nine leaders from both sides of the conflict had signed the treaty, the different responses of each signatory to the attack provide a lens through which to understand their perceived vulnerability during the current escalation of war.

After the attack on the Taylor and Parkinson households, both Lahai Serifoo and his ally Lahai Gorey received letters from the Government sternly reminding them of the treaty obligations they had made to protect British subjects, urging them to return the captives and goods and the "speedy arrest" of Vangang and his men.[41] Serifoo apologized to the Commandant, insisting that it was not his intention for the

"the war to go into the Queen's land" or capture the "Queen's people" in Mamaiah, though he did confess he had instructed Vangang and his men to raid the warehouse in Tom Cabbie Smith's town of Kambia outside of British jurisdiction.[42] He informed the Commandant that he had recovered some of the captives and goods from the Mamaiah raid who were now in his town of Mongray. In a clear effort to try and gain the diplomatic upper hand over his rival, Serifoo told the Commandant that Smith had recently sent one of his primary war men, Morry Lasarn, to "buy war" in the northern part of Bagru (likely within colonial territory) and that Smith's coalition of "Impereh Folkes" had violated one of the primary stipulations of the treaty by blockading the river and preventing trade from coming down. In his second letter he wrote that he was "everyday ready for peace" but that "Tom Cabby [*sic*] Smith is the identical person who refuses peace, my river was blockaded by him."[43]

Tom Cabbie Smith and his coalition of Imperri leaders firmly denied Lahai Serifoo's accusations. They insisted that it was he who had broken the conditions of the treaty by entering British territory and kidnapping Imperri women and children who had travelled there to be "under the protection of the British Government." Imperri leaders argued that not only should the colonial Government assist them militarily because of their treaty agreements, but because the land that Lahai Serifoo and his allies occupied "is ours in all respects, and we own its rights since the strangers prove ungrateful both to ourselves and to Her Majesty's Government . . . Mongray is a land that belonged to us, but was given to those people to be inhabited, as they were strangers to our elder people." In a separate letter, Tom Cabbie Smith reiterated the Imperri leaders' claims that the Mongray leaders were strangers, proclaiming that the "Mongray people are deceivers and plunderers." In a statement reminiscent of Thomas Stephen Caulker in 1861, Imperri leaders informed the Commandant that after meeting for a few days the previous week, they were collectively "determined to give up the Mongrayland to the British Government"—a statement that encompassed both an act of loyalty to the Crown and the bold assertion that they alone had the rightful authority to cede this section of land. Smith stated that "I and my allies are truly friends to the British Government and the Queen in anything . . . I am willing if the British Government will drive away the Mongray people from my country and then the country will be in peace."[44] This correspondence marks a pivotal shift in claim making that would continue into the Protectorate period. Autochthon treaty signatories increasingly used their ancestral lineage to claim rights to the land and mark "strangers" like Lahai Serifoo as mere "war captains" or outsiders who gained their position through illegitimate or immoral methods. In doing so, they created a new feature of legitimate authority in the eyes of the colonial state.

Military Expeditions and Punitive Measures

With war raging and trade at a standstill, a new Governor arrived in the Colony. Known as "old red breeches" by local people for the British military uniform he often wore while travelling in the interior, Dr. Samuel Rowe was remembered after his death as "rough but kindly, and unconventional in his habits of life."[45] Rowe fought in the Ashanti Wars in 1873 and had extensive experience as a magistrate, military doctor, and army captain in Lagos, the Gold Coast, and Gambia since 1866 and had been bestowed with several awards for his role in conflicts there. Drawing from what he believed was his strong understanding of the "African mind," Rowe brought a style of leadership that was a mix of benevolent paternalism and violent symbolism. His presence and policies would have a long-lasting impact on the legal framework in the region.

In response to raids along the borders of British territory, Rowe launched two unprecedented military campaigns to recover captives and capture those who had waged war in proximity to British jurisdiction. He and his men penetrated farther into the interior than any military campaign before it. Ignoring the advice of Lahai Serifoo, Rowe made his way up the Jong River to Mongray where he perhaps saw his first walled town. Sensing their importance, Rowe quickly made the destruction of stockades a hallmark of his campaigns, later incorporating their mandatory destruction into the articles of treaties and agreements he penned. Rowe explained to Lahai Serifoo that his actions were not intended to "hurt his people or his towns, but that [he] had come prepared for war, and was determined that the whole of them should thoroughly understand that, whatever their personal feuds may be, they must, in making their wars, take care not to infringe on the limits of British territory and respect the protection of the British flag."[46] While in the Jong, Rowe recovered all but two of the forty British subjects who had been kidnapped in the Jong and Mongray River, including Mrs. Parkinson, and returned to Bonthe to the great approval of the Krio public.[47] Returning from the Jong, he then travelled to the Bompeh, again burning village after village and tearing down stockaded towns.[48] He arrested John Caulker and two of his main war captains, claiming they were responsible for killing a colonial police officer and wounding Commandant Darnell

Davis in battle. Despite being the King of the Kpaa-Mende, and a clear colonial ally, Rowe had Gbanyah publicly whipped for allowing his people to take part in the war.[49] Upon reflecting on the events of 1875, Rowe stated that his primary intention was "to get the inhabitants to meet me, to see our force, and form some idea of it and of us, with a view to future peace."[50]

The treaties and agreements that concluded these two 1875 military campaigns were markedly different from those before. Treaties demanded the destruction of all walled towns, "fines" in the form of bushels of rice to "reimburse the colonial state" for the campaign, and the forced cession of the Shenge and Bompeh "the seaboard over which they have authority."[51] In May of 1876, more than thirty prominent leaders from throughout the region arrived in Bonthe and signed an "Agreement" drafted by Rowe himself. In it, the leaders publicly "begged for forgiveness" for "the insult offered by us to [the Queen] in thus disregarding the solemn promises" they had made in previous treaty signings.[52] The consequences of future disobedience laid out in the agreement left little room for interpretation: any person who signed the treaty and subsequently broke his word:

> shall be considered an enemy of the Queen's . . . [and] shall be considered to have forfeited his right to the government of his country . . . remove him from his government, confining him to Freetown or such other place as she may be pleased to assign, or punishing him in such other way as may seem good to her and taking possession of his country, which shall from that date become the Queen's country; or appointing another person to govern it according as she shall see fit.[53]

These terms established a new legal order that sanctioned the removal of signatories from their position if their actions ran contrary to British interests, establishing the prominent use of exile and deposing in the years ahead.

While diplomatic agreements like this are often viewed as a tool of European imperialism, the African leaders who signed these types of treaties clearly had their own reasons for agreeing to these more stringent terms. Some of this can be better understood by more deeply examining the names, towns, and ethnic breakdown of the leaders who agreed to these agreements and who did not. Of the thirty-four signatories of the Agreement of 1876, twenty-three signatories were ethnically Sherbro, while only eight were Mende, one was Foulah, one was Susu, and one is unknown.[54] Considering that ethnically Sherbro people made up only a small fraction of the overall population, the fact that they were the majority of signatories

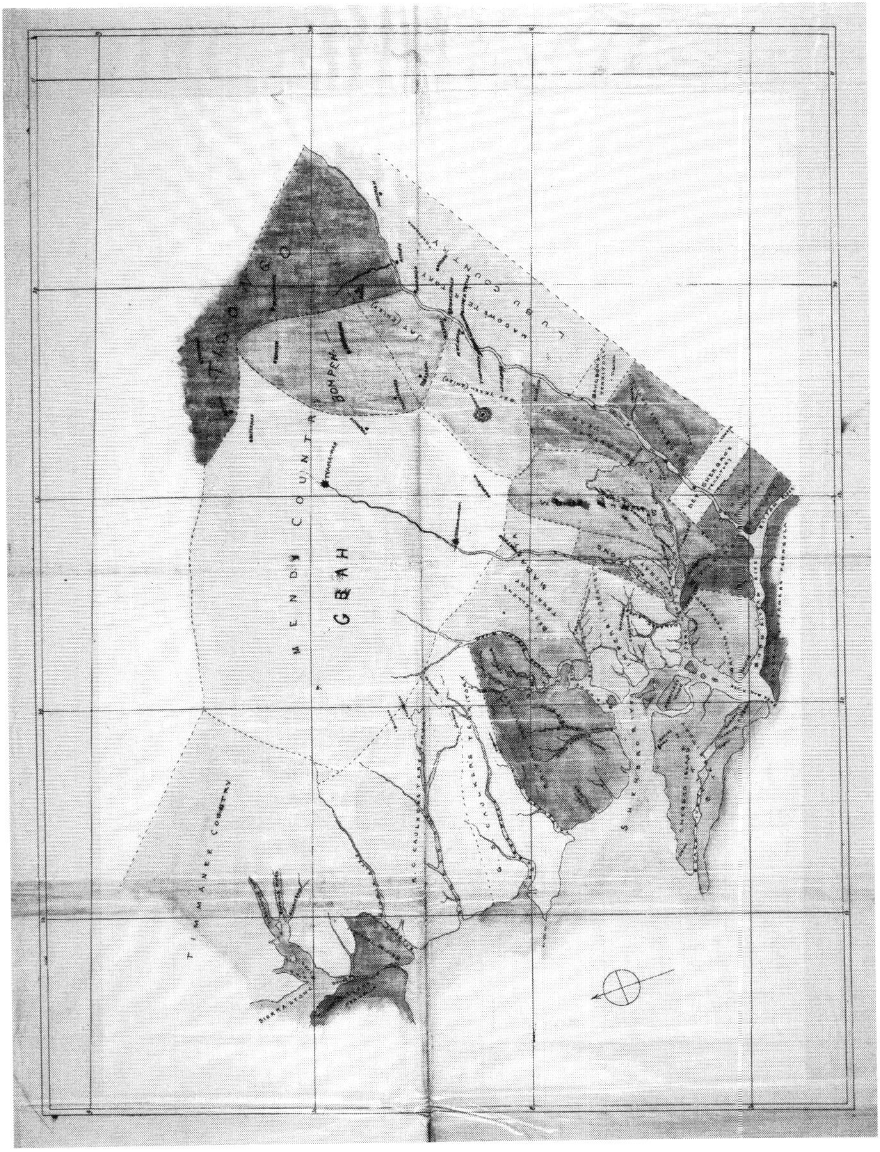

FIGURE 5. Sketch map of Sherbro Provinces and Beyond, 1876.

SOURCE: GOVERNOR ROWE TO COLONIAL OFFICE. MAY 13, 1876. BNA/CO 267/329/6908.

to this agreement sheds light on their waning political authority in the region. By charting their towns of origin, signatories also reveal the unevenness of colonial law and violence. Leaders who signed the agreement were predominantly from towns located in the four most strategic trading regions outside of British jurisdiction: the upper Bagru and Bompeh, the upper Boom River, Imperri province, and the Jong and Small Boom River region. As just over a third of the leaders who signed the agreement had never signed a treaty before, their participation also demonstrates how rapidly treaty making had expanded as a tool of political leverage against their competitors. From 1876 onwards, the majority of the "aligned" leaders were those who were unable to marshal the resources to fight back against an ever-growing confederacy in the interior that sought to displace imperial encroachment.

Signing the Agreement of 1876 was also a strategic way of solidifying the borders of individual leaders' territory. In a unique and fascinating map that accompanied the agreement to the Colonial Office in London, the dotted borders and colored zones indicate each titular or territorial province in the greater Sherbro region (figure 5). This geographic representation of the Sherbro is the only one of its kind in either the British or Sierra Leone Archives. In this map, almost every river and tributary is neatly labelled, as are towns situated alongside their banks. These identifiers confirm the centrality of rivers, visually reminding us of the uneven nature of British penetration outside the limits of formal jurisdiction. Similar maps from the period also focus on the political and topographies of rivers, highlighting them as economic and information highways from the coast to the interior.

Like treaties, sketch maps like this are rare snapshots of precolonial political and physical geography that were created through a collaboration between colonial officials and African leaders. In this way, we are reminded how colonial knowledge was contingent on the participation of African intermediaries. The map and the Agreement of 1876 exist in conversation with each other and shed further insight on the way territorial jurisdiction was claimed and contested amid intense political fragmentation.[55]

The final notable feature of this sketch map is the significant reduction of land marked "British Territory" when compared to the map of British Sherbro made in 1861 we saw in the previous chapter. By the mid-1870s, British territory appears confined to the region south of the Yaltucker River and bordered on the south and east of Bagru.[56] The most obvious difference is the status of Imperri. Despite it being clearly within the boundaries in the 1861 treaty in both the description of territory and signatories, it is probable that the strong coalition the Imperri had with neighboring communities like the Bompeh-Caulkers either prevented the British from establishing a firm control over the area or afforded them the advantage of not having to rely on the British for protection.[57]

From War Captains to Political Prisoners

While Governor Rowe's scorched earth campaigns left a considerable mark on the physical landscape, the political and legal fallout of his military expeditions were even more long-lasting. For the first time, leaders in the interior witnessed the firepower of the colonial state and the distance they were willing to go to protect their subjects outside the limits of British jurisdiction. For the first time since Whobay's trial in 1870, this included the use of capital punishment. To demonstrate to the crowd how any future enemy of the Crown would "be dealt with," Rowe publicly executed John Caulker and two of his war captains in makeshift gallows erected in Bonthe during the signing of the 1876 agreement. After their executions, Rowe made examples of three more "criminals" by taking them into British custody. The Chiefs of the Jong handed over Vangang, the man identified by Mrs. Taylor as the leader of the raid on Mamaiah the year before.[58] The second was Fahjongobah, a war captain who had been leading raids along the Boom River.[59] The leaders in the upper Boom River also handed over the man considered to be the most "notorious ruffian" of them all—Cannagboh: who had been an accomplice to Whobay and Ansumana Lolme six years prior during the raids on Bundooka.

The incarceration of these African subjects in British jails without a trial or formal charges was a pivotal moment in the legal history of the Sierra Leone hinterland. British military engagement allowed for the legal transformation of "war captains" into "political prisoners," a term that provided a legally cogent (at least, in the minds of British officials) solution for the ever-persistent problem of detaining non-British subjects in British custody.[60] The term "political prisoner" represents a shift in British definition of raiding as no longer a mere war between African communities, but a politically motivated act akin to sedition against the British state. As treaty making integrated British officials deeper into African conflicts, the number of "small wars" outside of colonial territory escalated.[61] The arrest and incarceration of these men was legitimated as part of the "state of exception" that occurred during active military campaigns.[62] The creation of this new category of prisoner ensured the legal and physical protection of British subjects and the imperial economy.

The incarceration of war captains was not only a tool of British imperialism. Close examination of the archives reveal how African leaders utilized this treaty stipulation as a tool to protect their own political sovereignty. "Delivering up" their rivals to the British became a strategy for vulnerable treaty signatories to rid themselves of their competitors, as well as demonstrate their "civilized" nature by participating in British law. Men who were delivered up to colonial authorities often came from difficult-to-reach areas, reminding us that their incarceration would have been impossible without the assistance of aligned African leaders. Letters to the colonial Government from local leaders specifically cite that they were turning over these "enemies" rather than using their own legal practices to punish them—a clear adherence to the more punitive treaty articles enacted after 1876. Through these processes, the legal culture of the region shifted, as British legal ideas and institutions were increasingly enfolded into strategies of African politics and warfare.

Colonial debates over the incarceration and eventual deportation of Sierra Leone's "political prisoners" represented the improvisational nature of imperialism on colonial frontiers. They reflected a blend of on-the-spot cultural and legal ideas about what rights non-British subjects living in "uncivilized spaces" had vis-à-vis the crown. Without legal rights or a formal trial, political prisoners were incarcerated for an undetermined amount of time. While a few eventually returned home, others were permanently deported to other British colonies in West Africa and died in exile. While the Governor of Sierra Leone admitted that the practice was "somewhat ultra vires," colonial officials in London condoned it in the name of imperial interests, stating that while the "proceedings . . . would be high-handed and unjustifiable in more civilized places [they] are sometimes necessary and must be overlooked in West Africa where wars which extend over large areas are ruined to trade, and the interests of our settlements, arise from such very small matters."[63]

By 1882, at least five African subjects who had committed crimes outside British territory were sitting in the Freetown jail as political prisoners.[64] Mapping where political prisoners came from and what leaders delivered them up shows that the majority were from the contentious trade corridors that lay along various jurisdictional boundaries. One of these leaders who participated in delivering up prisoners was Gbanyah who sought to align himself with the British to garner support for the Kpaa-Mende's territorial expansion westward into the Bompeh province. After his death in 1878, his heir Kong and his widow Madam Yoko continued this legacy by handing over two men who were aligned with King of Bompeh, Richard Canreba Caulker. In doing so, Kong was praised for showing a "great forbearance and a loyal desire to carry out the wishes of the Government by waiting patiently for a peaceful solution of the difficulty instead of taking the law into their own hands and making reprisals. This conduct is indeed the more praiseworthy by the fact that the Mendis, the tribe to which Chief Kong belongs, are warlike and quite able by force to maintain their rights and avenge their wrongs."[65]

The Kpaa-Mende leaders' attempts to position themselves as legitimate leaders in Bompeh occurred amidst renewed conflicts among Caulker family members. John Caulker's failed attempt to overthrow George Stephen Caulker of Shenge was taken up by his cousin William, a literate and litigious trader who had worked as a middleman for several prominent Krio and British mercantile houses. When William attempted a legal approach to dethrone George Stephen by accusing him of violating treaties and plundering British subjects, George Stephen had him arrested and bolted to a short wooden cross in a "dilapidated house" where he was "exposed to the rain and dew of Heaven for a full month."[66] After a great deal of debate, George Stephen and his other Sub-Chiefs agreed that handing William over to the Governor was the "best way of punishing him" and urged the Governor to execute him.[67] With the death of George Stephen shortly thereafter, his brother Thomas Neale Caulker was crowned leader of the Shenge by the British, despite protests that he had no valid claim to the title.[68] Although eventually released from prison in 1882, William's persistence in overthrowing the Shenge-Caulkers led to another arrest in 1888. This time, after a long and much publicized trial, he was executed in Freetown with some of his accomplices, while Richard Canreba Caulker was exiled to Gambia.

Delivering up war captains became a pervasive strategy for leaders to solidify diplomatic relations with the British administration and rid themselves of their competitors. Bound by treaty stipulations that prevented them from engaging in warfare, local leaders increasingly turned to British policing and prisons to obtain protection for themselves and their Krio tenants.[69] Of note, leaders who delivered up prisoners were those whose vulnerability required them to remain in the good graces of the colonial state. By the 1880s, the outward demonstrations of loyalty and support of British interests became increasingly important as regional leaders sought to consolidate their political rule. In the Jong, this resulted in a pitched battle between internal coalitions over who would ultimately claim the title of King—or Queen.

The "Rightful Owners of the Land": Queen Betsy Gaye, Lahsurrhu, and the Conflict over Mattru

Located on a bank about forty feet above the riverbank, the town of Mattru on the Jong River has a long and contested history. At the beginning of the nineteenth century, Mattru became inhabited by a group of Mende "refugees" who were said to have violated a law of a secret society in a town named Palima in the upper Boom River region. They settled there under a landlord-stranger agreement with the Do Farma, the titular leader of Mattru.[70] Upon their settlement, the Palima migrants tried to wrest control of the town, eventually making a deal with the titular leader of the Jong province, the Sei Kama, for them to remain.[71]

At mid-century, Mattru contained a diverse population of Mende, Muslim, Sherbro, and Krio people that reflected its importance in the palm oil trade. While its leader was listed as Bah Yegmbe in the Treaty of 1874, by 1879 leadership had reportedly been transferred to a man named Alikari, a Muslim. Colonial officials remarked that his legal and political authority was limited to the town and neighboring fakais, but that larger court cases were handled by the Sei Kama.[72] Alikari's rule over the town was a likely reflection of the consolidation of Muslim (Foulah and Susu) power in the region that resulted in the formation of Mongray.

By 1882 a man named Lahsurrhu was described as having "lately taken ascendency in the country" as headman of Mattru. Described as "a maker of charms and amulets, and is thought to possess supernatural powers . . . [whose] chief occupation is the organization and direction of marauding parties," Lahsurrhu was well known to the British administration.[73] During the treaty signing of 1874, he had been awarded a yearly stipend of "200 bars" for his "assistance and forbearance" in making peace during the conflict between Tom Cabbie Smith and Lahai Serifoo.[74] However, by 1881, Krio traders informed the Commandant that Lahsurrhu and his son had been enforcing a series of embargoes that had been enacted in the Poro bush that were "preventing them from pursuing our legitimate trade," threatening to

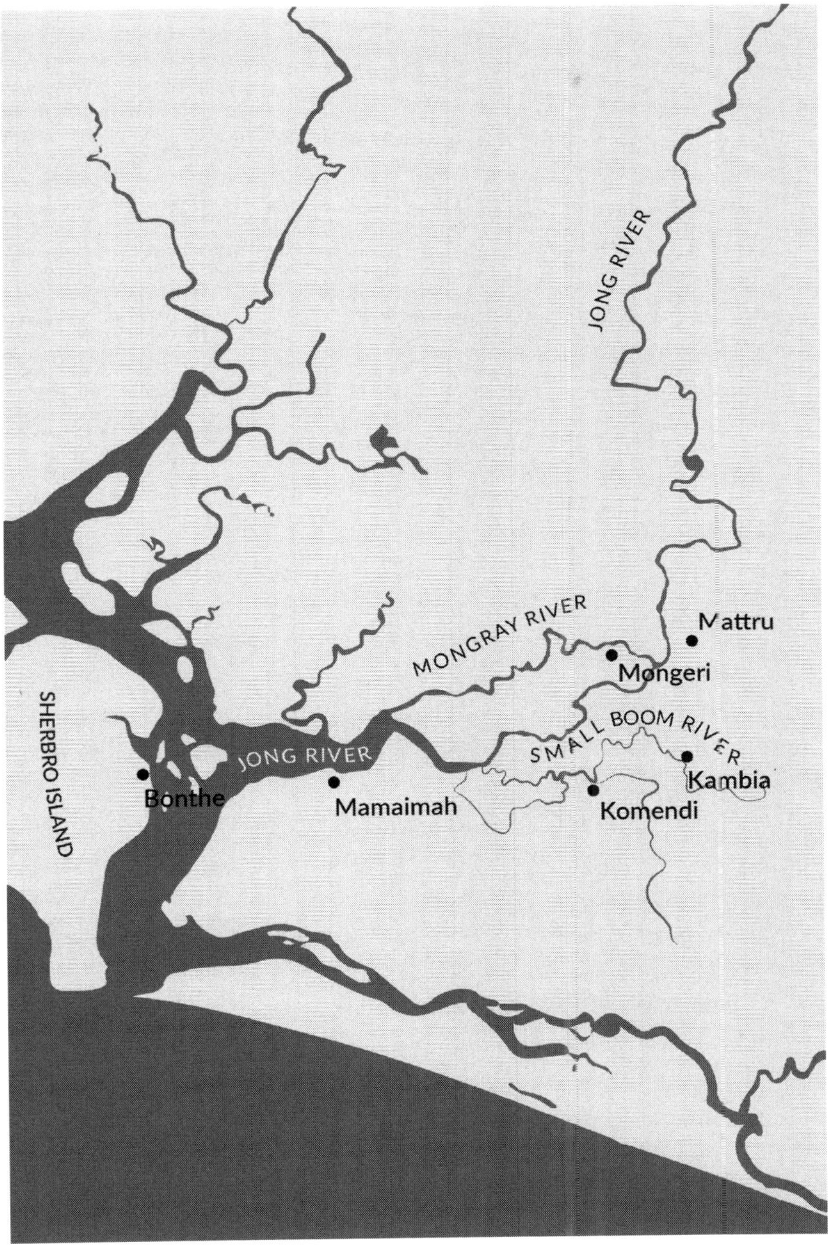

FIGURE 6. Major rivers and towns in the Jong region, circa 1882.

sell local laborers if they did work for them: "no one is to sell us even a fish on pain of being sold as a slave."[75] They reported to the Governor that these threats had their "desired effect, as there is not a single workman to be seen in all our places today."[76]

News of this trade embargo was accompanied by a letter informing the Government that leaders in Mattru were planning on crowning a new Sei Kama in April 1882. The invitation to this coronation was a surprise to the colonial Government and many living in the Jong River, as a King had already been reportedly crowned in the Jong River two years prior.[77] In particular, the events in Mattru appear to have alarmed an emerging new leader named Betsy Gaye who appeared on the Jong political scene in the wake of Tom Cabbie's death in 1878. Upon hearing about the formation of a Poro to elect a King in Mattru in early 1882, Gaye wrote a strongly worded letter to both Lahai Serifoo and Thomas Cleveland warning them to cease their actions and support her rule. The letter in its entirety reads as follows:

> Gentlemen,
> I herewith write this for your information that the Jong country which you are now inhabiting is my country, which I claim by right of my grandparents of which you are all aware, and that you were only strangers to them. But from the frequent wars in the country, my late mother deemed it necessary after the last war between Tom Kebbee and the Mongray territory to propose crowning a king (as she was very old) and that by crowning a king with the assistance of the British Government would create peace and a permanent peace in this country. But it appears you do not like her motive, owning to your dishonest practices, and many other proposals which my late mother put before you and on behalf of the British Government which you always oppose. And now you have made a "Purroh" without my notice, which I know for certain is a symptom of war. I now write this for your information that two days from this date I shall proceed to British Sherbro and report your conduct to the British Government and to come and take possession of my country claiming their protection, and that myself and all my families are in jeopardy. . . . So you can prepare yourselves to oppose me, that is, if you have more right to the Jong country.[78]

Little is known about Betsy Gaye's origins, but archival evidence suggests she was likely the daughter of Tom Cabby Smith and his head wife Kaifray Rigbah, though it is unclear who the "grandparents" are she refers to in the above letter.[79] By 1882, it is clear she had come to see herself as the rightful heir to the region. Her assertion that she will "claim their protection" by asking the British to "take possession of" a certain area of territory mirrors the language of the Imperri leaders in 1875, further suggesting that she had ties with that coalition. By claiming ties to this ancestral lineage, she used both political and kinship networks to curry favor with the British by drawing on a now well-established strategy of casting herself as the "rightful" leader amidst a group of strangers intent on disrupting trade and making war.

In September, Commandant Laborde arrived in Mattru accompanied by many British and Krio traders and police to present a gift to the newly elected King.[80] When he was told that the newly crowned King was still secluded in the Poro bush, Laborde decided to give an impromptu speech about the benefits of British rule. This speech was interrupted by the "heckles" of a man named "Mormordoo," identified in one account as the son of the newly crowned Sei Kama. Ordering Mormordoo to be arrested for his insolence, the men from the village told Laborde that he could not arrest anybody without the "sanction of their chief." At some point, Mormordoo was released by the crowd and his handcuffs were "beaten almost to a powder." At this point, the King emerged from the Poro bush and asked what the "uproar" was about and was "surprised to hear that the Commandant tried to arrest one unlawfully."[81] Laborde rushed back to the ship and found that his goods had been seized and that his boatsmen had been beaten. Fearing for his life, he escaped in a canoe and made his way back to Bonthe.

The Commandant was furious. He wrote Governor Havelock, accusing the people of Mattru of a "deliberate and prearranged plan." Several weeks later, the Governor arrived in Sherbro. Havelock, Laborde, Captain Henry Jackson, thirty-four constables, an interpreter, and a clerk set off up the Jong River. When they arrived in Mattru, they demanded Lahsurrhu answer for his and his people's actions. In one account of the event, Havelock was reported to have demanded that all "Natives surrender unarmed, otherwise he would destroy them and their country." When several men, including Lahsurrhu, boarded his ship, he reportedly tried to make them "prisoners of the state" and ordered them to "throw down their arms and kneel before them."[82] Amidst this chaos, a growing group of more than two hundred men armed with cutlasses, guns, and swords gathered. In the midst of the chaos, an undetermined shot was fired from the African crowd, and one of the constables shouted, "I am hit." Colonial forces opened fire on the African troops and community, launching rockets into the bush.

What followed was an attack aimed at shattering the political and legal framework of Mattru. A trader reported that the Governor gave orders for the destruction of the town and purposefully ordered that the Poro bush, "a place held sacred and where laws are always made," be destroyed. The result was a grisly scene where "no end of [the villagers] fell as victims to the devouring fire which burnt down the grove by the explosion of these destructive instruments of European warfare."[83] During this commotion, several of the prisoners escaped from the guardsmen, with only Lahsurrhu being recaptured.[84] He returned to Freetown with Governor Havelock and was locked in the Freetown jail. His incarceration as a former treaty signatory marked his demonstration of loyalty to the Sei Kama rather than Governor Havelock as seditious against the British crown.

As Lahsurrhu sat in the Freetown prison awaiting his fate, Betsy Gaye, Steven Cleveland, and several other leaders of the Jong River wrote to the Governor to express their deep regret for what had happened at the coronation and to ask for protection from the British Government. Therein, the authors of the letter strategically reiterated Gaye's earlier claims that they were the "rightful owners" of the land. The leaders reasserted that Lahsurrhu, Lahai Serifoo, and the other men who engaged in violence on Mattru were "strangers" to their land, whose "sole object seems to be to attain their personal advantages at any risk, to our great danger, because, ourselves, we are not powerful enough to expel them from the country."[85] Under traditional landlord-stranger laws, this break in loyalty to ones patron would have constituted the removal of the tenant (or non-renewal of their tenancy agreement), but the shift in the balance of power in the region prevented them from doing so. Nevertheless, even if they could muster up the funds to "buy war," the punitive measures now embedded in their treaty promises and the arrest of Lahsurrhu, signaled that retaliation was extremely risky. The paradox of protection was in full effect: limited by the threat of detention and being deposed from their positions, aligned treaty signatories were compelled to solicit the protection of the colonial state, or risk ending up the Freetown jail themselves.

Gaye and the other leaders' request for formal protection initiated a colonial debate on the limits and nature of British jurisdiction in the Jong. In search of a way to exercise dominion without formal colonization, Law Officers in England returned to the question of "Turner's Treaty," the 1825 treaty signed between Governor Turner and the "King of the Sherbro" which reportedly ceded a strip of the coastal area of Sherbro between Bendu and the mouth of the Kittam River. Although the treaty was rejected by Parliament in 1825 and never ratified, Governor Rowe insisted that the treaty ought to be recognized as though it had been. Though offering no proof for his claim, his justification was that political relations between the colonial administration and leaders in the region had continued as though it were valid, as African leaders had not been informed of Parliament's rejection of the agreement.

When Havelock asked the Governor Interpreter Thomas George Lawson to investigate the matter, Lawson insisted that Turner's Treaty omitted no part of the Sherbro region, including the Jong and its neighboring countries. Lawson justified this position through his understanding of local political structures, stating that "all the Chiefs in those places are tributary chiefs under the late Bey Sherbro who was considered the Supreme King over the whole of the Sherbro country."[86] Following Lawson's analysis, the Colonial Office concluded that there could be little debate: the Jong and Small Boom River region were part of the original 1825 treaty. Havelock was directed to explain to Betsy Gaye and other leaders that they were "already substantially in the position they desire . . . [and could] continue to enjoy the benefits of that position so long as they behave properly."[87] In one fell swoop, their land was annexed without a formal treaty, joining the hazy jurisdiction of "British Sherbro."

While the reinstatement of the Treaty of 1825 technically ceded even more territory under British rule, the Colonial Office privately warned Havelock that he was to "avoid increasing in any way our responsibilities in that quarter, and you should caution the Commandant of British Sherbro to have as little as possible to do with the affairs of the people in question."[88] Much like the Sherbro territory annexed in 1861 and the western coast that was ceded after Rowe's military campaign in 1875, the Jong and Small Boom River became a flexible legal space in which colonial administrators could acknowledge the land as British territory when convenient, but otherwise ignore it to avoid any financial or political responsibility.

For Jong leaders, placing themselves under the protection of the British state was a political gamble that they likely believed still favored them. Within a few years, Betsy Gaye began to consolidate her political authority over the entire Jong region. After making Mattru her primary residence, she frequently corresponded with the colonial Government on personal letterhead that proclaimed her "Queen of the Jong." While her rivalry with the Mongray appears to have been momentarily ceased after the death of Lahai Serifoo in 1884, renewed challenges to her rule were not over.[89] Ruling until her death in 1901, Gaye remained in power by securing a number of important Krio and Indigenous allies through trade and marriage to her daughters, while continually using her connection with the colonial state as leverage against those who threatened her position.

Conclusion

As Betsy Gaye ascended to power in the Jong, her enemy Lahsurrhu remained incarcerated in the Freetown prison. His six-year confinement and the shock and awe campaign launched against the town of Mattru forged a violent precedent that legitimated the burning of villages, murder of civilians, and deposing and deportation of anyone seen as disloyal or disruptive to British interests. After 1882, this practice was repeated in the upper Boom River when several central towns and villages were utterly destroyed by British forces; one campaign was so violent that it sparked an inquiry by the British Parliament.[90]

Breaking treaty stipulations became regarded as a demonstration of extreme disloyalty equivalent to treason. The evolution of this type of "protection talk" legitimated extra-legal practices that ultimately became woven into the judicial and legislative fabric of indirect rule itself.[91] Leaders who aligned themselves with the British hoping for physical and political protection were rendered even more vulnerable to colonial violence and territorial dispossession. In this way, treaties of peace and commerce produced even *more* insecurity by compelling signatories to refrain from retributive attacks, forcing them to tear down the walled fences around their towns, limit mediation to the Government, and protect and house British subjects and colonial police. Thus, while imperial alliances aided in consolidating autochthon political rule in coastal provinces like the Jong, this same political and territorial centralization ironically laid the foundation for their turbulent incorporation into the Protectorate.

Even as regional warfare subsided, British protection schemes intensified colonial involvement in Sherbro's coastal and riverine communities. As British law and policing increasingly clashed with African jurisprudence, a series of debates concerning the legitimacy of African legal authority and judicial procedures emerged. Although outside British jurisdiction, British officials' disregard and disdain for African courts allowed them to utilize the language of protection to justify further intervention in Imperri, the last independent coastal province in the Sherbro. British intervention in African law and courts on the frontier would have far-reaching impacts in the final decade before the Protectorate was declared, setting the stage for the criminalization of traditional ways of prosecuting "human leopards" in African courts.

CHAPTER THREE

African Courts and Tongo Trials

The Jurisdiction of Human Leopard Murder Cases, 1882–1892

In early 1890, rumors circulated throughout the town of Gbangbaia that a young boy had been attacked and killed by a "human leopard." Whispers throughout the town indicated that the boy had been taken at night by men who were dressed like or had shape-shifted into leopards and then killed the boy with a large, five-pronged, claw-shaped knife. The boy had been a member of the prominent African missionary and community leader Daniel Flickinger Wilberforce's household. The boy's death signaled the need for a new kind of protection against powerful antisocial medicines that threatened the lives and legitimacy of community leaders across the region.

Human leopards combined two prevalent fears that were deeply embedded in local culture: the established idea of shape-shifting witchcraft and the "harmful ritual action by malefactors."[1] While the belief that certain people possessed the supernatural ability to transform into animals had long existed in Sierra Leone, the death of the boy was attributed to a new medicine society of "human leopards," whose access to power objects bestowed supernatural sources of wealth and influence. The power object, or *hale nyamui* ("bad medicine") of what came to be known as the Human Leopard Society was the *borfima*. To maintain its strength, it was said the borfima had to be ritually recharged or "fed" through a process known as *boni hinda*, or "cannibal business" (Krio), a form of ritual murder to obtain human body parts or fluid to keep the borfima potent.[2] Rumors also suggested that members of the society also consumed the body of the ritual murder victim. It was said that once a member of a "cannibal society" consumed human flesh, they must be the next to offer up someone "he or she 'owns' [like a] slave, ward, or consanguineous descendent" as the next victim.[3] Like panyarring or Satta, the time limits placed on settling "debts" created a cyclical pattern of insecurity and violence as members were required to offer up new "victims."[4] The pervasive fear that women and children could be randomly snatched from the bush, road, field, or riverside recalled acts of kidnapping during recent warfare and raids that targeted the same vulnerable populations.[5]

The rise of the Human Leopard Society in the 1880s coincided with two important shifts in the political and economic landscape in southern Sierra Leone. The first was the firm establishment of the palm produce trade. This shift to "legitimate commerce" elevated the importance of domestic labor (most especially women and enslaved people), the circulation of hard cash, and securing land use for cultivation purposes. People purchased or captured in raids were settled in small communities outside of prominent towns called *fakkis*. There they would produce cash crops to sell on the open market or to finance warriors for additional protection. The second was a decline in regional warfare. While individual raiding was still reported, the increased use of colonial military forces, annexation of the coastal region, and pervasiveness of treaty making had broken up many regional coalitions. The combination of these two factors elevated the status of local African "Big Men" whose wealth enabled them to acquire and protect large numbers of dependents. As we saw in the previous chapter, this process challenged autochthon community leaders' authority that was traditionally derived from their ancestral connections to founding families or lineages. New emphasis on economic extraction exacerbated tensions between Big Men and traditional leaders in the riverine and coastal areas over land and labor.

These factors were highly woven into the emergence of the Human Leopard Society. While the connection between leopardism and Big Men continues to be debated among scholars, it seems clear that allegations of leopardism were directed at people suspected of hoarding wealth and "undermining society through excessive individualism."[6] Like other "new" forms of supernatural deviance that emerged in Africa in the late nineteenth and early twentieth century, human leopards represented the "embodiments of predation and of the 'cannibalistic' consumption of human productive and reproductive potential" that resulted from the alienation of labor, social consequences of a cash economy, and rural integration into global markets.[7] In southern Sierra Leone, incidents of human leopard murder were concentrated in regions that contained dense palm-rich forests, central transportation corridors like roads and rivers, and high levels of competition among Indigenous traders and between themselves and Krios merchants.

Beginning in the early 1880s, the frequency of these murders across the region prompted legal action by community elders. Drawing from a long tradition of ordealing in African courts to determine defendant's guilt, leaders hired a group known as the Tongo to use their esoteric knowledge and specialized divination skills to determine who was a human leopard.[8] For Sherbro leaders, seeking out and eliminating human leopards protected themselves and their communities. As human leopards were also frequently Big Men traders who challenged their rule, hiring the Tongo was a crucial protection strategy for retaining traditional leaders' access to land and political authority.

Clashes between Britons and Africans over these "supernatural detectives" produced a jurisdictional crisis that proved as difficult to solve as the persistent warfare in the decades before. From 1882 to 1892, the adjudication of human leopards in African courts by the Tongo was denounced by colonial officials as counter to treaty agreements and analogous to British crimes like fraud and larceny. British officials considered the execution through immolation as an act of "repugnancy" like other "inhumane" cultural or legal practices they criminalized in other imperial spaces.[9] Additionally, like the execution of war captains by their African enemies, the burning of accused human leopards was considered a threat to human security and British trading interests. Protection, again, provided the rationale for British control over life and death—particularly when it came to capital punishment.[10] This chapter traces how legal debates between African leaders and British officials over the punishment of human leopards was an extension of the promises of protection established through diplomacy on the frontier. Human leopardism prompted a reconfiguration of British protection schemes that centered on African legal practices, forging a new kind of legal order that further eroded African sovereignty through the formal annexation of Imperri, the enactment of new ordinances, and the establishment of permanent police in the interior. Ultimately, I show how conflict over African judicial practices led to the initial debates regarding formal colonization and the establishment of the Protectorate.

Several scholars have examined the emergence of the Human Leopard Society in the Sherbro region. While most historical studies have been limited to the colonial period, several anthropologists have especially demonstrated connections between the pervasive stories of cannibalism in the Sierra Leone hinterland and the extractive nature of the transatlantic slave trade.[11] They and other anthropologists' extensive field work have successfully identified and traced these Indigenous rhetorics of cannibalism across the precolonial, colonial, and postcolonial period.[12] Rosalind Shaw asserts that "witchcraft" must be understood as more than just an atemporal "corpus of traditional beliefs," but practices that are historically grounded in place and time.[13] This chapter extends Shaw's work by tracing how leopardism and the Tongo diviners reflected specific political and economic debates over protection in the 1880s and 1890s. To do this, I situate the rise of the human leopards and the development of the Tongo within the broader struggles over sovereignty and warfare during the previous decades. In this way, I show how debates over the human leopards and the Tongo were an extension of a longer struggle over legal and political jurisdiction of the southern coastal and riverine region both between Africans and themselves and Europeans.

Historicizing Early Human Leopard Trials: 1880–1889

On an ordinary day in January 1883, a letter landed on the desk of Thomas George Lawson. A Krio and longtime colonial employee, the Government Interpreter Lawson was responsible for all correspondence between African leaders and the colonial Government between 1861 and 1888. Decades of signing treaties, sending letters, and meeting with leaders in the interior and Freetown made him the deepest repository of African politics and customs, as well as colonial institutional knowledge.[14] Today, the Sierra Leone Public Archives literally contains thousands of pages of correspondence, memos, reports, and all other sundry items in his (very neat) handwriting, demonstrating the extent to which many Governors leaned on him for his expertise and advice in "interpreting" the "ancient customs" of the communities beyond the formal Colony.[15]

The author of the letter was Lawson's son-in-law, John Parker. A Krio, Parker had lived in one of the key trading towns in Kpaa-Mende for nineteen years and acted as an unofficial emissary by writing his father-in-law to keep him abreast of events in the interior. His letter from Sennehoo that January recounted how twenty-nine prominent leaders in the region had recently reported to him their plans to stop the "wicked practice going on in the country by certain persons who are cannibals always disguising themselves under leopard skins, seizing innocent persons for the purposes of eating them which they generally term 'human being transformed into leopards and alligators.'" Likely referring to their treaty promises to refrain from capital punishment, the letter cryptically stated that the leaders told Parker to convey to the Governor that he should "not be vexed with them should he hear that such persons are cruelly put to death."[16] Five months later, Lawson received another letter from Captain Henry Jackson who relayed a message from a number of Krio traders that the prominent leaders in Kpaa-Mende were currently away dealing with a serious "witch matter" concerning men who could shape-shift into "human leopards." He reported that some community leaders in the region had subsequently been burned with other "renowned men and women" and that, as a result, "many of their principal chiefs are in great fear themselves in this matter as they might be accused of having hands" in the Human Leopard Society.[17] When asked to explain their actions to the Governor, the Mende chefs confirmed that "the people who were burnt . . . were their own countrymen and family and from their own acknowledgement had killed nearly 70 innocent persons." Clearly acknowledging treaty promises to ensure all trade routes were free and open, they assured the Governor that "if they [the human leopards] were not punished in that manner, the roads would not be safe to anyone travelling through the country and people would not be able to bring down the produce as the Administrator wishes."[18]

The letters from John Parker and Captain Jackson represent some of the earliest archival references to both the human leopards and the Tongo. The Kpaa-Mende state region where the trials and burnings took place lay directly north-east of the Sherbro state. As we saw in previous chapters, the centralizing state of Kpaa-Mende was engaged in political expansion westward into Bompeh territory (ruled by Richard Canreba Calker until his exile in 1888) and southwards into the Bagru and Banta provinces. Krio and Indigenous traders established important centers of trade along the headwaters of the major rivers within those regions to facilitate the transportation of agricultural goods from Kpaa-Mende and Bompeh southwards through the Sherbro to the coast. Much of this political expansion occurred under the leadership of Gbanyah, a steady ally of the British and frequent treaty signatory. In 1878, Gbanyah died. Unable to command the authority of his father, his son faced a growing opposition of Mende leaders empowered by the wealth accumulated in the palm produce trade. For the next seven years, the political leadership of Kpaa-Mende was in a state of flux until Gbanyah's widow, Madam Yoko, assumed the title of "Queen of Senehun" through her keen political savvy, high ranking in the female sodality Sande, and close alliance with the colonial state.[19]

Leopard societies in Kpaa-Mende and elsewhere predominantly emerged in spaces of capitalist extraction like palm forests, rivers, and trading towns.[20] Accusations of being a "human leopard" were most often made against Indigenous traders or former war captains who had amassed considerable wealth and status in the community through the illegitimate use of labor, described in local parlance as "eating" people.[21] Moreover, many of them had acquired their wealth through alignment with foreign sources of capital like Krio traders. This connection suggests that the accused human leopards' mishandling of communal resources, made visible through connections with the imperial state or possession of foreign capital, was seen as sufficiently anti-social and that they posed a significant danger to the social, political, and even supernatural order of the region.[22]

Thus, like witches, human leopards represented a societal threat that required immediate legal intervention to stabilize the political and supernatural environment. Given the human leopard's possession of strong anti-social medicine, African courts counter-utilized their own supernatural resources through divination to determine the guilty party. Early court cases included a process known as ordealing. Among these was the "sasswood" ordeal that involved the consumption of a purgative liquid, the retrieval of iron rings at the bottom of a pot of hot oil, or a whip that would "sniff out" guilt by waving it around the accused.[23] In most cases, if the person subject to the ordeal was able to ingest the substance or complete a task in a certain way, they would be considered "not guilty" of their crime.

While single cases of witchcraft would have been heard in lower community-based courts, more serious matters that impacted or disturbed the peace of the broader region required adjudication by a larger collection of representatives. These upper courts were formed on an ad hoc basis and consisted of high-ranking men, titular leaders, and the heads of various Poro chapters.[24] After incidents of human leopardism in the 1880s and 1890s, archives recall large meetings where community leaders met to collectively solve this regional threat that impacted them all. Additionally, it appears that at times the nature of the crime and the high status of the alleged perpetrators required witch detectives.[25] Specialized diviners were hired to use supernatural methods to discover or "sniff" out the guilty. Diviners' use of such powerful medicines meant that their verdicts were rarely, if ever, challenged. As one Imperri leader simply stated in 1890, "The Tongoh [*sic*] people never make mistakes in finding out 'human leopards.'"[26]

A year after the human leopard burning in Kpaa-Mende, the Commandant of Sherbro received word of a similar "witch palaver," this time on the border between African and British territory. This incident took place in the town of Bengeh, a key trading town in the Bagru province that, like Sennehoo, housed several Krio traders. Initial reports closely resembled the earlier incident: a group of men "dressed in leopard skins" attacked over ten people; in some cases, "bodies [were] discovered half eaten" or "secretly wounded to death as if by claws of a leopard and left in the bush."[27] A representative of the leader of Bengeh, Banna Sokaka, told the Commandant that these events had prompted the "big people" of Bagru to send a message to "Tyama [Taiama] and Bompeh and brought *two medicine men* to discover the bad people and there are now about 25 persons detained in custody in Bengeh accused of witchcraft, male and female."[28] He informed the Government that while six of the accused had already confessed, "the rest had offered to prove their innocence by drinking 'sasswood water.'"[29]

Human leopard trials that involved ordealing or divination challenged the limits of what the British considered civilized legal practices.[30] For colonial officials, African evidentiary practices resembled a type of disorder akin to warfare that they believed prevented the development of trade. To remedy this, administrators attempted to apply the terms of treaties to legitimate colonial intervention. Like most warfare and raids that occurred in the hinterland, the location of these Tongo trials was outside of British territory. Because of this, British officials were compelled to rely on an established diplomatic language of "friendship," moral persuasion, and the threat of punitive measures to a punish crimes committed by non-British subjects. For example, in response to the Kpaa-Mende human leopard trials in 1883, Lawson informed the leaders that after hearing about the burning of those accused, the Governor "will not be a true friend to you after hearing such acts. . . . You are considered by him as friends, if so, you are equally friends to the Queen of England who and her Government abhor such cruel and horrible practice." Much like treaty negotiations, Lawson told leaders that the Governor "has no desire to interfere in your laws . . . [but] as a friend advises you to leave off burning people. There are many ways of punishing evil-doers instead of torturing them. The Queen's law never permits it, but has a milder way of punishing offenders and hopes to hear from your own messengers that you have taken this friendly advice."[31]

The majority of the leaders from Kpaa-Mende and Bengah who had informed the Government of their human leopard problems had previously signed treaties or had assisted the colonial Government in military campaigns.[32] It is clear in their initial responses to British inquiries concerning human leopard trials that they saw no contradiction in treaty promises and trying the accused in their own courts, except perhaps in the method of execution. In Bengeh, leaders informed the colonial Government of their human leopard trials by sending a representative to Bonthe to relay the details of events, including an invitation for the Government to participate by "send[ing] an officer to be present when the sasswood drink will be administered."[33] In a clear statement of compromise that was reminiscent of the capture of war captains or enemies, leaders promised to change the type of punishment in the future, despite their stated belief that they "dread" the British practice of hanging.[34] In July, Lawson reported to the Governor that one leader, Karjoie, had "passed a law . . . that no man is to be burnt for being accused of being a witch."[35]

Gesturing to the treaty agreements, Kpaa-Mende leaders explained that the execution of the human leopards was critical for the protection of their people and Krio traders, emphasizing that "people are afraid to go to their farms or to gather palm nuts [as] there is so much danger to be apprehended from the leopard men."[36] These descriptions were confirmed by outsider accounts of "cannibals roaming the countryside" in Krio correspondence and newspaper articles. Several articles of the *Early Dawn*, a missionary newspaper published in Bonthe, confirmed the description of men dressed as leopards stalking the riversides and roadways, stating that the situation was so dire, "a person dare not walk alone a distance of half a mile. He or she will not return except [if] 3 or 4 persons walk together."[37] Publications reported the inclusion of the specific details of individual cases. Resembling their calls for protection from raids, they implored the colonial Government to intervene and eliminate the human leopards.[38]

British legal response to these reports must be situated within a longer history of protection and treaty agreements. In a manner similar to early war captains like Whobay, it appears the British initially arrested and tried some of the alleged human leopards in colonial courts. Fragmentary evidence in local newspapers suggests that prior to 1890, the colonial Government arrested and tried three cases of "cannibalism" in British courts: in 1883, 1887, and 1888.[39] Details of these trials are extremely sparse, though it appears in one case (1887) the defendant was found guilty and received ten years of imprisonment as his sentence. In a newspaper article the following June, the writer ironically condemns the Government's leniency in the case, stating that penal punishment alone will not "make an impression on the minds of the native," rather, that "unless they are made to feel what capital punishment or death by hanging is then and not till then will the lives of men be held sacred." He closed hoping that the punishment of the new prisoner who was tried in Freetown the following month would "cast a lasting impression on the minds of those who are perpetrating the same deeds."[40]

While reports of cannibalism and ritual murder were not condoned, this 1888 article and other correspondence between leaders and the British administration in the same period confirms that it was the manner and circumstances of African judicial procedure (divination followed by immolation) that British officials found particularly repugnant. Clearly confused about how to proceed, increasing numbers of leaders who were aligned with the British Government stepped forward to share their "leopard problems" and seek advice about whether they could use the Tongo. In 1889, Gbannah Will Caulker, a member of the Caulker family who had been temporarily appointed "Chief of the Bompeh" by the British after the arrest and exile of Richard Canreba Caulker, reported that human leopards were causing "havoc" in his territory. In his letter describing the incidents, he told the Governor that he would not punish the human leopards "without first reporting things and ask you to point out what course to pursue . . . it is therefore necessary that something be done to assure them [his people] of safety; but I must look to you for instructions. If you will allow us to investigate matters in our old way, I am almost sure that a stop will be put to these things."[41] Less than a month later, the Governor received a similar request from another aligned leader, Thomas Neale Caulker of Shenge, asking if he might use country customs to prevent cannibalism there.[42] In June 1890, two leaders in the Mano Bagru (likely just on the other side of the Bagru River from Gbangbaia) requested they be able to use their "country customs" to deal with their human leopards.[43] These strikingly similar requests suggest a Sherbro-wide paradox pondered by community leaders throughout the region: how do demonstrate loyalty to the colonial state while also effectively eliminating the human leopards? Little did they know in that the answer to that question would be debated well into the period of Protectorate rule.

Imperri and the Tongo Trials of 1890

While pinpointing the origins of the Human Leopard Society is an almost impossible task, several accounts in the archives link its emergence with specific places, people, and events. In 1895, Thomas Joshua Alldridge, a palm oil trader turned colonial official, recounted the origin of the Human Leopard Society that he heard from the Krio trader J. C. Maccaulay.[44] He stated that in the mid-1870s, the leader of Taiama tried to strike a deal with a war captain to assist him in attacking Beah Boom, the leader of Gbangbaia in Imperri.[45] Ultimately, however, the deal between the leader of Taiama and the war captain did not hold, as the war captain was said to be Beah Boom's brother. The Chief of Taiama was soon deceived when the war captain revealed his plan to Beah Boom. When the warriors of Taiama attacked, the people of Gbangbaia were ready and nearly all the "war-boys" from Taiama were killed. As a result of this deceit, the people of Taiama vowed revenge upon the Imperri people. Through the assistance of a "Fetish man," a powerful "medicine" called borfima was introduced to Imperri. It was said that although the borfima had been previously "fed" with goat's fat to maintain its powers, when it was "brought into operation in the Imperri," the people were told that human fat had to be used to maintain its strength. It was said that the ultimate goal of introducing it was to "compel the Imperri people to kill themselves."[46] Since then, Alldridge stated, the borfima had become "a fetiche [*sic*] or everything."

Taiama was one of the most important cities of the Kpaa-Mende confederacy and, as we saw earlier, the site of one of the first cases of human leopards in 1883. During the wars of the 1870s and 1880s, the Kpaa-Mende were in a large regional coalition that frequently fought against the Imperri people.[47] The only named person in Alldridge's story—Beah Boom—was a well-known and formidable leader in Imperri, having signed numerous treaties with the British and housing Krio traders. To protect his political authority, however, he chose to align himself with leaders who increasingly opposed British encroachment in the region like Tom Cabbie Smith, Richard Canreba Caulker, and a series of war leaders in the upper Boom River. This coalition also included the prominent war captain and former political prisoner Cannagboh, who is likely the "brother" of Beah Boom recounted in Alldridge's story.[48]

Many human leopard cases after 1890 were located in or involved people from Imperri.[49] In subsequent years, it was frequently referred to by officials as the "great centre of the institution."[50] Alldridge states that after the introduction of borfima to Imperri, the people soon became "infatuated by the supposed infallibility of the 'medicine,' formed themselves into Secret Societies for the purpose of providing the victims from their own families and relations . . . and so the custom had spread through the whole Imperri land."[51] One way to interpret these accounts is that while leopardism had its origins in Kpaa-Mende, it was likely in Imperri that a more formal "medicine society" was created to manage the borfima.[52] In fact, later twentieth-century accounts suggested that the "Mother Borfima," the central source from which all other borfimas were created, was housed in Imperri.[53]

Centrally located near major rivers yet outside of British jurisdiction, Imperri was a highly desirable site for Krio and Indigenous trading factories. Its coastal shoreline was home to several European mercantile firms, and Krio traders established trading depots along its major rivers. The province of Imperri was traditionally ruled by the titular leader known as the Sokong. As previously discussed, with the Sokong's death in 1870, an extended period of interregnum created a massive political fracture between local leaders that prevented the consensus needed to elect a new one. In 1888, the leader referenced in Alldridge's story, Beah Boom of Gbangbaia, died. His passing likely further exacerbated the political cleavage between community leaders. He also left behind several wealthy Krio tenants who had heavily relied on his patronage and support. It is likely that the province's continued independence throughout the 1880s was a draw for many Krio traders who wanted to remain close to Bonthe but avoid import and export taxes or engage in smuggling. Relationships with Krio traders, however, often placed local Africans in various types of debt, resulting in raids and other forms of violence to recover them. As seen in the previous chapters, the possession of imperial cash was essential for protection from panyarring or other raids to recover outstanding loans.

Several Imperri leaders leased large tracts of land to Krio traders throughout the 1880s as a means of securing a steady flow of cash to retain the services of Mende and Muslim war captains and their men.[54] Among these was S. B. A. MacFoy, arguably the wealthiest Krio merchant operating in the Sherbro region, who established as many as ten separate trading factories in Imperri. Throughout the late 1880s, the colonial Government received several reports that MacFoy had been aggressively attempting to retrieve debts owed to him from the time of Beah Boom, even threatening people with involving a lawyer in Freetown.

Imperri leaders who had signed treaties with the colonial Government reported on MacFoy's aggressive behavior. They complained that his actions were directly interfering in their internal affairs and "our own laws in this country"—likely a

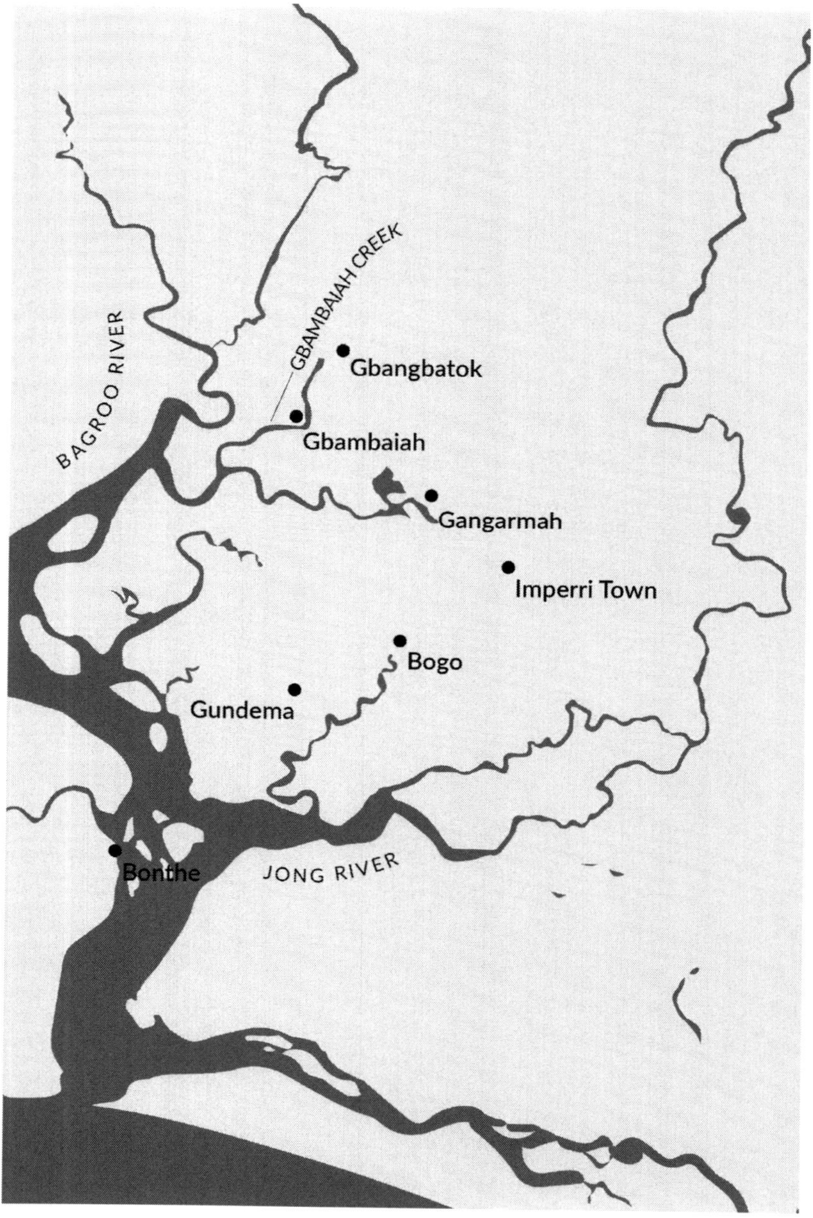

FIGURE 7. Map of Imperri region, circa 1890.

reference to the landlord-stranger agreement that MacFoy, as an outsider, was traditionally bound by.[55] When their initial complaints were not addressed, they turned to the assistance of Reverend Daniel Flickinger Wilberforce, Beah Boom's nephew and the man whose boy was murdered at the beginning of this chapter. Wilberforce was a well-known missionary who was born on Sherbro Island in 1857 to Christian converts. In his youth, he travelled to the United States for his secondary and post-secondary education, returning to his birthplace with his American wife in 1878 to open a mission station in Imperri and proselytize to his people.[56] Writing on behalf of Imperri leaders, Reverend Wilberforce informed the British that some inhabitants had sold MacFoy land north and south of the Gbangbaia River because of their inability to pay their debt to him. For those who refused to settle their debts, MacFoy reportedly deployed several rounds of heavy artillery and burned a series of homes. Presumably satisfied, MacFoy left his local proxy, Tuah Yeamie, the leader of Gbangbaia, in charge of his affairs and returned to Freetown.

Tuah Yeamie was not the only Imperri leader who aligned himself with MacFoy. In February 1890, five months before the human leopard trials, Reverend Wilberforce and a number of other leaders complained to the Commandant that a leader named Gbanna Bunjay had recently "made over Gangarmah"—a town less than ten miles from Gbangbaia—"and its *fackis*," an accusation that seems to point to him giving up the town in a lease or sale (presumably to MacFoy).[57] The colonial administration was well acquainted with Gbanna Bunjay. He was a wealthy trader who had signed several treaty agreements, collected a stipend, and met with colonial officials on several occasions. Earlier in the year when another Krio trader named Mr. Parkinson had been plundered, Gbanna Bunjay aided in his protection by providing some young men to assist in retrieving his stolen goods. When only some of his property was recovered, Gbanna Bunjay paid Parkinson the remaining £96 that was missing—a considerable amount of money in that period.[58] These instances indicate that Bunjay's wealth and "Big Man" status was visibly connected to the British through stipends, the protection of the colonial state, and Krio traders through the sale of land and foreign goods.

In response to these events, Imperri leaders gathered for a palaver with J. C. E. Parkes, the secretary of the newly formed Department of Native Affairs. At the meeting, leaders argued that Bunjay's sale of the land in Gangamah exceeded his status, having "no right to do what he had done . . . without consulting himself and the other old chiefs." They informed the Commandant that as a result of Bunjay's actions, which included an unsolicited raid on MacFoy's trading factory, Bunjay had been deposed from his position as "Speaker" and advised the colonial Government to withdraw his annual stipend. As the letter writer, Wilberforce relayed that the leaders in Imperri intended to make a "Sokong during the rains," which the Commandant approved, stating that at present it was "extremely difficult to do business with any country which had no recognized leader." This act was clearly controversial. While Wilberforce and others insisted that the rightful Sokong was a man named Burboh, on the other side of the political divide, Gbanna Bunjay insisted that he was "the speaker and acting Sokong of Imperreh."[59] The battle over leadership escalated.

Perhaps predictably, Bunjay denied the charges laid against him. In April 1890, he sent a letter to the Commandant denying he had led the raid, instead accusing the leader of Bogo who he claimed had summoned his warboys to raid MacFoy. Demonstrating his savviness of how to play the game, Bunjay requested that the Governor send police to help settle the issue. His narrative of events of the previous few months was distinctly contrary to how the other leaders reported several months prior: that MacFoy had every right to the land as he (Bunjay) and the "late Beah Bome [*sic*] gave him the country with the presence of we Chiefs and with our consent and Sierra Leone people present" some years back.[60] His alignment with MacFoy, however, was dangerous and insinuated wrongdoings. MacFoy's proxy, Tuah Yeamie, was arrested and held in the Bonthe jail for raiding yet another Imperri leader.[61]

By mid-1890, the struggle between Imperri leaders was roughly divided into three major issues: who the rightful Sokong of Imperri was, the validity of MacFoy and other Krio traders' leases on Imperri land, and the legitimacy of the violence used to recover debts. Within this context, rumors spread to the Commandant of the murder of at least four people by human leopards, including Wilberforce's boy at Gbangbaia.[62] Alongside these struggles over land and leadership, leaders in Imperri informed the Commandant that they were currently taking steps to "stamp out cannibalism which had existed to a considerable extent in their country."[63] In May, leaders as far as the neighboring Jong province were invited to a regional Poro to discuss the problem of the human leopards. As recounted in the story that opened this chapter, the group decided to summon the Tongo from Kpaa-Mende to use their divination skills to seek out the "human leopards" who had been terrorizing their towns.

Arriving sometime in July, the Tongo started their investigation in Gbangbaia, then moved onto Gbanna Bunjay's town of Gangarmah. Upon their arrival, the Tongo and local leaders went into the Poro bush. One by one, men who were accused of being human leopards were called out. At the mention of each name, the Tongo men applied a horn full of medicine to the chest of a woman. If the horn stuck to the woman's chest when the person's name was called, the person was declared a human leopard. Most of the men accused of being human leopards were wealthy traders or Big Men. They were placed into stocks, and their property was confiscated. While two men were able to use their wealth to pay off the accusers and evade punishment, the rest were taken out to the middle of the town and beaten. After this, seventy of the accused were gathered and burned en masse in a huge pyre, making it the largest human leopard trial ever reported.[64]

Among the men identified as a human leopard by the Tongo was Gbanna Bunjay, even though he was part of the group that originally summoned them. Another was the former war captain and "brother" of Beah Boom, Cannagboh, who was reportedly able to use his wealth to pay off the accusers (either the Chiefs or the Tongo) and evade punishment. Bunjay was not as lucky. He joined the other accused men and met the same fate as the human leopards before him. His property and the other accused men's property was seized and redistributed to other community members. The redistribution of his and the other human leopard's wealth represented a social and economic reckoning: a return of the communities' collective resources that had been illegitimately hoarded for selfish purposes.

The execution of Gbanna Bunjay and the other accused human leopards in Imperri sparked an unprecedented legal crisis between colonial administrators and Imperri leaders. When rumors of Bunjay's death began to circulate in June 1890, colonial officials debated how to intervene and whether it should be permissible to allow local leaders to seek out and execute human leopards using their "country customs." Far removed from the events and people of Imperri, the Colonial Office in London initially held its well-worn policy of maintaining strict jurisdictional boundaries: "as Imperri was not within British territory," one secretary stated in his notes, "I think the Gov't can only put pressure on the chiefs outside of jurisdiction to execute their cannibals in a more humane manner."[65] However, when a June 1890 report contained rumors of even more executions of human leopards, Governor James Shaw Hay countered London's stance, justifying that his administration's intervention was based on enforcing "treaty agreements," which did not permit the use of "torture" or enslavement.[66] Hay asserted that he "deemed it his duty to write to the Chief requesting that they stop this cruel mode of punishment *at once* and have threatened to hold them responsible should any more cases be referred to me." He further stated to the Colonial Office that he had also "led" Imperri leaders to "believe that I may even arrest those who take part in such proceedings and have invited the chiefs to meet with me in Bonthe early next month so that I may, if possible, make a most careful inquiry into the matter."[67]

It appears that Hay could not wait. Following established treaty protocol, the three men who were "implicated" in Bunjay's death were arrested as political prisoners and imprisoned in Bonthe, much like war captains or "disloyal" signatories before them.[68] As details emerged that up to thirty more men had been executed, a full investigation into the burnings was conducted by Sherbro Commandant Bennett and the Queen's Advocate Reginald Brett. The men travelled to Imperri and interviewed over thirty residents of various statuses, producing an incredibly detailed historical record of the Tongo. Their concluding assessment—that Imperri leaders had "conspired together to plunder, torture and murder a number of their fellow countrymen"—prompted them to demand that the Imperri Chiefs who committed these "crimes," as well as the members of the Tongo, come to the law courts in Bonthe to defend their actions.[69] The rest of the leaders were forced to sign a treaty-like agreement to not engage in any human leopard trials until the matter was resolved. A month later, fifteen Imperri leaders arrived in Bonthe to answer to the charges.

The "trial" conducted in Bonthe by Commandant Bennett allowed leaders to fully articulate the circumstances leading up to the Tongo's arrival, and in the process, produced an incredible archival source for historians. In their deposition, the leaders stated that the men were killed because they "belonged to a secret society called the 'Human Leopards' and were known to be cannibals whose existence among them was a source of terror and danger to the whole community."[70] The men further explained that they had hired the Tongo because of their proficiency in making the "proper discovery" and that they had only "killed those who were pointed out by the Tongoh [*sic*] people as having been guilty of such practices." As Ba Sin of Bogo testified, "If I had been accused by the Tongoh [*sic*] people, I would have been killed all the same though I may have been innocent of the charge. Nobody would have believed me if I had protested."[71] Imperri leaders insisted that they had acted "in good faith" and that they reasonably expected to be allowed to engage in their "Native Customs"—a right which they had been assured of numerous times by colonial officials. As one leader bluntly stated in the courtroom in Bonthe, "We decided upon doing this business without any reference to the Government. All the chiefs had 'one word.' I mean, we all agreed in this matter."[72]

For local leaders, the Tongo's process of seeking out human leopards and cannibals was valid and legitimate: well-known and established experts were brought in and paid for their divination skills. In contrast, the British characterized the process of hiring the Tongo as "taking the law into their own hands." While at no time did the colonial administration deny the existence of human leopards, colonial officials concluded that the Imperri leaders took advantage of the "prevailing feeling of terror" to justify their actions. One colonial report summed up this sentiment by stating:

> The Tongoh [*sic*] people are impostors and Tongoism as practiced in Imperri is a conspiracy on the part of the Chiefs of Imperri to kill people and enrich themselves by plundering the effects of the people whom they kill, that the visit of the Tongoh [*sic*] people to Imperri and the aforesaid atrocities committed under colour of their pretended supernatural powers have done nothing whatever toward putting down cannibalism, that it has not touched the fringe of this wickedness, but has largely added to the previous insecurity of life and property in that unfortunate country.[73]

Contrary to how divination operated in African courts, colonial officials came to support the opinion that the leaders who summoned the Tongo preselected the "victims" before the Tongo arrived. This notion would be repeated frequently in the decade and a half that followed, perpetuating the idea that Imperri leaders were distrustful and despotic.[74] Colonial officials came to believe that the other leaders secretly arranged with the Tongo to have Bunjay killed "under the *pretext* of being a cannibal" and that his personal wealth also made him a target of jealousy. Brett concluded that as Bunjay was a "wealthy man in the eyes of his fellow Chiefs . . . the probability amounting to a certainty, in my opinion, that it had been previously arranged by a majority of the chiefs in collusion with the Tongohs [*sic*], that . . . his property might be confiscated, and his relatives plundered in the manner I have described."[75] Whether Bunjay and the other accused men were shape-shifting human leopards or simply convenient political targets, the events of 1890 suddenly placed Imperri's political power struggles at the center of British protection schemes. The disparity between British and African law created the ideal opening to justify British legal intervention in the last province to be incorporated in the colonized coastal region.

After a follow up trip to Imperri in late 1890, Brett concluded that the emergence of human leopards was the result of a lack of "individual governing power" in Imperri. Like many colonial officials before him, his observation was that while each village had a Chief or headman, there was no "supreme authority."[76] This absence, he concluded, led to the creation of "troubles amongst themselves for the sake of plunder or are at the mercy of any one choosing to either beguile or menace them."[77] However, instead of encouraging a coronation of a Sokong like many an administrator before him, Brett recommended that the forty square miles that made up the Imperri should be formally colonized, asserting that a strong colonial presence would enable the Government to pacify the region and keep it free from "all internal derangement."[78] Like the other Sherbro provinces that surrounded it, the rhetoric of protection provided the justification for intervention despite the Colonial Office's insistence they refrain from interfering in local matters.

Annexing Imperri: "Protecting" Africans and the Criminalization of the Tongo

After more than twenty years of treaty making, military expeditions, and moral persuasion, British officials failed to assert the influence and control over the hinterland that they desired. This was particularly true of Imperri. Despite the inclusion of Imperri in treaties of annexation in 1825 and 1861, and numerous treaties and agreements of peace and commerce (1872, 1875, 1876), the region remained impervious to British control.[79] Although they had signed treaties, autochthon Imperri leaders formed coalitions with states that had strong military forces, including many war captains and their "warboys." Unlike many of their neighbors, Imperri's central place in the palm produce trade (which clearly attracted many Krios) allowed Imperri traders to acquire enough wealth to implement their own forms of protection as evidenced by the fortification of their towns with walls and wooden palisades. The decision to engage in their own "country customs" to investigate and punish human leopards was the ultimate declaration of their sovereignty in the context of imperial encroachment, and it was perceived by the British as an active challenge to their growing hegemony in the region. The human leopard trials in

Gbangbaia represented decades of Imperri resistance against British protection schemes, particularly through their decision to assert their right to engage in capital punishment. The immolation of dozens of "cannibals" less than twenty miles from British territory, potentially condoned by a Christian missionary and several African allies and treaty signatories, was a symbol of British failure to achieve their aims of "pacifying" the interior simply through contact with British culture or commerce.

Brett's suggestion of annexation marked the development of a new protection scheme that placed more emphasis on formal colonization rather than moral persuasion through treaty making. Protection was reframed as the duty of the Crown to protect the everyday African from their own leaders, a notion that would eventually be extended into the framework of indirect rule. Governor Hay wrote to the Colonial Office that annexation was the only logical course of action as the lessor "chiefs" and everyday people had no one to "apply [to] for advice or redress" and thus "*require to be protected from themselve*s, being at present the victims of evil advisors, but they are also the prey of unprincipled persons ready to take advantage of their ignorance to obtain possession of their land to gain their own ends."[80] Embedded in this statement was a new formulation of protection that shifted away from the protection of British subjects, who themselves were increasingly viewed as the cause of chaos and corruption in the interior.

On October 25, 1890, Imperri was officially incorporated into British Sherbro. It was the first territory to be annexed without request or direct correspondence with local leaders. The following week, Governor Hay travelled to Imperri to announce to a large group of leaders that they were now under the Government's protection and "under the laws and of England," expressing hope that they would "assist the Government faithfully obeying all orders issued by it."[81] During his speech, he handed each leader a copy of the Proclamation and ordered the leaders to immediately cease from burning human leopards using the Tongo.[82] British rule, he declared, would restore the order and prosperity that had been stagnated by fear of travelling on roads, a lack of attention to agriculture, and the "illegal" mortgaging of local villages for profit.[83]

British annexation of Imperri was also representative of changes in European ideas about race and the capacity of Africans to represent "nation states" as treaty signatories. As legal historian Antony Anghie has written, this shift can be attributed to a decline in the belief of "universal laws" based on human reason and natural law. In this new legal reasoning, colonial administrators and jurists increasingly embraced "positivist jurisprudence," the belief that civilized nation states could be the only principal actors in the making of treaties or other forms of international law.[84] This shift allowed European empires to justify the rejection of the terms of treaties with "non-civilized" people on the basis of their supposed limited intellectual capacity as Africans, a turn that legally facilitated the annexation of the rest of the continent in the "Scramble for Africa" and set the parameters of indirect rule. The annexation of Imperri in 1890 was a foreshadowing of things to come in 1896, not only in terms of the reasons given for formal annexation, but by forging a legal precedent of ceding land without the consultation of local leaders. To be sure, the establishment of colonial protectorates would not have been possible without this shift in the legal status of African nations within international legal norms.

Despite formal colonization in 1890, Imperri was administered in a haphazard and uneven manner like the rest of British Sherbro. This hazy assertion of British jurisdiction was compounded by the construction of a frontier road that connected the headwaters of the major rivers through African and British territory and the stationing of a para-military police called the "Frontier Force" along it. These measures aimed to solve the decades-long problem of safely transporting people and goods along Sherbro's rivers, a feat that was consistently made unpredictable by warfare and weather. As one colonial official bluntly stated, the road scheme would be "almost as beneficial to the country as comprised within the area of annexation, without the responsibilities that annexation would incur."[85] When Frontier Forces began to be stationed along the 350-mile-long road in 1890, one of their permanent stations was in Gbangbaia. Leaders in Imperri were explicitly told by the Governor that the police and roads were there to "afford due protection to traders" but that the police were not to "interfer[e] in the domestic institutions so long as the country were not disturbed."[86] In private correspondence between Hay and the new leader of Gbangbaia, MacFoy's old partner Tuah Yeamie, it was reiterated that "it was not the wish of the Government to interfere with their domestic institutions, more than absolutely necessary."[87] However, what those limits were was entirely at the discretion of the colonial Government; on one hand, the frontier road and police represented a continuum of the protection schemes established in the decades before, on the other hand they represented a new extension of British law and violence.

While Krios initially supported Hay's road and the stationing of Frontier Forces, newspapers quickly criticized their ineffectiveness at preventing the threat of human leopards. One columnist in the *Sierra Leone Times* wrote that without firmer intervention of the British, Krio traders would soon become the dinner of some "savage gourmand," noting that at present, traders needed to protect themselves from the "greedy propensity of blood-thirsty savages."[88] Articles became increasingly more graphic, describing grisly scenes where the corpses of "human alligator" victims daily floated down the Boom and Kittam River, while the Inspector of Police "pass[ed] his time in idleness at Bonthe" while "cannibals prevent the aborigines from collecting produce for the European market." Like warfare in the decades before, economic disorder attributed to the human leopards led the Krio population to push for harsher punishments and annexation, arguing that British law was simply not effective enough to deal with the human leopards—an accusation that would reverberate even after protectorate rule was established. One newspaper article summed up this conundrum by stating that: "It has been repeatedly pointed out that civilized laws . . . cannot satisfactorily deal with the question: than what is to be done? Shall we deliver up the aborigines to the jealousy and malignity of their compeers to be tried by superstitious ordeals of which more enlightened nations have found by self-experience to be unavailing? Or, if reason and law answer in the negative, shall we then declare the impotency of Government to arrest the evil?"[89]

To add to British problems, news of another set of Tongo trials in Imperri—and with it, questions about the capacity of British law to handle the "spread of cannibalism"—moved beyond the confines of the Freetown press. One British newspaper in Liverpool described "Black Jack the Rippers" who continued to operate in the recently "taken over territory" The article stated that while the spread of human leopards had previously been kept "in check for some time by country law or what the natives call country medicine" since "taking over the country by the Sierra Leone colony the 'medicine law' [Tongo] had ceased and the crimes have again begun." Human leopard murders in both the local and international press were described in exceedingly grisly terms, highlighting the inability of the British to maintain control and authority in the region.[90]

Colonial intervention in African courts also diminished African allies' belief in the British as effective protectors. In deeming the Tongo's detection and punishment of crime inadmissible, the British unwittily appeared to be "protecting" the human leopards themselves—a problem that administrators would encounter elsewhere in the empire in terms of witches or other supernatural deviants.[91] Less than a month after the annexation of their territory, the same Imperri leaders who had been "arrested" in 1890 submitted a petition imploring that they be "allowed and permitted to adopt our native course in finding out and treating these Cannibals, as provided by our native policy." Not only did leaders draw from treaty stipulations to emphasize their plea, arguing that cannibals prevented the "free traveling for the purpose of trade, or farming" and were "especially endangering the lives and safety of our wives and children," but stated emphatically that these "clubs of cannibals taking shelter from the lenient treatment of the British Government in cases brought before their notice are becoming bold, and destructive to our lives, welfare and interest."[92] Imperri leaders emphasized how their African methods were the best form of protection for trade and their own people, gesturing to British law as too "lenient." However, the "repugnancy" of both the investigation and punishment techniques of the Tongo prevented Governor Hay from conceding to these requests, responding that while he was willing to consider "legitimate" ways of getting rid of the human leopards, he could not give permission to use their customs to do it. Instead, he told them to assist the Frontier Force in arresting and collecting evidence of anyone they "suspect of being a cannibal."[93] The colonial state's order seemed to have been largely ignored by Imperri leaders, demonstrating that they saw human leopards as more of a threat than the colonial Government itself.

News in April 1892 of a second mass burning of more than one hundred human leopards directly along the frontier road in Bogo again brought the Tongo to the forefront of colonial concern.[94] Much like the Gbangbaia case two years prior, Commandant Mr. Huggins sailed up the Bagru River in search of answers.[95] Over a fifteen day investigation, Huggins interviewed twenty-three people, which included the family of victims, an Islamic teacher, farmers, a blacksmith, and several Krio traders. The depositions were as contradictory and confusing as British jurisdiction itself. While some witnesses recounted that the Tongo were summoned from Taiama by several important leaders in Imperri, others attributed their arrival solely to "the great leader of Imperri" Ba Sin of Bogo, who himself had been accused of leopardism and burned.[96] Neppoh, the leader of the Tongo, defended his actions by saying that prior to the burning, several white men had told him to dress up as he did when he did the Tongo play so that he could photograph him, while other witnesses suggested that another white man had told the Tongo that they could do their investigation, but that when they caught the leopards, a "letter must be sent to the white man who would then come up and see about the matter."[97] Another statement suggested that leaders had written either Captain Campbell or Captain Cockburn (both European) of the Frontier Forces a letter asking if they could burn their leopards, of which they received no reply.[98] Another from a Krio trader stated that Campbell had actually given them permission, while others suggested that the act of photographing Neppoh and giving him a tumbler of rum while doing it "sanctioned his actions," suggesting to onlookers that his presence and purpose was legitimate.[99] Other depositions described how leaders knew they were in the wrong when they sanctioned the executions, describing how Neppoh and others hid the accused in a house when the white man's boat approached so they could be burned at a later time. Not knowing what version to trust, Colonel Ellis ordered that Neppoh be arrested at once and sent to Bonthe.

The presence of police stationed directly in Bogo added another layer to British inability to control the territory. Frontier Force members were rumored to have aided in beating the victims or "dancing the Tongo dance" while people burned, making this case particularly embarrassing for the colonial administration.[100] After the investigation was complete, much debate was undertaken as to whether Sub-Inspector Sawyerr, the African officer in charge of the detachment, had neglected his duties and allowed the Tongo to proceed. Pleading his case, Sawyerr stated that his lack of interference in the Tongo trials was attributed to his ignorance that the town was within "active jurisdiction." He insisted he had been ordered not to "interfere with native matters," as doing so "might lead to native wars or other complications."[101] His defense again lay bare the way Britain haphazardly applied British law to regions that had been formally annexed.

While Governor Hay had been comfortable with the uneven application of rule in Imperri, his replacement in 1892 was much less so. Sir Francis Fleming, a man of considerably different character than either Rowe or Hay, had built his early colonial career as a lawyer, judge, Attorney General, and colonial secretary and had been stationed throughout the empire stretching from Barbados, Jamaica, Ceylon, Mauritius, and Hong Kong. This administrative and legal background did not necessarily compliment the usual ad hoc, military-based policy of the Sherbro hinterland. As the inheritor of Hay's road and police scheme, the human leopard question in Imperri prompted Fleming to question the difference in how British law was applied in territory within the "British sphere of influence" versus places under "direct jurisdiction." The major problem, as Fleming saw it, was in the administration of the latter, where some areas were ruled in a "direct way" (Freetown, Sherbro Island, and the coastline) and others (such as Imperri, the Jong River, and Tucker's territory) were "really within British jurisdiction in name only . . . those who commit offenses therein are amenable to our laws, but the chiefs manage their own affairs and things go on much the same as they did before the District was taken over by the Government."[102]

Observing the Tongo trials in Bogo, Fleming stated the obvious question—"Are we to make the native chiefs responsible for the good order of territory which actually belongs to us or are we to do this ourselves?" In a rather heated circular memorandum between the Colonial Office in London, Governor Fleming, and the Secretary of Native Affairs J. C. E. Parkes, participants debated the primary contradictions of formal colonization in Imperri and other similar places on the coast; namely, what aspects of African law, from Tongo trials to domestic slavery, were to be permitted or criminalized under formal British rule.[103] Seemingly predicting the the troubles that would arise in the future Protectorate, colonial officials debated how to assert rule while still maintaining the cooperation of African leaders who had been the center of British protection schemes since the 1860s. Officials expressed concerns that if practices like domestic slavery were criminalized or leaders perceived that their jurisdiction over courts were significantly diminished, they would be less likely to uphold British economic policies. As one article in the *Sierra Leone Times* noted, "It is indeed unfair that the Government should not only neglect to give her Majesty's subjects in that District [Imperri] the protection to which they are entitled, but should also deny them the necessary protection afforded to them by their native Laws and Customs."[104]

Colonial policy that limited African legality extended the paradox of protection by limiting African leaders' ability to enact particular forms of punishment , not the criminalization of the human leopards themselves. Enacted in 1893, the Tongo Ordinance stated that the Tongo, "being contrary to law, must at once cease throughout the colony. That every Tongo person is hereby enjoined and required to quit the Colony within twenty-one days from the date of this Proclamation on pain of being arrested, detained and deported as a Political Prisoner."[105] While the legislation that criminalized leopard burnings aimed to stabilize and bolster individual Indigenous leaders (still a considerable issue in Imperri as a Sokong had not yet been crowned), it ironically delegitimated local authority by forcing them to use an ineffective British legal system. The Tongo Ordinance represented the first of a series of ordinances passed by the Legislative Council on the eve of the Protectorate that straddled the line between asserting active rule and nonintervention. The legislation's language was clearly an extension of previous British protection schemes on the frontier, signaled by its use of the legal category of "political prisoner" as a means of detaining and exiling non-British subjects, as well as legally sanctioning the bypassing of the British courts to exile the accused. These legal strategies continued to be woven into policies in the interior, and, as we will see in the next chapter, the legal framework of the Protectorate itself.

Conclusion

While no evidence exists that the Tongo Ordinance was ever enforced, its legitimacy as a tool for eliminating human leopards continued to be debated by the Freetown public well into the Protectorate era. Directly after it was enacted, the *Sierra Leone Times* published a scathing critique of it, stating that "We cannot say we agree in the principles of the measure nor its provisions. We do not mean by this to say we are in favour of the burning of persons for the offence of cannibalism, but it must be remembered that not many hundreds of years ago our teachers of today followed exactly the same course in dealing with those whom they considered witches." The author practically accuses the colonial Government of not having the guts to burn the human leopards themselves, having opted to target the "quack practitioner" instead. Speaking to the threat that the human leopards continued to pose: "it is a well-known fact that whenever the Tongo man appeared on the scene, acts of murder and cannibalism decreased."[106] In 1893, colonial officials could not predict that the criminalization of the Tongo would lead to decades of human leopard trials in their own criminal courts. The resurgence of the Human Leopard Society in the twentieth century raised the same concerns of the *Sierra Leone Times* author in 1893; namely, whether the criminalization of such an "effective means" of eliminating the "cannibals" had been the right course of action.[107]

For Governor Francis Fleming, the obvious solution to eliminating both the Tongo and the human leopards was direct rule. For him, the Tongo trials had exposed the ineffectiveness of informal British protection schemes like treaties and diplomacy. As he saw it, the only type of legislative authority that could facilitate the shift from moral to physical persuasion was "taking as much of their country as possible as we can not only under our sphere of influence, but under our direct authority."[108]

In less than three years, the annexation of the entire Sierra Leone hinterland would facilitate the reordering of African judicial and political institutions based on Britain's long engagement over the past four decades. While beneficial for

British interests, formal annexation shocked the empire's closest African allies. The widespread protests by African leaders against the imposition of the protectorate underscores the belief that these agreements were meant to offer protection rather than threaten their sovereignty. Their anger produced the opposite of the intended impact of indirect rule. Instead of producing stability, it created the conditions for a regional Insurrection. And so, the paradox continued.

CHAPTER FOUR

These Laws Are Too Strong for Us

Petitions, Poros, and Puugwei (the White Man's War), 1896–1898

AFTER MANY DAYS OF DELIBERATION IN THE PORO BUSH, THE "CRY" OF THE BAHUN signaled the election of the first Sokong in twenty-five years.[1] Upon being unanimously declared King of the Imperri in 1895, Humpa Karwonjoe was ceremoniously hit from all directions by palm fronds by the important men and Poro elders who surrounded him; together they chanted "Minta libeh, Minta libeh": "You must learn to endure the duties and trials of a King."[2] The Sokong and his Lavari (his Speaker) were then seized and taken to an enclosure to begin their seclusion for three months. During that time, important men from throughout the country visited the new Sokong in the Poro bush "instructing them on the country laws" and describing what his obligations were as the new leader of his people. Sworn on country medicine, the Sokong was declared no longer a member of his family, but a "guardian of all his subjects who must always impartially administer justice to all people, no matter whence they come or what nationality they may be."[3] Rather than a sword, he was now to hold a scepter and a white cloth, symbols that he was now a "man of peace" and not war.

While attending the event, the above group photograph was taken by Thomas J. Alldridge, a British trader, colonial official, and author who was well acquainted with the Imperri people. The image is a fascinating reflection of the legal and

FIGURE 8. The coronation of the Sokong of Imperri, 1895.

SOURCE: THOMAS JOSHUA ALLDRIDGE, *A TRANSFORMED COLONY, SIERRA LEONE, AS IT WAS, AND AS IT IS: ITS PROGRESS, PEOPLES, NATIVE CUSTOMS AND UNDEVELOPED WEALTH* (J. B. LIPPINCOTT, 1910), 271.

cultural pluralism that had evolved in the Sherbro region over the preceding century. Donning their bowlers, top hats, and British staffs of office, it is evident that Sherbro leaders' political symbolism was woven into their long engagement with European hallmarks of power and authority. The King of the Sherbro, Beh Sherbro, the man in the cocked hat standing between the Sokong and his Lavari, wears a large silver medal that had been given to his grandfather in 1811 by King George III. The ceremony also embodied hundreds of years of African tradition. Wearing the bones of their ancestors, the four Tasso men that flank the central figures were said to each represent a Poro group from the Imperri community. The presence of the Tasso, the Beh Sherbro, and the centrality of events in the Poro bush at the coronation confirm the continued role that Poro had in Sherbro law and governance.

While the colonial Government had previously encouraged coronations as a way of centralizing African rule, the crowning of this Sokong in the final decade of the nineteenth century provoked a new kind of debate that questioned the role of African royalty in a recently annexed British territory. While many in London held no objection to "making use of the Native Chiefs to regulate native affairs," one colonial official insisted that "it should be explained to [the Sokong] that the district is part of the Colony."[4] As we saw in the previous chapter, Imperri had been declared part of British territory in 1890, making the coronation of this Sokong, as another colonial official pointed out, "not altogether consistent with the Queen's Sovereignty."[5] Memos between London and Freetown now asked new questions: To what extent should African states and communities be allowed to select their own leaders? What political jurisdiction did these leaders have versus the British crown? These queries lay at the definition of changing ideas of dominion throughout the British Empire that protectorates and the structure of indirect rule aimed to resolve.

This chapter traces the tumultuous first three years of the Sierra Leone Protectorate. During this time, the Sokong's promise to peacefully rule over the Imperri was not easily achieved. Fifteen months after his coronation, a Protectorate was declared over the entire Sierra Leone hinterland without the consultation of him or any other African sovereign. The annexation of the Sierra Leone Protectorate in 1896 without any debate or formal treaty making was a complete betrayal of the relationship African leaders and their forefathers had forged with the colonial state over the past four decades. Responding to this unprecedented seizure of their sovereignty, I show how African leaders drew from their own political framework to reunite the Sherbro state under the leadership of the Beh Sherbro and titular leaders like the Sokong. While initially engaging in peaceful protest that drew from a long history of palavers, petitions, and the use of Poro embargoes, struggles over the sovereignty of the region ultimately resulted in one of the bloodiest Insurrections in British Africa.

The Insurrection of 1898 reflected the apogee of the paradox of protection.[6] Negotiations over protectorate rule were the result of the abrupt withdrawal of promises of protection that colonial treaties had proclaimed. This fact especially explains why so many of the leaders of the rebellion had been long aligned with the British. Using the extraordinary ability of the Poro to collectively organize and communicate with each other throughout the entire southern hinterland, high-ranking Poro men induced their people to try and eliminate any "white men": Krios, missionaries, and anyone else connected to the colonial state. For many, these "rebellious" actions would be paid for with their lives.

The rationale for the Sierra Leone Protectorate was much the same as it was elsewhere in the empire: British control over a particular foreign (and usually rural) territory was in the best interests of the Crown and the "native" population that resided there. Occupation of foreign territory on the part of the "Protector State" was legitimated through the belief in the racial and cultural superiority of the West, the idea that Europeans possessed the highest level of civilization through industrialization, the rule of law, free trade, and Christianity. Coded as tutelage, the establishment of protectorates throughout Africa rested on the pervasive notion that without British surveillance, African populations would further revert to a state of barbarism, slavery, and warfare.

Histories of African protectorates typically attribute the framework of indirect rule to Sir Frederick Lugard, a British administrator whose book *The Dual Mandate*, published in 1922, provided reflection on his implementation of indirect rule in Nigeria and acted as a guideline for implementing it elsewhere. While Lugard's text was essential reading material for District Commissioners in the 1920s, its publication has caused scholars to overlook how the political and legal order of protectorates were informed by the long engagement between British officials and African leaders during the period of informal rule. This chapter shows how protection remained the central legal concept through which Africans and Britons debated the transition into formal rule. Protectorate laws, I argue, were an extension of treaties and diplomacy: colonial administrators purported to be safeguarding African customs while simultaneously seeking to alter them when British interests were challenged. African leaders throughout Sierra Leone were not easily duped by this rhetoric and quickly understood the protectorate rule as a dispossession of their territory. Instead, they argued that the treaty agreements their ancestors had signed were promises of protection, not a sale of their land. In an effort to secure their rights, leaders fought back using a wide range of British and African legal strategies, including armed resistance.

As this chapter shows, protection language especially justified the implementation of a severe top-down style of governance that constrained community leaders through physical and juridical violence. This was evident in the colonial response to the Insurrection of 1898. Colonial administrators enacted several ordinances that replicated the extra-legal measures that had been developed on the frontier. Martial law legalized the further stripping of the basic rights of Protectorate residents. Backed by the violent legislative and judicial power of the colonial state, leaders whose authority transcended that of the colonial state were incarcerated, deported, and executed as political prisoners and "insurgents."

From Protection Schemes to Protectorate Rule

Sailing into Freetown in 1894, the newly appointed Governor Sir Frederick Cardew arrived at a very different port than the one Thomas Ellis had sailed away from fifty years before. By the end of the nineteenth century, Freetown had become a bustling capital city. The intermarriage of the children of the original settlers, Liberated

Africans, and other African sojourners to the Colony had created a recognizable and self-defined Krio population. Highly educated, many were entrepreneurs, churchman, artisans, police officers, teachers, and clerks in the colonial administration. Those who were particularly successful built large homes filled with domestic help and furnished with imported goods. Those who could afford it sent their children to school in England. Some left Freetown and formed elite African communities in places like Banjul, Lagos, and Accra. While the majority of Krios maintained a physical and cultural distance between themselves and the Indigenous populations in the hinterland, by the end of the nineteenth century, around three to four thousand Krios were living "upcountry" as traders or middlemen for larger mercantile houses.[7]

While many Governors had maintained good working relationships with the Freetown population, the same could not be said for Governor Cardew. His dispatches to the Colonial Office only thinly veiled his disdain for Krios, a negative position on urban black populations that were increasingly held by European administrators and travelers in the late Victorian era. Ideas of rural Africans were also changing, transforming the image of Africans from "ferocious savages" to "child savages."[8] This type of colonial paternalism not only shaped everyday advertising and books in Britain, but informed a new set of policies that imagined Africans as less evolved societies that required the tutelage of Europeans to transition from primitive to civilized peoples.

No stranger to Africa, Cardew had been a lifelong soldier and colonial administrator. Like Frederick Lugard, Cardew was born in India and joined the colonial troops as a young man. Prior to arriving in Sierra Leone, he served in South Africa as the Resident Commissioner in Zululand. From almost the moment he arrived in Sierra Leone, Cardew's preference for rural spaces guided his extensive travels in the interior. As he met with leaders throughout the hinterland, he formed a strong personal vision for the future of the Colony that centered on the establishment of a Protectorate and the construction of a railway through the interior. Cardew's attitude and approach embodied the common belief that contact with European culture had corrupted African people's "traditional" way of life, which needed to be restored, but that repugnant practices like slave trading or witchcraft also needed to be rooted out for the sake of peace and economic progress.

Following this logic, frontier spaces became seen as "protected states" with their natural resources held in "trust" and their populations in perpetual tutelage. Protectorates throughout the British Empire justified their existence by claiming to safeguard local populations from external aggression (like other European Empires or foreign concession companies), as well as internal "exploitation" like their own despotic leaders, slave trading, and repugnant legal practices. According to the Foreign Jurisdiction Act of 1890, declaring a protectorate allowed for a seamless transition from a "sphere of influence" into a space where European Empires could exercise the same jurisdiction as if such had been acquired by the conquest or cession of such territories.[9] During the Berlin Conference and subsequent meetings, the sovereignty of African states was disregarded on the basis of those states being "semi-civilized," rendering the treaties they had signed with Europeans invalid. Essentially deemed minors under international law, declaring protectorates allowed European Empires to implement legislation written in the Colony without the participation of the African subjects living there.[10]

Protectorate rule in Sierra Leone was informed by these European legal ideas. By 1896, treaties and military campaigns were described as failed methods for asserting imperial control over the region. In declaring a Protectorate, colonial officials could effectively made licit extra-legal strategies like policing, incarceration, and the deportation of political prisoners, strategies whose legitimacy had been increasingly questioned by some colonial lawmakers as the century wore on. Like many other colonial spaces, the Protectorate Ordinance in Sierra Leone implemented a system of "indirect rule" whereby rural populations were "governed as far as possible, through the chiefs and in accordance with native laws and customs as far as they are consistent with humanity and civilization."[11] Community leaders of all ranks were transformed into "Paramount Chiefs" and were responsible for collecting taxes and acting as judges in local courts using "customary law." Unlike a formal Colony, Protectorate residents were legally classified as "natives" rather than "British subjects," a status that formally differentiated them from Krios and white Britons. While simultaneously claiming to protect African customs, this clause justified the alteration of any African institutions that ran contrary to European notions of civilization.

Petitions and Protests: The Initial Response of Sherbro Leaders to the Protectorate

"My good friend, I am directed by His Excellency the Governor to write and inform you that a law has passed under which your country has now become part of the protectorate."[12] This was the first line of the short circular that Governor Cardew directed Secretary of the Department of Native Affairs, Krio J. C. E. Parkes, to give to African leaders throughout the hinterland. Unbeknownst to them, their territory had been annexed and placed "under the Protection of Her Majesty" two months prior to Parkes' visit without their consultation. Local leaders were not the only ones Cardew had not notified; in fact, the first draft of the Protectorate Ordinance had been passed without even submitting a draft to the Colonial Office in London for approval.

Attaching a copy of the Protectorate Ordinance, Parkes sent an accompanying letter to Indigenous leaders outlining the new laws using a sort of local parlance adopted from decades of communication. The letter begins by explaining the change in the jurisdiction of local courts, stating that "all debt and other small palavers will be in the Chief's Court but big palavers like murder, 'slave palavers,' 'man-eating Leopard and Alligator palavers' shall be tried by the District Commissioner and the Chiefs . . . cases arising out of fights between different sections of your tribes shall be by the District Commissioner alone."[13] The letter also relayed that the Governor had the sole right to remove any Chief who was seen as "unfit for his position and appoint a fit and proper person to be Chief in his place." Leaders were told that they would now be required to pay the Government a "hut tax" each year: ten shillings for every house with four or more rooms, and five shillings for every house with three rooms or less. The penalty for individuals who did not pay was a fine three times the amount of the tax they owed. Leaders were told in no uncertain terms that continued disobedience would be viewed as criminal: "anyone who resists or obstructs officers in the performance of their duties shall be guilty of an offence."[14] Deportations, the letter warned, would be ordered for anyone who disrupted the "peace and security" of the region.

The imposition of protectorate rule caused shockwaves throughout the hinterland. Leaders immediately saw how these new laws undermined their authority with their slaves and wives, deprived them of roles as judges in their own courts (including the collection of court fees), stripped them of economic power, and—perhaps most importantly—dispossessed them of their sovereign rights to their own land. Letters directed at Parkes and Cardew expressed that the "laws were too strong," with one stating that the conditions of the Ordinance produced "such a terrible cry and noise over the country."[15] In particular, many cited their disbelief that the ordinance had not been discussed with them prior to its enactment, not knowing it was to happen "till we see it all of a surden [*sic*]."[16] Leaders expressed their anger by stating, "Every other law [in the past] has come through them to us: the law has jumped over them and come to us."[17]

The vast majority of the African leaders who wrote these responses were the colonial state's strongest allies, often framing their protest by citing how the Ordinance contradicted the terms of the treaties they and their forefathers had signed.[18] For them, the Protectorate represented a complete betrayal of British promises on the frontier that they would not interfere with African sovereignty. For instance, in a letter to the Governor from leaders in Mafwe on the lower Boom River, former treaty signatories expressed their frustration of not being included in negotiations over the terms of the Protectorate, as they would have been during former treaty negotiations. One petition sent from the leaders on the Small Boom River wrote that while they had "received and carefully perused the notice," and pledged to honor the basic articles of previous treaties such as keeping peace and "not destroying lives and property," they were not able to abide to the new instructions, such as the paying of the Land Tax and House Tax.[19] In a similar letter written by sixty of their neighbors in the south, leaders expressed their incredulity of the new Protectorate Ordinance and its incompatibility with the terms that they had previously agreed upon. They wrote:

> He [Governor Havelock] gave us law to clean the roads and not to fight or make any war or to kill willfully; we agree to all that laws, but now we see ourselves in bondage, we are not free, we know that our country did not take by conquest only we gave the queen to protect it, we find now she took it from us, but not only protection. If we know that such will be the case, we might not agree to sign treaty [*sic*] with His Excellency Governor Havelock, we ask him all these things, he deny that such will not take place. We know that H. M. Queen Victoria is a merciful queen and, she will not take another man country by force, thats [*sic*] why we agree.[20]

Both letters directly address protection, confirming that while they had agreed to British intervention in their wars or to refrain from engaging in the transatlantic slave trade, these treaty terms did not mean that their rights to the land had been forfeited. As we have seen, the process of forming a coalition with a more powerful leader in the precolonial period did not mean the severing of one's ancestral claims to the land.

Responses to the Protectorate testify to the transmission of the content of treaties from generation to generation. Treaties occurring during Governor Havelock's rule mentioned above, would have been signed between 1881 and 1884, a time when many of the men signing this petition had not yet assumed leadership positions. Those that were older and present at treaty signings clearly distinguished different eras by the Governors they had met. As Chief Gberri from the Boom River testified in 1898 after the insurrection was over, "Governor Rowe explained to us that the Queen did not want us to deal in slaves, and we agreed to that, or to sell or pawn our children, and we agreed we were willing to abide by that. Governor Havelock told us the same thing, and we were willing. Governor Hay said the same thing and we were content."[21] A petition to the Governor from a group of leaders from outside Sherbro in the Karene District embodied many of the same grievances of their southern counterparts: "Our forefathers were good friends with the Government . . . our forefathers did not sell this country to the Government; it was a friendship what belongs to us belongs to you as a friend."[22] Statements like this testify to the fact that leaders understood treaties as collective agreements between sovereign states.

Even the colonial Government's closest allies expressed their concerns about the tax. Madam Yoko, by then the leader of the Kpaa-Mende region for at least a decade, wrote the Governor asking that he "be gracious to us, by lesson [*sic*] the strength [of the laws] a bit, as we are country people."[23] Similar to the leaders mentioned, Yoko expressed confusion that her cooperation in "terminating" local wars in the region had essentially been met with even harsher measures. Careful to not be too critical, she writes that:

> [as this is a] new Ordinance which we are not accustom with we shall make a trial of it for we do not yet know what it is like yet. But if we find any that it be two [*sic*] strong for us, I think that if we ask His Excellency that an amendment should be made for us, as we are country people, he will be gracious to us and our request, as we are protectorate under the Government.[24]

Like many others who protested protectorate rule, her letter suggests that she believed the terms of the ordinance were flexible and could be negotiated with the Governor. Allies like Thomas Neale Caulker, who, like Madam Yoko, also owed their position to the support of the British Government, also expressed their hesitation at paying taxes which they feared were a dispossession of the land.[25] This fear was likely compounded by the fact that the majority of the allies of the colonial Government had ancestral lineage as "owners of the land," which already rendered them particularly vulnerable over the past two decades. The tax structure of the new Protectorate was essentially a reversal of the stipend system established by treaties (seen as a kind of rent from a stranger—the British—to their African landlord), and leaders feared that the payment indicated the unlawful "sale" of their ancestral territory to the colonial state.

Understanding this perspective helps us reconcile why Governor Cardew's outright rejection to negotiate the terms of the Protectorate (as countless Governors had with treaties) led to an unimaginable fear and anger that no archival record can truly capture. Perhaps the disbelief that such a massive territorial annexation could even occur without treaty negotiations further explains the initial response of leaders to engage in peaceful forms of protest to revoke the articles they found most unacceptable. As Governor Cardew rejected their requests one-by-one, African leaders regrouped to plan their next course of action.

Beh Sherbro and the Poro as a Form of Protest

Almost immediately after the announcement of the Protectorate, hundreds of Sherbro leaders gathered in the small town of Yoni on Sherbro Island, about five miles from the colonial headquarters of Bonthe. Leaders were summoned there by a man named Gbanna Lewis who held the title of Beh Sherbro or "King of all the Sherbro" since 1879.[26] Lewis was the grandson of Kong Kuba, the previous Beh Sherbro who had famously signed Turner's Treaty in 1825, the legal loophole that had allowed the colonial Government to annex places like Jong and other coastal regions that had been traditionally under his jurisdiction. Attendees to the meeting reflected the heterogenous population of the Sherbro and included important leaders from the entire coastal and riverine region. Beh Sherbro's authority over the titular provinces of the Sherbro state (and perhaps even beyond) stemmed from his elected title, his royal lineage, and his very high rank in the Poro.[27] Thus, while he lived on Sherbro Island, a region that was technically still the formal Colony and was not subject to protectorate laws or the hut tax, his role as the King of Sherbro facilitated his ability to form a massive Poro to discuss this unprecedented political crisis.

What was said at that meeting in November 1896 remains unknown. Afterwards, however, messengers were reportedly sent throughout the southern Protectorate requesting travel funds for Beh Sherbro to go to Freetown and "for the purposes of making a collection to employ a lawyer."[28] Rumors swirled that over £500 had been collected from the Sokong of Imperri, Queen Betsy Gaye of the Jong, and even leaders as far as the Bandajuma District.[29] On February 2, 1897, the funds were put to use. Beh Sherbro's arrival in Freetown caused quite a stir, particularly because he arrived with two hundred followers in tow.[30] This substantial delegation included representatives from the Imperri, Krim, Jong, Timdale, Boom River, and Bompeh regions. Among the important leaders present were the Sokong of Imperri and Adolphus Dick, the longtime representative and son-in-law of Queen Betsy Gaye.[31] In a later deposition, one of the delegates explained, we went to "see the Governor as a friend, and to express our opinion to him . . . [as] the laws have not been explained to us; we have only heard of them."[32] Leaders from the Jong read a letter from Queen Betsy Gaye that begged the Governor to "take pity on us poor natives . . . that they may please to abolish the paying of this tax ec [*sic*] as we are worth nothing and we cannot go against the government but we come humbly and beseeching to you."[33] After reading their statements out loud, one of the leaders present later recalled that the Governor responded by taking out a copy of the Protectorate Ordinance and "read[ing] a good deal of it out loud." He then told them that if they "require to trade, you will have to pay a trade license; and everyone who builds houses shall be asked to pay tax for the houses." He then explained the court system and reiterated that if "anyone makes a disturbance he will be transported."[34]

Cardew uniformly dismissed the complaints of Sherbro and other African leaders as the irrational response of "people that are practically savages—some are cannibals—quite illiterate and very degraded by ignorance and gross superstition."[35] His dismissal of their concerns reflected the pervasive notion that Africans were unable to comprehend the benefits that colonization would bring. Reading the archives today, however, reveals that leaders in the southern Protectorate were quite informed about the impact of colonial policies on their communities, particularly on issues of trade and the economy.[36] For example, colonial administrators misconstrued leaders' protests regarding their slaves as a cultural issue, rather than an economic one. While the export of palm kernels increased in the latter half of the 1890s, palm oil decreased substantially.[37] Trade licenses and fixed produce prices impacted the ability of leaders to obtain the labor needed to harvest and transport palm produce from forests to their town (to make palm oil) or carry palm kernels to the coast. The abolition of the internal slave trade in these palm-rich parts of the Protectorate must have additionally prompted African leaders' fears that their access to enslaved labor would soon be gone too, despite the fact that leaders were assured that domestic slavery would not be abolished.[38] Still, leaders were well aware that enslaved men and women had been travelling to the formal Colony or other centers of British authority like police stations to obtain their freedom for decades. In the year before protectorate rule was declared, the construction of the new railway enticed many young men to leave home in search of wage labor, instead of staying in their home villages.

African leaders' assertions over access to women's labor were also economic. Enslaved women, pawns, wives, and daughters were primarily responsible for the harvesting and production of palm oil. The significant decline in the export revenue of palm oil between 1895 and 1897 may be attributed to a decrease in accessible labor in conjunction with a declining global market and local constraints on harvest.[39] As we saw in previous chapters, women and children were the primary people kidnapped during raids. However, this form of acquiring both reproductive labor had largely been cut off with the establishment of Protectorate rule. According to some leaders, women were leaving their husbands in favor of partnering with Frontier Forces or other men who had access to hard cash and wage-based work (this may have also been true of enslaved women).[40] All of these changes served to challenge the patriarchal authority of men who had traditionally claimed almost exclusive rights to people, labor, and land.[41]

Much evidence suggests that local populations were also facing significant economic losses as the result of Krio traders' unfair practices. The District Commissioner received a report in 1896 that Krio trading houses had been using raids and seizures to recover their debts.[42] Many Sherbro leaders had come to resent the presence of Krio traders who failed to adhere to landlord-stranger agreements, bypassing them in favor of dealing directly with producers, and were rumored to have inflicted violence on their servants or refused to pay their laborers.[43] Hinterland populations came to regard all Krios as "white men" or the Government's *pikin* (Krio: children) and were seen as inseparable from the implementation of Government interference. African leaders focused their complaints on how the need to obtain licenses on trade and canoes seriously impacted their profit margin, particularly because the colonial Government refused to alter the price of palm kernels per bushel.[44] Krio traders upcountry were refusing to pay more than four shillings for a bushel of palm kernel, when the producers were asking for seven .[45] Thus, despite the fact that the export of palm kernels actually increased around three thousand tons from 1895 to 1897, constant agitation occurred between African producers and Krio traders.[46]

Africans understood these economic hardships were the result of imperial protection schemes that had been implemented over the past few decades. The lack of redress from the colonial Government in their first trip to Freetown compelled Sherbro leaders to regroup in Beh Sherbro's town of Yoni in February 1897. Together they debated how to proceed and unanimously agreed to revive one of the most powerful tools of the Poro: an embargo on agricultural products like timber or palm kernels or a ban on certain kinds of labor. Poro embargoes were an effective tool for pushing back against imperial trade conditions as they could stop the flow of trade along a particular river or impose sanctions on various groups or new kinds of fines and fees associated with trade.[47]

This was not the first time this type of embargo had been used against the encroachment of the imperial economy. During wars in the Sherbro in the early 1870s, reports of a series of fines, fees, and other bans that sought to limit the actions of British subject traders at the headwaters of the major rivers began to emerge.[48] Evidence suggests these pre-Protectorate embargoes originated in the upper Boom river, then travelled westwards to other members of their coalition in the Kpaa-Mende and upper Jong River region.[49] In 1881, John Parker, a longtime resident in Kpaa-Mende and son-in-law to Thomas George Lawson, reported that traders were complaining about a stoppage in "trading transactions by causing the Porroh customs to interfere with their callings."[50] As we recall from a previous chapter, these embargos were enforced by Lahsurrhu in Mattru in 1882 and were one of the primary causes of consternation that led to his arrest and incarceration. All of these poro embargoes aimed to regulate the market and counter the advantages that Krio traders had gained through special rights acquired in treaty agreements. By acting in concert, autochthon leaders from the headwater's regions demonstrated their ability to form a powerful confederacy that used Poro law as a means of acquiring resources and labor.

Twenty years later, they did it again. The Poro embargo in 1897 was remarkably effective. As Krio trader Moses Zacchaeus Macaulay recounted in 1898, the meeting in Yoni produced a "great change" in the Jong River: "All the men stopped working and they told me they had made a Porro [*sic*] law not to cut kernels . . . they said they would not cut them until they had got a note about the tax from the Governor in Freetown."[51] Beginning on the coastal shoreline, Krio and European traders complained bitterly that they were unable to obtain local laborers Palm kernels were prevented from being transported across the water to Bonthe along the side of Sherbro Island where Beh Sherbro lived.[52] The trade in palm oil dwindled as palm kernels reportedly lay rotting on the ground. As 1897 progressed, the embargo spread northwards. Trade was limited to local people only; no provisions or goods were to be sold to "Sierra Leoneans" and no laborers provided to them for trade. When Macaulay asked his landlord Queen Betsy Gaye what the reason for the poro was, she replied that she "told us we had no right to pay licenses in their country and that by paying license in their country we were giving the *Government ahold on it and they would soon be driven away* from the whole country."[53] By mid-1897, trade embargoes enacted along all the major southern river corridors ground trade to a halt.[54] Deputations of British, French, and Krio merchants located on the coast showed up on District Commissioner Thomas J. Alldridge's doorstep in Bonthe to inform him that produce was not being brought down as usual, and that they had been obliged to send their own laborers upriver to obtain palm kernels.

Colonial administrators immediately denounced the embargo as an act of despotic leaders hell-bent on destroying the economy through secretive and barbaric mind control. This position was epitomized in Alldridge's strongly worded memo to the Governor entitled "One-Word Poro." Here, he claimed:

> [while the] precise obligations attached to it [the one-word-poro] are carefully veiled there is, I am of the opinion, no doubt that whatever the mystery is, it is to no good purpose, is antagonistic to the interest of the Government and calls for the immediate remedied measure to at once deal with those badly disposed persons who are seeking to exercise undue influence over the minds of the ignorant and superstitious country people by Fetich [*sic*] artifices and by savage country customs.[55]

Alldridge's report emphasized the ability for the Poro to use these "savage country customs" to manipulate everyday people to do their bidding. Alldridge identified Beh Sherbro as the primary instigator and the Sokong of Imperri as his "main puppet." The coordination of local leaders defied British attempts to impose strict boundaries between the Colony and Protectorate and exposed the Poro's ability to coordinate between the chiefdoms in the five newly created Districts. Beh Sherbro's leadership further contravened the place of the District Commissioner in the political hierarchy of the new system.

Throughout 1897, colonial officials continually harassed the two men in an attempt to force them to remove the ban. Alldridge travelled to Yoni, rousing a sick Beh Sherbro from bed to give him a lecture on the proper respect due to "his good friend" the Governor. In Imperri, the newly appointed Assistant District Commissioner, a Krio named William Hughes, frequently terrorized the Sokong, even threatening him with the destruction of the sacred Poro bush if he did not lift the embargo. These reports and personal experiences led Alldridge to argue that these men's presence in the region disrupted the "welfare and permanent security" of the people and impaired the "general advancement of the country." He suggested that the removal of Beh Sherbro and the Sokong "for a time" to Freetown as political prisoners would produce "a most beneficial effect in the country."[56]

The Krio population also put pressure on the colonial Government to limit the actions of the Poro and other "secret societies" who they believed were working in tandem. In June 1897, a contributor to the *Sierra Leone Weekly News* alleged that members of the Human Alligator Society were working in tandem with the Poro by murdering anyone who dared cross the river to their farms or attempted to convey "produce for sale to the merchants or traders." This and other articles emphasized the barbaric and dangerous qualities of "secret societies," reiterating the common trope that all of the Poro leaders in this part of the country were "cannibals."[57] Not surprisingly, the article also identified Beh Sherbro as public enemy number one:

> The Chief of Yonnie [*sic*] who has practically assumed the character of O'Donnel to free his country from the British Government as is the belief of the untutored natives, has suddenly become all important and all his plans against the Merchants and Traders, in short, against the Government have met with support at the hands of mostly all the chiefs in the Jurisdiction, and in the Protectorate, backed by the native charms that were called into requisition.[58]

Like Alldridge's report, this article emphasized how the Poro and its "native charms" deprived people of their free will.[59] To put a stop to these acts and protect the general population, the article urged the Government to assert full jurisdiction over Sherbro Island and eliminate the title of "Chief" for any leaders living in British territory. Unlike the Protectorate, they argued, the laws of British Sherbro decreed that "all the natives here within the Colony-proper are British subjects . . . but when some of them are styled chiefs, they consider themselves as having subjects who are bound to obey them to the prejudice of, and in preference to, the British Government."[60] The control that leaders like Beh Sherbro had over his people (which perhaps might extend to leaders throughout the Protectorate) posed a dangerous threat to

British rule.[61] The continued status of the Sherbro Island or Imperri as part of the formal Colony (due to their respective annexations in 1861 and 1890 continued to blur both the physical and conceptual lines between colonial and protectorate rule.

The uneven application of British jurisdiction in the Protectorate produced a legal conundrum that was evident in colonial debates regarding the Poro. While residence within colonial territory technically guaranteed its inhabitants the protection of the British crown, it proved a double-edged sword when solving the issue of the "one-word-poro." Beh Sherbro and the Sokong could not simply be deported because their status as British subjects ironically protected them from being incarcerated without evidence and formal charges—special legislation was required to detain political prisoners who resided in the Colony. Therefore, in June 1897, the Executive Council empowered Attorney General Smyly to draft legislation to deport Beh Sherbro in the event of his refusal to remove the poro.[62]

After months of diplomatic attempts, the Legislative Council reconvened in November to pass the "Poro Ordinance" which made it an offence "for any person by any kind of 'Poro' laws or Customs or fetish to intimidate or hinder any other person from carrying on his trade." Rather than criminalizing the formation of a Poro, the ordinance made it illegal to "assault, intimidate or threaten any other person with intent to deter or hinder him from gathering produce." Anyone who "permits, encourages, aids, abets, incites or is concerned in placing or imposing Poro Laws or Customs" to block trade would also be found guilty as well as those who failed to report the formation of a Poro to the police. Leaders who were called to remove a Poro and refused would be found in violation of the Ordinance.[63] Because of the continued confusion over the boundaries in the south, the bill passed as the first law that was simultaneously applicable in both the Colony and the Protectorate. At the time the "Poro Ordinance" passed, J. C. E. Parkes, now retired from the Department of Native Affairs, warned the Governor of the futility of the new law. Well versed in Sherbro religion and politics, he warned Cardew that it was "no use to make a law against a secret society."[64]

Puugwei or "the White Man's War"

In December 1897, Cardew steamed up the Bagru River in the colonial steamer *Countess of Derby* to meet with the Sokong, Beh Sherbro, and other leaders of the area. The petitions and Poro embargo had been a source of extreme consternation

FIGURE 9. Group of Imperri chiefs photographed at Gbangbaia, Imperri, Sherbro, 1898.

SOURCE: T. ALLDRIDGE (2004). GROUP OF IMPERRI CHIEFS PHOTOGRAPHED AT BAMBAIA, IMPERRI, SHERBRO, FOUR AND A HALF MONTHS BEFORE THE NATIVE RISING OF 1898. [IMAGE]. ROYAL COMMONWEALTH SOCIETY LIBRARY. CAMBRIDGE UNIVERSITY LIBRARY. UNIVERSITY OF CAMBRIDGE.

for Cardew. Upon his arrival, six hundred people gathered and presented him with yet another petition outlining their grievances with the British Government, which included that their "slaves and wives . . . had become no longer amenable to their orders and were frequently deserting them."[65] Cardew recalled in a later dispatch that he had explained to the petitioners that since Imperri was within the jurisdiction of the Colony and not the Protectorate, it was bound by colonial laws which made slavery an offence. He told them that their concerns about the Hut Tax were unfounded "for the same reason, they had no jurisdiction as Chief except in the portions of their territories lying in the Protectorate."[66] Like the meeting the previous year, he dismissed their concern as a reluctance to give up their barbaric ways and embrace civilization.[67]

While Cardew did not record the exact response of local leaders on his trip, Thomas Joshua Alldridge, always at the ready with his camera, took a photograph of some of the leaders who had gathered. The image is a striking contrast from the more formal photograph he took two years before at the Sokong's coronation that opened this chapter. In the 1897 image, the Sokong's hand rests thoughtfully on his chin, looking directly at the camera (figure 9). He and the other leaders' sober stares seem to reveal their escalating frustration with the colonial Government's intervention and surveillance in their political and legal affairs. The powerful men of the country—the Sokong, his Speaker, Beh Sherbro and their fellow countrymen symbolically stand shoulder to shoulder and are literally backed with what appears to be a large crowd of Indigenous residents and Krios. Unlike the 1895 group portrait, not a white official is in sight.

Despite fifteen months of peaceful petitions and trade embargoes, the collection of the hut tax commenced on schedule in January 1898. Leaders realized that the legal means they had been pursuing were not going to be enough. Something drastic needed to be done. Large palavers like the one in Yoni formed throughout the countryside. In Mafwe, one Krio trader reported a meeting of one thousand people led by some of the colonial Government's closest allies, including a representative from Queen Betsy Gaye. In the Ronietta District, Beh Sherbro called another meeting in Kwelu.

When word spread of these meetings, the District Commissioner of both regions arrested the leaders for their "insolence" and refusal to pay their taxes. Not surprisingly, among the detained was Beh Sherbro, despite the fact that his residence on Sherbro Island precluded him from actually paying the hut tax. Other important leaders were rounded up, "seized by police men and roughly handled." Pa Nembana and Beh Sherbro were transported to the Freetown jail, while leaders from Mafwe were held in the Bandajuma prison.[68] In a deposition he gave after the Insurrection, Beh Sherbro stated his arrest was shocking, as he "did not expect to be treated the way that he was," owing that he had been "crowned by the Government."[69] The violence of these and other arrests of the Protectorate's most respected leaders disturbed people greatly. Rumors swirled that the Frontier Forces were indiscriminately murdering people for not paying their taxes, beating people, raping women, and in one case forcing a man to eat his own beard after shaving it off.[70]

In a secret location somewhere in the upper Boom River, several important men met covertly in March or early April of 1898. As it had been in the past, the region was an ideal location to convene such an important meeting, as it lay far from the prying eyes of the colonial Government. It is unclear whether this Poro was arranged independently or whether the meeting was orchestrated from afar by Beh Sherbro, as one later newspaper article alleged.[71] As a bell made from a giant turtle shell rang out, the Poro began. Leaders consulted their ancestors and debated the merits of going to war. What had occurred over the past two years must have been discussed and debated thoroughly before a "one-word-poro," a total consensus to go to war, was agreed upon. Poro elders assembled their messengers to circulate news of the decision they made. With them, messengers carried the sign of war: a burnt palm leaf and a bag of rocks. Messengers would throw one rock out of the bag on their journey each day and then instructed their allies to do the same upon receiving it. The day the last rock was thrown signaled the day to attack.

It is unclear whether subsequent meetings were held along the Jong, Bagru, and lower Boom River.[72] Regardless, the attack began simultaneously throughout the region. When the day arrived, many people observed that there appeared to be two separate waves of warboys; one that travelled south from the upper to lower Boom River, eventually attacking Mafwe, and another that travelled southwest towards the Jong and Imperri Chiefdoms. Some villagers reported that the insurgents used the word "Bumpe" as a password to identify themselves to fellow Poro members, perhaps further evidence that the final war Poro was held in that chiefdom.

On April 25, 1898, the sound of war horns was heard throughout the land. Warboys shouted "Koibia! Koibia!" meaning "war open!" as they attacked towns dressed in all white with a white headband and palm leaves wound around their neck and wrists.[73] The men referred to themselves as *wobaimbbay*, meaning "a flock of birds that does not stop in one place" in Mende.[74] Armed with "cutlasses, sticks, bill-hooks, and flint guns," they charged into villages believing they were protected from British bullets by the amulets or bags of medicines that they wore around their arms, neck, or feet.[75] These power objects would have been distributed by the various morimen that were hired by war captains and other powerful Chiefs to lead the various campaigns. Warriors raided villages in much the same manner as attacks recounted in previous chapters—plundering trade goods, destroying palm produce, killing men, and capturing women. Some important traders and missionaries were taken as prisoners (perhaps with the hopes of collecting ransom), and a few were later released after negotiations with District Commissioners.

All "white men" associated with the British were targeted, including Krio traders, missionaries, and Frontier Forces. Some accounts after the war suggest that even local people who had converted to Christianity or lived in mission stations were killed. As news of the violent "Mende Uprising" reached Freetown, Krios struggled to explain the events unfolding upcountry. Prominent Krio lawyer, Sir Samuel Lewis, believed that Krios were targeted by rebels because of the perceived relationship with the Frontier Force, who had become increasingly hated since the tax collection had commenced.[76] Thus, while around thirty European and American missionaries were killed, the Krio trader population was the hardest hit; likely somewhere between three and five hundred people were killed. In Imperri, Mr. Hughes, the Acting District Commissioner of the Sherbro who had had such an antagonistic relationship with the Sokong and his people, was tortured and then shot along with his wife days after he had preached about the benefits of the tax.[77]

Not every community leader participated in the Insurrection. After the Insurrection was quelled, Madam Yoko suggested that two of the waves of warboys from the upper Boom River region had directly targeted her and Nancy Tucker, the unpopular Paramount Chief of Bagru whom the Government had appointed the year before.[78] Yoko, Tucker, and others who owed their position to the colonial Government requested assistance and police protection. With the help of the Frontier Forces, both women escaped to colonial territory. Queen Betsy Gaye, who had initially been opposed to the Protectorate, also escaped to safety, though her main speaker Adolphus Dick had been arrested in Mafwe.[79] Thomas Neale Caulker of Shenge was not as lucky. Rumors circulated that he was killed by a man named Alfred Doomabay, a war captain of his longtime rival Francis Caulker, who had vied for Thomas Neale's position for at least a decade.[80] These targets suggest that rebels used the Insurrection to settle much older conflicts concerning colonial alignment with illegitimate leaders.

Courts and Commissions: The Legal Aftermath of the Insurrection

In the months following the first waves of attacks in the southern Protectorate, hundreds of Krio refugees arrived in Freetown. Their eyewitness accounts provided much content for the two major newspapers operated by Krios, the *Sierra Leone Weekly News* and the *Sierra Leone Times*. As they had for decades, the journalists offered pointed criticism and policy suggestions for the Government based on their long-standing relationship to the interior and their essential role in establishing trade there. While most articles were published anonymously, the level of detail speaks to firsthand knowledge of the events of the Insurrection, including the major players and towns. Accounts recall how Krios had been killed as innocent victims, emphasizing the murder of missionaries, women, and "suckling children" who died "praying, fixed and unmovable while the barbarians were tearing their flesh with cutlasses."[81] Some authors described villages strewn with bodies and corpses floating in the rivers. Other articles reprinted the long-held stereotype of the Mende as a particularly brutal and "bloodthirsty" people.[82]

Colonial reactions to the attacks in the interior were swift and severe.[83] Members of the Frontier Force led the charge, backed by the West African Regiment, the West Indian Regiment, and the Royal Navy.[84] Many prominent community leaders were arrested and placed in temporary holds throughout the Protectorate. Others were brought to the permanent prison in Bonthe on Sherbro Island or the main Government jail in Freetown. According to many witnesses, the arrests of local leaders included severe beatings, humiliation, and even death. Recalling previous military campaigns in the Sherbro, whole villages were burned, stockades destroyed, and civilians were forcibly conscripted to act as labor, turn over food for troops, or house battalions. This violence and the poor treatment of respected members of the community continued to fan the flames of resistance.

In addition to the deployment of colonial troops, Governor Cardew drew from a series of legal precedents from the frontier to punish the rebels. Cardew's "counter insurgency" ordinances imposed a series of emergency measures in the Protectorate. These new laws allowed him to arrest and detain the "insurgents" as political prisoners without formal charges. He requested special permission via telegram to conduct a court "trial of insurgent bands for capital punishment by Special Commission."[85] The Colonial Office did not immediately grant Cardew's request for a special court, asking for clarification on his request. In a telegram, Chamberlain asked:

> For what offences and by what virtue of what Ordinance do you propose to try insurgent bands by Special Commission? Send full particulars. Capital Punishment will not be allowed for any cause less than murder. Corporal punishment must not be inflicted on account of refusal to pay hut tax, as I consider that it would be illegal to inflict corporal punishment under existing Ordinances."[86]

Cardew's response to Chamberlain reveals a clear attempt to ensure that the "insurgents" he arrested were swiftly convicted and executed. His rationale for this special legal body was justified by his conviction that "there is no other mode of bringing offenders to justice in the cases where they have been concerned in the killing of Europeans and persons not native." Despite the number of Krios killed in the Insurrection, Cardew believed that any trial that would be conducted in Freetown with Krio men on the jury would not result in a successful conviction, as the "feeling is very strong against direct taxation in this Colony and the majority of the people sympathize in consequence with the cause of the insurgents."[87]

Colonial legal responses to the Insurrection of 1898 wove the paradox of protection into the judicial framework of the Protectorate. Cardew's ambitions were drafted by the Attorney General of Sierra Leone and sent to the Colonial Office at the beginning of April 1898. The "Protectorate Commission Inquiry Ordinance" allowed for the creation of a separate court, free of Krio jurors or lawyers. It was approved and passed into law on May 27, 1898. Additional ordinances were enacted to create a Travelling Assessors Court at the end of August and beginning of September.[88] Finally, the "Insurgent's Temporary Detention Ordinance" allowed for hundreds of people to be incarcerated without evidence. While these two ordinances were unique due to the circumstances of the Insurrection, these wartime measures built on a precedent of the *ad hominum* legislation that detained and deported local leaders or war captains on the frontier. Likewise, capital punishment was used directly after the military campaign as a demonstration of Britain's sovereign power, regardless of the executed man's subjecthood.

By October 1898, 180 men were tried by courts enacted specially for Insurrection prisoners. Of the 180, 67 men were acquitted and 112 convicted. Sixty-six of those men were executed. Almost a third of those executed were leaders from Imperri, including the Sokong, his Speaker, and likely many of the other men from Alldridge's photographs.[89] We know at least some of these men were no strangers to colonial courts—two had been accused of being the "principal instigators" of summoning the Tongo almost a decade before. After a short trial, twenty-one men were found guilty of the murder of Assistant District Commissioner Mr. Hughes. In the days after their sentencing, the prisoners desperately tried everything to avoid being executed, even "send[ing] for some persons to intercede for them" the day preceding their last in the world. While four of the prisoners had their sentences commuted at the last minute, the other seventeen men "went on the gallows, and on the verge of eternity, persisted in saying they were guiltless" and then dropped eight feet to their instantaneous death.[90] Following this, a series of special "Political Prisoners Ordinances" passed in early 1899 and seven of the suspected main leaders of the Insurrection were further detained without evidence in the Freetown jail.

Alongside these trials, another kind of legal intervention was occurring. The Colonial Office in London appointed Sir David Patrick Chalmers as a Royal Commissioner to investigate what the Colonial Office how new dubbed the "Hut Tax War" and the state of affairs in the Colony. From July to November of 1898,

Chalmers interviewed 272 witnesses, examined more than 40 historical documents, and produced a series of tables and charts outlining the economic history of the region. Printed in January 1899, the Commission consisted of 867 pages of observations, recommendations, interviews, historical documents, and data and is remarkably condemnatory in tone. It exposes the extreme and violent measures taken by colonial administrators to not only collect the "hut tax," but in policing the region more generally. In the conclusion of his report, Chalmers wrote that the Insurrection was caused by a deep "sense of personal wrong and injustice from the illegal and degrading severities made use of in enforcing the Tax, coupled with the aversion to the Tax in itself."[91] The collection of this tax, he insists, was tantamount to "legalized plunder," and he spends much of the Commission recounting stories of assault, torture, and murder on both sides of the conflict.[92] Chalmers attributes the rebels' actions to rational causes and the result of their particularly long and oppressive relationship with colonial police, traders, and merchants.

The Commission exposed many of the contradictions concerning the operation of British law within African territory that had been debated for decades. Unlike Cardew, Chalmers asserted that British jurisdiction over the Protectorate bestowed all residents the rights of British subjects, even if they did not technically possess the same legal status. His vocation as a lawyer and a judge made him particularly sensitive to what he saw as the legal oppression of the Protectorate's population. In the section of the Commission entitled "The Mendi Uprising," Chalmers expressed that "it would be impossible to do otherwise than conclude that there were very many examples of cruel and flagrant abuse of authority, utterly unsanctioned by the law."[93] Throughout the Commission, Chalmers asserted that Protectorate residents readily understood the principles of European legality, stating that the "native mind has a strong grasp of the idea of individual liberty" and that the tax represented a "taking away of the right of the people in their own country."[94] Chalmers characterized the Insurrection as a rational reaction to an infringement on their legal rights. The military response of leaders and their people was merely an extension of this assertion of sovereignty, as one of the leaders he interviewed stated, "paying for a thing in your country means you had no original right to it; so it seems as if they had no right to their homes."[95] The Insurrection, Chalmers concluded, represented a fight for their "home," something they had always been assured they possessed in previous decades.

Embodying the notion of protection, Chalmers reminds his readers that regardless of their race, the Protectorate population is "under the British flag. We impose restrictions and liabilities upon them. Reciprocally we are morally bound to do no violence to their rights."[96] His statement embodies a framework of "imperial legal universalism" that many colonial lawmakers increasingly held in the late nineteenth and early twentieth century. This position sought to accommodate and contain African differences within a global legality that aimed to bring all colonies under the same legal framework.[97] This vision for colonial rule in the Protectorate represented a particular set of liberal aims where indirect rule, unlike frontier imperialism, was structured through "settled laws . . . [and] settled legal principles and not by mere views of temporary expediency." Rule in the Sierra Leone Protectorate, Chalmers concluded, should be centered on repairing relations with African leaders by ceasing all punitive expeditions and providing amnesty for all combatants, including "the continuance of arrests, prosecutions, and even military promenades [that continue to] have the effect of unsettling and terrorizing," a repeal of the Insurgents Temporary Detention Ordinance.[98] Above all else, Chalmers recommended a gradual and benevolent form of rule in the Protectorate that emphasized partnership, trust, and understanding of the specific customs and practices of the people living there.

Making amends would be difficult considering the continued detention of the "primary instigators" in the Insurrection. Along with Bai Bureh, the leader of the northern rebellion, Beh Sherbro and Beh Kelleh of Banta sat in the Freetown jail without formal charges. Gberry and Nyagua, two prominent war captains who had previously been aligned with the colonial state, were imprisoned too, along with Richard Canreba Caulker—the Paramount Chief of the Bompeh District who had only just returned from exile as a political prisoner in 1894 to resume leadership over his chiefdom. Held as "political prisoners," separate legislation was drafted to deport Beh Sherbro, Nyagua, and Bai Bureh to the Gold Coast, paving the way for subsequent "troublemakers" who disturbed the peace of the Protectorate. The rest of the men died in prison and were buried in a Freetown cemetery far from their homeland and ancestors.[99]

Conclusion

The response of Cardew and other members of the colonial administration in Freetown to African protests highlighted broader debates about the definition of a Protectorate and the rights of the Africans living within it. Upon reflection of his initial draft of the Protectorate Ordinance, Cardew admitted freely that he had given little thought to bestowing Protectorate residents the status of "native' rather than British subject. For him, the two different statuses were self-evident and indicative of the lack of "civilization" that "natives" possessed compared to "a European or Sierra Leonian [*sic*]" who should not be "subject to the jurisdiction of a tribunal composed of persons quite uncivilised."[100] Just as policies of extraterritoriality had been written into treaties, the denial of British subjecthood to Protectorate residents permitted the colonial state to simultaneously extract resources and deny its residents the same rights of people born in the formal Colony. As we will see in the next two chapters, this legal loophole became a central tool of colonial law enforcement and justification of violence during the period of indirect rule.

The concomitant acts of violence conducted by Cardew and an investigative truth-seeking Royal Commission represent two sides of the protection spectrum, and reflect what historian Martin Weiner has identified as the "tension between everyday racial inequality evident throughout the Empire and the deep-rooted liberal premise of British justice that extended everywhere in the Empire."[101] The emergence of scientific racism reshaped how colonial officials thought about precolonial past, including Africans' capacity for signing treaties and their ability to act as effective intermediaries within the framework of indirect rule. These ideas shaped the legal structure of Protectorates, in particular informing colonial policies that sought to reorder African political and legal structures.

For Africans living in the Protectorate, the legal aftermath of the Insurrection represented both a continuity with the past and a new and uncertain future. Though most of Chalmers' recommendations fell on deaf ears, the colonial administration did engage in a series of centralizing reforms in the Protectorate that formalized the position of Paramount Chiefs and established bordered chiefdoms. These restructuring efforts ushered in a new era of extreme political instability, as African leaders and their competitors scrambled to establish and protect their lineages' right to rule and favorably maximize borders of their "chiefdom." As the political and territorial constraints of British rule commenced, existing conflicts over land and legitimacy that stretched far back into the precolonial period now had to be settled in a new political sphere.

CHAPTER FIVE

Making Paramount Chiefs and Chiefdoms

Conflicts over Land and Leadership in the Protectorate, 1899–1915

In February 1901, the newly appointed Governor Charles King-Harman commenced his first tour of the Sierra Leone Protectorate. With the Insurrection of 1898 looming in the not-so-distant past, one of his main aims was to foster good working relationships between the colonial administration and the local African leaders that the British relied so heavily on. Travelling on the newly built railway, one of King-Harman's stops was the town of Moyamba. Days before the Governor's arrival, the town's leader Madam Yoko gave strict orders to clean the roads and make repairs to the Officer's Quarters, the Court House, and the District Hospital. Madam Yoko had been an important ally to the British both before and during the Insurrection, and her loyalty had undoubtedly secured her position within the new governmental framework of the Sierra Leone Protectorate. On the days before his arrival, much discussion and rumor circulated among the townspeople about this new Governor who was said to love "justice and truth . . . irrespective of colour and race."[1]

When the Governor finally arrived, he was greeted by Madam Yoko, another Paramount Chief Nancy Tucker of Bagru, and hundreds of townspeople, Krio traders, and Big Men who had made the journey to Moyamba to see what the Governor had to say. King-Harman stood in the crowded Court House and laid out his vision for the relationship between the colonial Government and the Chiefs. Reminiscent of decades past, he asked the Chiefs to embrace him as a "friend" they could trust and not fear, emphasizing the British Government's "desire before all things that you and your property and people shall be protected." The recent death of the Queen of England, he proclaimed, would not impact the governance of the Protectorate, for the new King would continue to "protect this country . . . preserve the people with peace, and prevent war." While he expressed that the protection of the people would remain the primary aim of the Crown, in this new era, leaders were told they could not expect the people of England to pay for the security and benefits they now possessed. Referencing the Insurrection, King-Harman assured the people that the tax they paid was the "smallest tax paid by anyone in the world . . . for the peace and security which they have under her protection." Speaking to the leaders directly, King-Harman informed them that taxes were collected for the benefit of their own security, allowing them to "trade without fear of war and need no fear of having their villages burnt and their women and children taken as captives."[2]

King-Harman's visit was clearly a chance for Madam Yoko, Nancy Tucker, and their Sub-Chiefs to demonstrate their loyalty and secure their position in the Protectorate. The extreme violence of the Insurrection of 1898 and its aftermath surely signaled to them the permanence of British rule, and with it, a radical transformation of power and authority. Establishing oneself as a legitimate leader in the eyes of both the Government and one's own people in southern Sierra Leone proved to be an extremely precarious endeavor. Fierce competition between ruling families and ambitious competitors, many of which were extensions of these same contests for power in the pre-Protectorate period, were exacerbated by the new political constraints of Protectorate rule.

As elsewhere in colonial Africa, the imposition of indirect rule, a system of rule through African institutions and intermediaries supervised by European officials, aimed to stabilize rural African populations to produce optimal conditions for economic development. The framework of indirect rule began with the assumption that there once existed a time of extreme stability in Africa's precolonial (pre-slave trade, pre-imperialism) past. Then, Britons believed, Africans lived in small communities ruled by the complete authority of male leaders (Chiefs, Kings, etc.). Indirect rule sought to replicate this imagined past by instituting a new vertical bureaucracy and codified "customary law" that were entirely overseen by British District Commissioners, judges, and other administrators.

Two elements were at the center of political reform in the Sierra Leone Protectorate in the years following the Insurrection of 1898. With the aim of restoring "peace

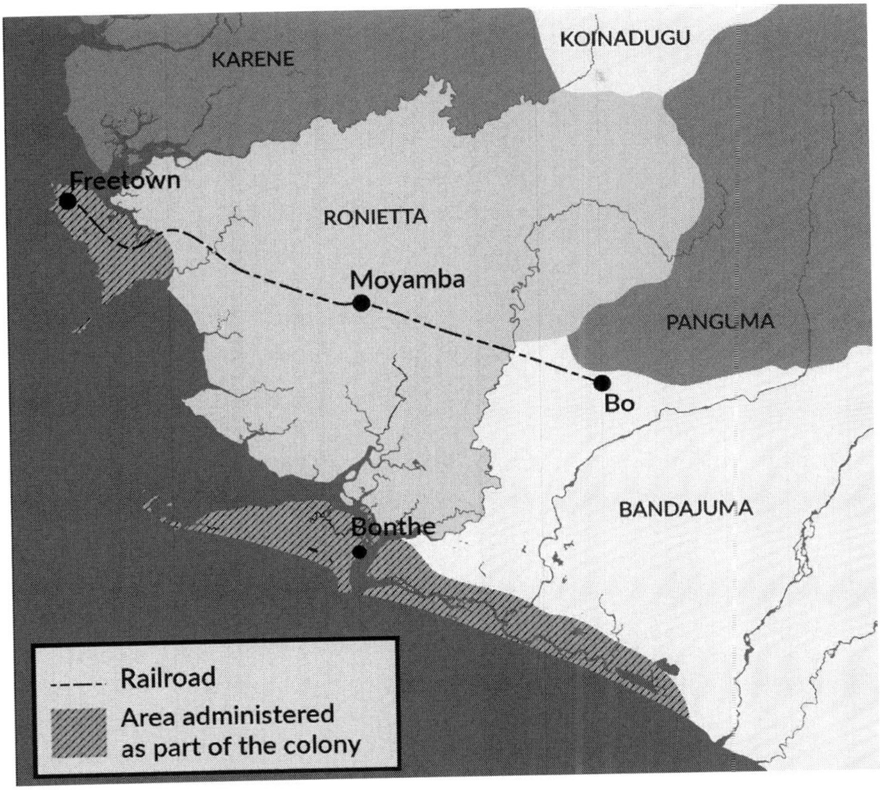

FIGURE 10. Map, Sierra Leone Protectorate Districts, 1900.

and security" to the region, administrators sought to reorder the political landscape by creating a "Paramount Chief" who would be assigned to rule a corresponding bordered "chiefdom." This chapter traces the selection and implementation of Paramount Chiefs and their chiefdoms, revealing how the formalization of these two new political forms compelled local leaders to construct legal claims to land and leadership that blended older narratives of founders and strangers with colonial notions of sovereignty and self-determination. This contestation occurred within the framework of colonial policies that placed considerable constraints on these imperial intermediaries, including limiting candidates to members of ancestral or founding families and strict political and legal control over Paramount Chiefs' access to wealth, labor, and resources. Given the Sherbro region's heterogeneity and flexible definitions of leadership, these policies created intense debates over what constituted legitimate authority over people and land, principles that, as we have seen in previous chapters, had transformed considerably over the last one hundred years.

Initially, the southern Sherbro region that this study has concentrated on bridged two of the five new Protectorate Districts: the Ronietta and the Bandajuma—later amalgamated as the Northern Sherbro District—while a few coastal areas that had been annexed in 1861 remained part of the formal Colony.[3] While the borders between Sherbro's southern titular provinces had gradually become more fixed through British annexation and African political consolidation, Protectorate rule altered the meaning and function of these boundaries. By reformulating these spaces into bounded "chiefdoms," the colonial state aimed to constrain Paramount Chiefs' ability to form regional coalitions or project power across multiple regions as they had during warfare or the Insurrection. Competing political claims over space frequently included complex narratives that went back several generations using the language of settlement and strangers. As colonial rule rerouted people and resources towards the interests of the British state, the political power of the Paramount Chiefs became constrained within the boundaries of their chiefdoms.

So far, this book has traced how British desire to create order and security ironically lead to a paradox of protection: vulnerable leaders who aligned themselves with the colonial state became increasingly vulnerable to violence and political rivalry from competitors and strangers. The creation of the Sierra Leone Protectorate essentially codified this paradox by creating a formal structure of rule that limited or criminalized Indigenous protection strategies but did not replace them with sufficient social or economic capital to assert legible authority over their people. In doing so, the new framework of indirect rule generated unprecedented levels of social and political turmoil. The incorporation of frontier practices like deposing and deportation worked directly against British aims to impose a stable group of imperial intermediaries and instead created political chaos and frequent interregnums. In the Ronietta District alone, Paramount chieftaincies changed hands within chiefdoms an average of three times in fifteen years, the majority of which were the result of community accusations of corruption, illegitimacy, despotism, or human leopardism.

While Protectorate laws, like frontier protection schemes, were created by the British, they could not simply be imposed without the "contingent accommodation" of African intermediaries.[4] As Moses Ochonu writes, the concept of protection in African Protectorates was "not a phenomenon made up simply of European protectors on the one hand and protected subalterns on the other, but rather as an enterprise that involved a range of actors and gradations of power."[5] As this chapter shows, African and British contestation over what constituted protection, and who had the authority to bestow it, continued to shape the colonial legal order in the era of formal rule in fundamental ways. The frequent election of new Paramount Chiefs occurred alongside a multitude of claims over land and legitimacy from incumbent ruling families, their competitors, and community members. By closely examining two cases studies in the Kagboro and Jong chiefdoms, this chapter shows how debates over territorial jurisdiction and political succession integrated local definitions of chiefly authority and protection into Protectorate law. Over time, I argue that these contestations over power produced new political and geographic structures that transformed the institution of Paramount Chiefs and their chiefdoms into meaningful and durable features of indirect rule.

Making Paramount Chiefs

The impact of colonial rule on African political institutions is one of the most pervasive topics debated by anthropologists, historians, economists, and political scientists.[6] Sierra Leone is no exception. On one hand, some scholars have argued that the decision of the colonial Government to select Paramount Chiefs from leaders with demonstratable connections to ancestral lineages fostered a certain continuity from the pre-colonial to Protectorate period in that it favored candidates who descended from rulers and families prior to 1896. In the words of one historian, the "resurrection of the old criteria for chieftaincy" in Sherbro facilitated the election of the grandsons and granddaughters of previous titular leaders into the position of Paramount Chiefs.[7] This continuity has lent some scholars to conclude that the institution of Paramount Chieftaincy (and to some extent territorial chiefdoms themselves) in Sierra Leone was not "invented," but an approximate extension of the precolonial political institutions and territories that had previously existed.[8] One aspect of continuity that has been particularly debated is the role of women rulers in the precolonial period.[9] Historian Lynda Day asserts that rather than the "achievement-oriented criterion of military prowess" that arose during the wars of the 1870s and 1880s, the "reconstitution" of chiefly authority on the basis of one's ancestral lineage in the Protectorate "proved to be a pathway for females to formal positions of authority."[10] Female Paramount Chiefs elected after 1896, she argues, represented a return to an earlier time when women held important positions of community leadership based on their lineage, personal aptitude, connection to Sande, and role as mediators. While she does admit that some features of legitimate authority did change (including wealth and the size of territorial holdings), many aspects of the "system of landholding families" persisted. Day's findings have been echoed by a number of social scientists, many of whom conclude that "the creation of colonial chieftaincies did not disrupt the strength of these families" who claimed original occupation.[11]

On the other hand, some scholars have asserted that Protectorate rule "radically transformed power relations" through the destruction of precolonial states, the transformation of local authority, and the disproportional political power given to Paramount Chiefs.[12] Historian Arthur Abraham characterizes the 1896 period as a "high velocity" shift that "blurred our understanding of the precolonial system" and "distorted the true traditions of the people."[13] Indirect rule, he argues, appointed leaders who did not possess the necessary qualifications for legitimate rule, while simultaneously diminishing the Poro from intervening in local politics. In the words of Abraham, "pre-colonial chiefdomship belonged to the past; a new kind of chiefship was now the order of the day."[14] In contrast to Day's position on female Paramount Chiefs, Abraham argues that women like Madam Yoko and Nancy Tucker were "colonial products" that entirely owed their position to the British.[15]

In a sense, neither of these positions are entirely right or wrong. While some precolonial Kings or Queens and their descendants did become Paramount Chiefs, the line from precolonial to Protectorate is not necessarily as straight and clear as some scholars (or members of those families today) surmise it was. In the southern hinterland, some of the "Founding Families" that became recognized by the colonial state (and, indeed the Government of Sierra Leone today) were often the result of treaties and the distinct set of "aligned" leaders they produced. This process was highly contingent on political geography. As leadership in the former Sherbro state was considered relatively "weak" compared to areas elsewhere (like the former Kpaa-Mende state), the colonial Government took a more forceful approach in appointing and guiding their elections. Particularly after the Insurrection in 1898, the colonial Government sought to select leaders in southern Ronietta more for their loyalty, rather than their legitimacy. The legacy of diplomacy and the sheer number of leaders who had signed treaties shaped which leaders were initially appointed as Paramount Chief and, subsequently, which ancestral lineages were able to establish themselves as "Founding Families." This process was similar for the borders of precolonial states and provinces. For example, while the Mende political states north of Sherbro were eventually balkanized to limit the power of former warrior Chiefs, the titular provinces of southern Sherbro remained fairly intact. In part, this geographic stability in the south can be attributed to the precolonial political structure of Sherbro and the territorial consolidation the had been occurring since the 1860s.

The long engagement between Sherbro leaders and the British state had a significant impact on how leadership was viewed and how indirect rule was implemented. For at least a century, British officials attributed two main factors to the instability of the region: the lack of centralized authority and "fetish" worship or other "heathen" customs. Wars between leaders were dismissed as "petty" conflicts or "tribal disputes" that were the result of Africans being in a "comparatively primitive stage of development [with] too little organized industry."[16] Furthermore, increased visibility of secret societies like the Human Leopard Society and the role of the Poro in the events of the Insurrection in 1898 compounded British impressions of African leaders as subversive and secretive. Governor Cardew, the initial architect of the Protectorate, characterized the leaders' in these communities as "only just emerging from barbarism . . . in many respects he is but a grown-up child and requires the Government to think and act for him." For Cardew, it was the British Empire's "moral obligation to civilize, educate, and raise to a higher standard of life . . . [and] protect the native from corrupting influences."[17] To do this Colonial Governors and administrators focused on reforming institutions connected to African leadership, believing that "it is through the Chiefs alone that we can help the people to raise themselves into the position of citizens of the Empire."[18] Customs and practices that were seen as potential sites of insurgency or disorder were criminalized in an effort to prevent them from challenging the authority of British rule.[19] Over time, subsequent Governors came to see themselves as a sort of "wise and experienced native Paramount Chief" themselves.[20]

The notion of protection guided British administrators' aim to centralize and civilize this imaginary past. Despite experiences over the previous decades that demonstrated the opposite, British administrators held the deeply engrained belief of the stability and static nature of African society which included a patriarchal Chief who held authority over a single ethnic "tribe." Paramount Chiefs were viewed as illusory figures whose authority had been disrupted by the transatlantic slave trade, the introduction of imperial commerce, and "modernity" in general. Dynamism in African rural societies was largely seen as cultural, rather than driven by political or legal institutions, which was seen as fundamentally irrational. Indirect rule aimed to stabilize and codify Africans "traditions," which in theory would prevent Africans from modernizing at too rapid a pace or being exploited from outsiders or other empires.[21]

To further limit the power of Poro elders and regional Kings like the Beh Sherbro, the Protectorate Ordinance dictated that Paramount Chiefs were directly answerable to a European District Commissioner and could not be "subordinate in his ordinary jurisdiction to any other chief." This article aimed to flatten the complexity of the nature of leadership by limiting the political jurisdiction of any titular ruler or King who could project power across wide regional spaces.[22] Put another way, the position of Paramount Chief was structured such that each one was on the same rung of the political hierarchy. Subordinate to the District Commissioner, Paramount Chiefs were responsible for the collection of hut tax, judging cases in "customary court," and providing service and insight as assessors to the District Commissioner in the "Mixed Court" (later the Circuit Court). In exchange, they continued to receive their precolonial stipends, were provided with a 5 percent cut of the tax they collected, and were given an additional rebate if they collected the tax in coin.[23] They were also able to retain fees and fines they obtained as judges and collected a standardized annual £1– £2 "gift" from strangers who settled on their land.[24] In 1905, revised laws expanded the power of Paramount Chiefs to obtain labor from their people for cultivation and public works, including the building of their compounds.[25]

While the formal policy was to select Paramount Chiefs from "Founding Families," their appointment was highly contingent on the relationship they established with the British prior to 1896. This can be seen in the initial years of the implementation of indirect rule.[26] In fact, the term "Paramount Chief" was rarely used in colonial correspondence or Freetown newspapers in the first two years.[27] An original list of "Paramount Chiefs" is printed as an appendix in the Royal Commission in 1899 after the Insurrection, likely compiled by J. C. E. Parkes specifically for David Chalmers' purposes. The various ways that leadership is accounted for in each region reveals the haphazard nature of indirect rule in its early years. Each Protectorate District had its own unique organizational structure, with some merely listing a single leader and the villages (not leaders) they had jurisdiction over.[28] The chart for Bandajuma lists eleven Paramount Chiefs and Chieftainesses and twelve other "chiefs and chieftainesses" alongside various "Native Districts or Towns."[29] In Ronietta, the district that encompassed the majority of the region covered in this book, ten Paramount Chiefs are listed, along with fourteen Chiefs, one Sub-Chief, and one "Ex-Chief" (Richard Canreba Caulker).[30] Some leaders labeled Paramount Chiefs are listed as rulers of what would become chiefdoms (like Ben Sherbro of Yoni), while others are only identified by their town of residence. Furthermore, some of the leaders listed as "Sub-Chiefs" in 1898, like So Lokko of Mano Bagru, somehow became official Paramount Chiefs of those "native districts" the following year.[31]

The Insurrection of 1898 had a profound impact on the structure of Paramount Chieftaincy.[32] The high number of Krio and British deaths during the so-called "Mende Rising" in July 1898 fueled administrators' desire to assert a firmer control over this region. As we saw in the previous chapter, Governor Cardew used the Insurrection as an opportunity to stage something akin to a military "conquering" of the southern Protectorate by exiling and executing leaders he deemed antithetical to the interests of the state. Cardew and subsequent Governors rejected David Chalmers' recommendations to "restore to the Chiefs the privileges they formerly enjoyed" in favor of a more rigid system of leaders and chiefdoms that emphasized British law, order, and protection.[33] To aid in this new schema, J. C. E. Parkes and the District Commissioners embarked on a Protectorate-wide accounting and evaluation of leaders and their territory in 1899.[34] The result is a unique volume that still sits in the Sierra Leone Archives that became one of the foundational documents for establishing Paramount Chiefs and their corresponding chiefdoms. Each entry lists the name of a single Paramount Chief, the name of chiefdom, and details of their rule ranging from one sentence to a page and a half of text.

Despite a paucity of detail in some of the entries, most descriptions emphasize the history of the leader before the creation of the Protectorate, a sense of their character and reception by their people, and their loyalty during the Insurrection. Read as a whole, the volume reflects British preoccupation of installing leaders who had some degree of legitimate authority but did not have the means to challenge British hegemony like their predecessors. Thus, even after the Insurrection, the majority of the Paramount Chiefs in Ronietta and Bandajuma were men and women who had already established relationships with the British through treaty signing and collecting stipends—some cases even if they had participated in the Insurrection.[35] Perhaps more so than other districts, southern coastal leaders where the Insurrection had been concentrated tended to have more tenuous connections to ancestral lineage than their northern counterparts.

In the two case studies discussed next, we return to families and regions that we closely examined in the previous chapters. To establish their legitimacy as rulers and stake claim to land and resources in the new Protectorate, their stories show how Paramount Chiefs and their competitors were compelled to invent and unearth narratives of strangers and settlers that stretched back hundreds of years.

Caulkers and Sosants: Conflict over Leadership in the Kagboro Chiefdom

In precolonial Shenge, negotiations over authority and territory were particularly fraught among Britain's oldest allies. As seen in previous chapters, the Caulker family underwent a series of political and economic challenges during the transition from the transatlantic slave trade to agricultural commerce. Beginning in the 1820s, Caulker leaders used diplomacy and treaty making with the British as a means of securing political and economic leverage in the region over older autochthon groups, stranger migrants, and even their own family members. Caulker signatures are found on over ten individual treaties throughout the nineteenth century, all of which varied in their promises of protection, annexation, and peace. In signing these treaties, Caulker leaders believed themselves to be asserting their exclusive rights to their territory, even though other ruling families continued to claim that they were "strangers."

Upon the establishment of the Protectorate in 1896, Thomas Neale Caulker transitioned from the title of King of the Shenge and Cockboro to Paramount Chief of Kagboro Chiefdom. Since his coronation in 1881, Thomas Neale had proven himself to be "decidedly aligned" to British interests. Though regarded as an illegitimate leader and "son of a slave" by some Caulker family members, the British had protected him from being overthrown by the "old people whom the country really belonged to," a label that was a vague foreshadowing of events to come.[36] Thomas Neale was well connected to Krio traders and overseas missionaries, as well as Krio colonial officials like Thomas George Lawson with whom he had attended school in Freetown during their youth. Literate and a professed Christian, his connection to the British state and collection of the hut tax made him a target of insurgents, leading to his murder which was said to be revenge for his connections with the British that led to the execution of William Caulker in 1888.[37]

Thomas Neale's death exacerbated old rivalries between the descendants of the Shenge-Caulkers and another "Ruling Family," the Sosant, who claimed it was their ancestors who had been the original founders of the region. The Sosant's proposed candidate for Paramount Chief was Madam Neighbo, a woman who had been married to Thomas Neale Caulker, but had long separated from him on account of a dispute between the two families.[38] Perhaps sensing her claims to Shenge would not be approved, in 1901, Madam Neighbo declared her intentions to the Governor to form a separate chiefdom east of Shenge where she would be Paramount Chief.[39] Her request and the territory she claimed was noted in an early colonial map sketching out the borders of two new chiefdoms—one that was ruled by the Caulkers in the area surrounding Shenge, and the other northeast of that in the territory that surrounded the Sosant capital of Mocobo.

Her pronouncement prompted loud protests by the Caulker Family. Their intent was to elect Thomas Neale's widow, Sophia Neale Caulker, as Paramount Chief. After much debate among colonial officials, Madam Neighbo's demands were rejected on the grounds that Sophia Neale Caulker's combined ancestral connection as the granddaughter of George Stephen Caulker and as the widow of the former Paramount Chief secured her title and territory of the whole region.[40] The land that Madam Neighbo proposed form a separate chiefdom was incorporated into Sophia Neale Caulker's holdings and formed a single chiefdom called the Kagboro. These new colonial borders now made the Sosant family mere Sub-Chiefs in what they saw was their rightful territory.

The election of Sophia Neale as Paramount Chief was typical of how the British initially "appointed" Paramount Chiefs in the early years of Protectorate rule in the southern coastal region. Sophia Neale's lineage and demonstrated loyalty to the colonial state disregarded claims over rulership over the chiefdom from other groups that had not substantially engaged in diplomacy with the British prior to 1896. Despite this early leadership struggle, relations between the Sosants and Caulkers appeared to have been officially quiet for seven years.[41] However, the death of Paramount Chief Nancy Tucker and the election of So Lokko, the grandson of the precolonial leader in the adjacent Bagru chiefdom, reinvigorated tensions between them. The Sosant family's attendance of the coronation of this "ancient family" prompted them to renew their own claims to a separate chiefdom. In April 1908, they wrote the District Commissioner to declare their wish to "have their country independent to ourselves . . . [and not to] a foreigner not belonging to our tribe neither family as if to say we are all dead." Sosant elders denounced the treaties the Caulkers had signed with the British in the past as having been signed "without consenting them [*sic*] and taking advantage of their being ignorant of book learning." To rectify a great "oppression in our land," the Sosant Chiefs sent a bold invitation to the District Commissioner, requesting his attendance at the "coronation" of their "own paramount chief" in Mocobo."[42]

Throughout the remainder of 1908, a series of antagonistic letters were sent between Shenge and Mocobo. The Sosant leaders accused Sophia and her family of being "strangers" whose forefathers had actually been the tenants of *their* direct descendent, the Ya Cumba. Sophia penned scathing letters back, threatening them with arrest and declaring with unshakable insistence that her family had ruled the Kagboro since "time immemorial." In one letter, she wrote with confidence that she was "not afraid of your presented claims. I know you are only making an empty noise . . . I close with the advice that you will please have less to do with my chiefdom until you prove your pretended claims, It is not your district, it is mine, If it is yours please to prove it."[43] At stake was whether or not a Caulker had the right to assume the position of Paramount Chief, given that the founding ancestor of their family, Thomas Corker, had been a stranger and a tenant to the Ya Cumba. Countering these claims, Sophia forwarded a number of treaties and correspondence between the Caulkers and the British from 1820 to 1899 as "proof" of her and her family's right to hold the title and territory. By the end of the year, the threats volleyed between the two sides alarmed the British to the extent that the Governor decided to intervene, lest the letter writing dissolve into armed conflict.

The conflict between the Caulker and Sosant family reveals that the recognition of a Founding Family in the Protectorate necessarily hinged on defining who was a "stranger." The colonial policy of selecting Paramount Chiefs from existing Founding Families required those who claimed ancestral connections to the land to demonstrate (and potentially invent) settlement narratives to cement their access to political power. These claims included both narrower and more expanded definitions of "owners of the land" and "strangers," depending on who was making the claim. In the past, strangers to the land were required to secure the permission of the existing settlers who had rights to the land to hunt, trade, or settle. To strengthen their ties to the land, high-status stranger-tenants like Thomas Corker often married the daughter of their landlord or the ruling elite to secure their tenure to the land and gain a place in society for their children and subsequent descendants. Particularly among the Sherbro people, subsequent generations of children born of this type of union were in the position to possess land-use rights through their mother's lineage. As the marriage of Thomas Neale to both Madam Neighbo and Sophia Neale indicates, the merging of families clearly did not end with the settlement of the initial "stranger," but continued throughout subsequent generations as a way of maintaining peaceful political and social relations. In this sense, the consequences of accepting an initial stranger or strangers were more than a "simple economic agreement"; they involved the merging of families and a commitment to certain interpersonal relations, a pathway to social and political belonging, and a projection of future relations based on successful reciprocity.[44]

While this way of accommodating strangers helped peacefully incorporate newcomers into the political structure of Sherbro in the past, it muddied claims to land and leadership in the Protectorate. The framework of indirect rule reshaped leaders' relationships to the land and resources by legislatively fusing ancestral lineage and rights to land in ways that were considerably less flexible than the precolonial period. The Sosant family's assertion that the Caulkers were "strangers" was a clear strategy to seize political control, but was also supported by their perceived break in the landlord-stranger reciprocity. This was especially seen in the way that the Sosant's frequently emphasized that Caulker rule was extortive and did not adhere to ancestral ways.[45] As they stated in 1908, it was "*unlawful* to see strangers in command of the country" who do not "seek the intress [*sic*] of it while the right owners of the country are available to be in command."[46] In a subsequent letter, they further stated that "we know that the Caulkers at Shengeh are strangers even for that spot of ground which inhabit by them. We can prove that our forefathers brother or near relation a Chief by the name of Ya Cumba station at a town call Tarsoh who gave the Caulkers Shengeh to reside as strangers." Confidently, they assert that "now we have the Government who is just and will give us our right." They wished to place "the Caulkers of Shenge [in] their right place by the native sistem [*sic*]."[47]

Throughout the documents, it is notable that the Sosant cite illiteracy as the primary reason they have not been able to assert political control over the region. In 1908, various Sosant leaders wrote the colonial administration stating that the Caulkers insisted that because they were a "lettered people . . . [they would] instruct us the right way of obeying the Government." This suggests that the Shenge-Caulkers' visibly distinct outsider status through their English language, conversion to Christianity, adoption of other British cultural traits, and mixed-race heritage placed them in a position of permeant cultural intermediary between local people and European traders.[48] It is also possible that the Sosant's assertion that the Caulkers were "strangers" stemmed from resentment in their involvement in the slave trade. In the 1960s, one member of the Sosant family told a visiting anthropologist that the Caulkers had sold their descendants to European slave ships after being tricked into going to the Plantain Islands and poisoned by "knock-out" powder.[49] For the Caulkers, their claims to the land were supported by Corker's initial marriage to the Ya Cumba's daughter (forming the Ya Cumba-Caulker line), which ultimately allowed them to claim ancestral control through matrilineal descent.[50]

In December 1908, Governor Probyn travelled to the Protectorate to try to unravel these contradictory claims. While in Shenge, Sophia Neale Caulker's Speaker George Domingo recounted the long history of Caulker rule in the region. His narrative was clearly aimed at discrediting Sosant claims to rule over the Kagboro chiefdom. In one story, Domingo downplayed the relationship of the Ya Cumba to the Caulker family, stating that at the signing of the Treaty of 1825, the woman described as the Ya Cumba was actually a "subchief" and "ought not have signed as queen."[51] His account also aimed to discredit the "character" of the Macobo leaders, describing them as "troublesome" and "warlike," even relating these qualities as the primary cause of Governor Rowe's military expedition in 1875. In more recent history, Domingo also claimed that the Sosant had also been the ones to murder Thomas Neale and that lately, Madam Neighbo had been imprisoned for confiscating hut tax. All of these stories were presented as evidence that Mocobo people were not worthy of rule.

While these historical arguments were clearly integral for the Africans gathered at the meeting, Governor Probyn seemed to be unmoved by them. Instead, he fixated on the current state of the chiefdom and Sophia Neale Caulker herself. Probyn seemed highly disturbed by Domingo's vocation as a trader, which he believed prevented him from being able to judge cases in customary court impartially. Probyn's report to the Colonial Office characterized Domingo as a puppet master over the "old" and "weak" Chief Sophia, whom he frequently described as suffering from a sort of dementia. In his final speech, he imparted to the gathering that Sophia should be deposed on the grounds that her "mind is so upset that she cannot remember things . . . she cannot do business." He explained to those assembled that deposing her would "leave the country free after it is settled down to choose a Paramount Chief," to which the people agreed.[52]

The deposing of Sophia Neale Caulker was the final opening the Sosant leaders needed to claim the title. In 1907, Madam Neighbo's brother Sei Lebbi became the Paramount Chief of Kagboro and moved the capital to Mococbo. In Sei Lebbi's three years as Paramount Chief, the Caulker and Domingo family relentlessly tried to undermine his authority.[53] In May 1910, Sophia Neale and ninety-seven other Caulker family members, Shenge residents, traders, and merchants submitted an extensive six-page petition that reiterated their claims to exclusive rule over the

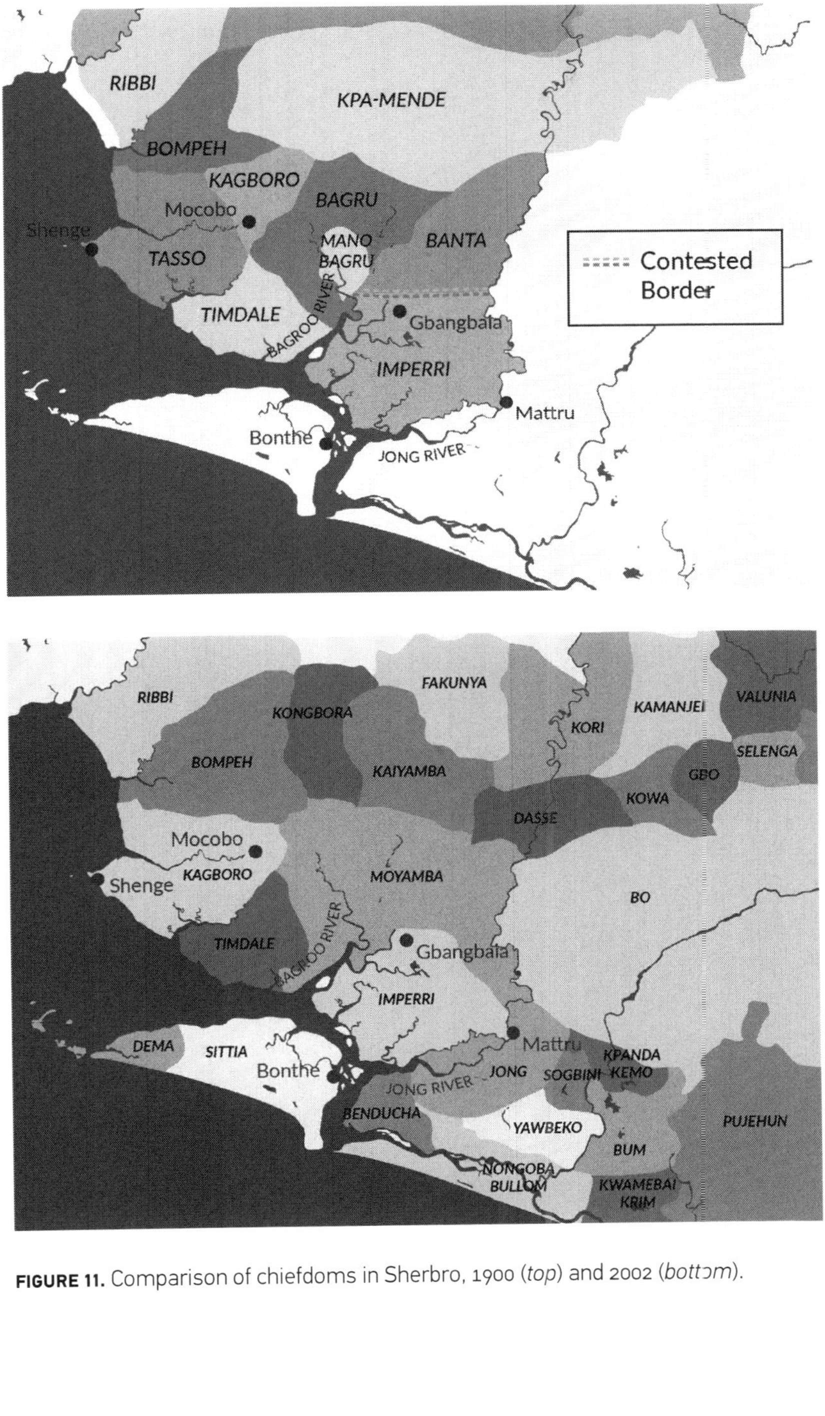

FIGURE 11. Comparison of chiefdoms in Sherbro, 1900 (*top*) and 2002 (*bottom*).

Kagboro Chiefdom. The petition described each of the treaties that the Caulkers signed and included excerpts of correspondence between the Caulker family and various colonial officials that, in their eyes, positively confirmed the extent of their territory. When the petition was reviewed by the Attorney General, he flatly rejected its claims on the basis that the establishment of any Protectorate made treaties null and void; acknowledging the sovereignty of the Caulkers would "seriously hamper the protecting power in carrying out the various duties for which it made itself responsible when the Protectorate was proclaimed but which is entirely foreign to the modern conception of what is implied by a protectorate over semi-civilized or barbarous peoples." Treaties, he asserted "were entered into while the modern conception of what is meant and understood by the establishment of a Protectorate was still in process of evolution" when "the various tribal rulers were probably regarded by those then representing the British government as being hereditary sovereigns with rights vested in their families in respect of the territories over which they exercised authority."[54] Simply put, treaties were now to be considered a vestige of the past, mere scraps of paper signed in a time of European ignorance of "native laws and custom." In the famous words of the architect of indirect rule Lord Frederick Lugard, "the old treaties were dead."[55]

The Attorney General's report was likely based on another decision made two years earlier. When the nephew of Canreba Caulker, Thomas Canreba Caulker, became Paramount Chief of Bompeh Chiefdom 1907, he also submitted a petition directly after his coronation citing treaties as evidence of the historic boundaries of their chiefdom. His initiative was also based on a dispute over boundaries of his chiefdom, claiming that his land had been "usurped" by Madam Yoko, a leader he describes as a stranger and refugee to the region. Like the Shenge leaders, the Bompeh-Caulker leaders' requests to expand the boundaries of their chiefdom were rejected based on the perceived "unrest and disorder" colonial officials imagined would ensue by redrawing the border. Thus, in both Caulker Kagboro and Bompeh territories, colonial law ruled that the family were operating under the "false assumption" that they had exclusive sovereign rights to either chiefdom.[56]

Attempts by the Caulkers to claim exclusive authority in their respective chiefdoms can be directly tied to their early efforts to engage in reciprocal protection arrangements with the British almost one hundred years before Protectorate rule. Their tenuous control of the land (both because of inter-family and external competitors) likely compelled them to be some of the region's earliest treaty signatories. As seen in the previous chapters, those who challenged Caulker authorities were among the first men executed after military campaigns or detained and deported as political prisoners. However, in the end the accusation by the Sosant family that the Caulkers were "strangers" simply did not matter to the British, so long as they remained loyal to British interests. If they didn't, they would end up like John, William, or Richard Canreba Caulker—on the wrong side of the law.

While Africans saw treaties as evidence of their rights over titles and territory, the British did not see it that way. Similar to treaties, the legal flexibility of indirect rule enabled the continual reinterpretation of African law to serve British interests. Protectorate policies utilized the language of protection only to uphold African leaders and pre-colonial polities in ways they believed would uphold British hegemony, rather than shield African rural communities from the encroachment of modernity (as they sometimes claimed). In the end, as Governor Probyn wrote, the "interests of the people, were of greater importance than the rights of the family from whom, in normal times, the people would select as a Chief."[57] Throughout the Protectorate, colonial officials consistently opted for leaders and territorial configurations they believed would usher in the most economic stability with the least amount of friction from leaders and their people.

The method of selecting Paramount Chiefs often had the opposite effect. Selecting leaders who were loyal over those who the people saw as legitimate frequently lead to a Paramount Chief being deposed either by the Government or by criminal charges connected to corruption or human leopardism. This perpetuated a cycle of political insecurity that was at complete odds with British aims for stability. This example of the paradox of protection can clearly be seen in the battle over the Kagboro. In Shenge, conflicts over leadership between the Sosant and Caulkers went on for decades after Sei Lebbi's coronation. After a succession of several Sosant leaders and a long period of interregnum, the grandson of Thomas Stephen Caulker, Samuel Africanus Caulker, was made Paramount Chief in 1919. Despite major challenges to his rule, family history cites that he was able to protect his power using native medicines and power objects to place a curse on his competitors.[58] Like the Paramount Chieftaincy in Bompeh Chiefdom, leadership of Kagboro remained in Caulker hands for the remainder of the colonial period and beyond.

Contesting Borders, Proposing Chiefdoms: Returning to the Imperri, Jong, and Mongray

The creation of the Protectorate spurred several territorial reconfigurations.[59] Some resulted from border disputes between Paramount Chiefs, while others were attempts by communities to establish new chiefdoms based on the claim that they had historically constituted a separate polity.[60] With the imposition of colonial rule, the mediation of jurisdictional disputes was no longer the authority of the Poro but was now in the hands of the colonial Government. In 1901, Governor King-Harman remarked that the majority of complaints directed at him by Protectorate leaders concerned land—either the "absence of boundaries" or the "encroachment on each other's territories."[61] Two years later, he frustratedly wrote that many of these conflicts remained unresolved, despite them being of "vital concern" to leaders. Rectifying these disputes, he admitted to the Colonial Office, was "exceedingly difficult to unravel; the rival claimants for territory always being ready to produce any amount of evidence in support of their respective contentions."[62]

Border disputes involved protracted debates between leaders and elders that unearthed long histories going several generations back, often coalescing along the same border and transportation hubs as the previous century. Land disputes emerged to rectify inconsistences based on the rights of past settlement, competing family lineages, and unsettled inter-community conflicts. After having served five years as District Commissioner of Ronietta, George Page wrote in 1909 that petitions to settle border disputes often "divulge secrets frequently long hid and bare the conditions of the country as it existed fifty and more years ago with a precision and a reality quite startling in its vividness . . . this adds immensely to one's fund of information concerning the District one is called upon to administer."[63] By this point, African leaders in Ronietta were requesting that the colonial Government place "artificial marks" on the "physical features of the ground [that] were always used as landmarks."[64]

Prior to the creation of the Protectorate, legitimate authority was demonstrated by a leader's ability to protect large amounts of dependents. Leaders amassed the resources to do this as far as their trade and kinship networks stretched, sometimes connecting people and places of a considerable distance. The imposition of formal chiefdom borders in 1900, however, limited leaders' abilities to engage in the reciprocity expected between clients and patrons. This may have been particularly true in the Sherbro region for a couple of significant reasons. The first was the construction of a railway that connected the headwaters of the major rivers at the beginning of the century. This new transportation corridor redirected trade directly to Freetown rather than down the rivers to Bonthe and the other custom houses on the coast. Moreover, Protectorate laws that mirrored treaty stipulations and other punitive measures continued to constrain these same leaders' abilities to project meaningful political power. The second was that chiefdoms that did not contain large tracts of palm forests or the rivers to transport those goods were at a considerable disadvantage from those that did.

Soon after his Protectorate tour that opened this chapter, Governor Charles King-Harman realized that the appointment of former allies had not resulted in the type of centralizing power structure the colonial state had hoped. This failure, ironically, stemmed from the execution and exile of many of the leaders of the Insurrection of 1898. For example there can be little doubt that the deportation of Beh Sherbro (the "King" of the Sherbro) had been deliberate attempt to limit his executive power. Despite numerous petitions insisting he be allowed to return like other political prisoners, he died in the Gold Coast in exile. His predecessor, Fama Yanni, lacked legitimacy and was eventually deposed and deported for the possession of illegal objects connected to the Human Leopard Society.[65] Thus, the inability for Paramount Chiefs like Fama Yanni to assert control over their communities was a direct result of the policies of indirect rule. In his report to the Colonial Office in London, King-Harman remarked that "the Chiefs of Sherbro are men of no great influence or position. They do not in any great degree command the respect of their people." This weakness, he noted, gave them "neither the energy nor the power to do much either of good or of harm in their country."[66]

While this may be a surprising statement given that this same group of leaders organized a large-scale rebellion less than three years prior, King-Harman's confident statement undoubtedly stemmed from his observation that the majority of the Paramount Chiefs in Sherbro needed "constant support" to maintain their position, especially as the Government had limited the overt use of the Poro.[67] Despite this, Paramount Chiefs continued to utilize the Poro to control their people on a number of occasions, such as preventing young men from deserting the chiefdom or preventing the importation of "powerful medicines" from Liberia.[68] While some colonial officials continued to question the legality of the Poro (no doubt as the memory of the Insurrection lingered), officials did lessen their criticism when it was used to uphold the authority of (especially colonial appointed) Paramount Chiefs.[69] Taking a cue from these Indigenous laws, colonial administrators imposed their own ordinances that limited the mobility or labor of young people or criminalized destructive medicines in an attempt to empower Paramount Chiefs in these matters.[70] And still, despite these efforts, political instability persisted as the authority of Paramount Chiefs was continually challenged by their competitors, Big Men, and their own communities.

Perhaps not surprisingly, one of those politically volatile regions was the Jong Chiefdom. As we saw in previous chapters, the population along the banks of the Jong River historically consisted of an ethnically diverse population. Strangers from afar offered resources, trade connections, and supernatural services to the local community. When they intermarried with local populations and established their own towns, they connected local leaders with trade routes that ran deep into the interior. In the nineteenth century, one group of Susu migrants arrived in search of trade opportunities.[71] In chapter two, we saw how the leadership of one of those descendants, Lahai Serifoo, challenged emergent Big Men traders like Tom Cabbie Smith who had become wealthy through their participation in the palm oil and kernel trade. Conflict between the two leaders precipitated a long-standing conflict in the 1870s and early 1880s between the "Mongray people" of whom Lahai Serifoo belonged, and a broad alliance of Imperri, Jong, and Small Boom leaders. In 1882, the conflict over the political control of Mattru resulted in a British military campaign and the emergence of Betsy Gaye as "Queen of the Jong" through her ancestral connections. By 1888, she moved to Matrru and became a clear ally of the British Government, frequently calling on them to protect her during raids from her enemies. In 1890, the frontier road was built through her town and police were permanently stationed there.

Maps in this period reflect this territorial turmoil. Historically, the territorial states and titular provinces in Sherbro possessed geographic boundaries that were marked by natural features and manmade markers.[72] In the south, these borders—which one historian has referred to as "territorial"—tended to remain static no matter who was in power. However, while several maps in 1853 and 1861 clearly label a region named the "Jong," by 1876 the Jong province was bisected with a territory labelled "Jong" in the north and "Mongray" in the south. However, by 1882 the placement of the town of Mattru outside the Jong province foreshadowed the intense battle over that place.[73] By the mid-1880s, the standardized map created by the War Office of the region completely omitted any territory called "Jong." This may have been because it became incorporated into British territory, although other similar regions like Bagru and Imperri that had been annexed by that time remain on the map, so it is unclear why the Jong is missing.[74] In the Protectorate, the titular province became the "Jong Chiefdom," returning roughly to its precolonial borders.

The successful territorial transition from precolonial state to chiefdom can likely be attributed to the diplomatic prowess of Betsy Gaye. Like Madam Yoko, Gaye was one of the female leaders in the southern coastal region to successfully navigate the transition from informal to formal rule in the Protectorate. Despite her involvement in protesting the hut tax, she somehow remained in power after the Insurrection and was listed as the "Paramount Chieftainess" of Jong in the Royal Commission.[75] Land disputes between the Jong and Imperri first appear in the colonial record following the election of the Sokong of Imperri in 1895. As described in the opening of the previous chapter, Humper Karwonjoe's coronation marked the end of a twenty-five-year interregnum that had produced internal political strife that impacted the entire surrounding region. After the new Sokong was pulled from the Poro bush, the Speaker called out the names of the of villages he believed were within Imperri territory, following the custom that those assembled would have the opportunity to either agree or protest by raising their hands.[76] When the towns of Banka, Mocharge, and Kabati were called out, Betsy Gaye's representative, a man named Sessi Temmi, put up his hands in protest to indicate his dissent. His actions indicated that he believed that the towns belonged to the Jong and not the Imperri.

Jurisdictional disputes that could not be reconciled at a coronation would typically be mediated by a third person, most likely another titular leader or the Beh Sherbro himself. If those means failed, raiding, as we saw in Gundema after the death of the Sokong in 1870, could be used to forcefully reclaim a town or region. Likely unwilling to risk a raid due to her alliance with the British, Betsy Gaye attempted to lean on her long-standing connections with the colonial Government. Upon Sessi Temmi's return, Gaye wrote the District Commissioner in 1894 to inform him that the Sokong had "took it upon himself to make an encroachment into a portion of my territory by compelling the people of the town of Gbanka (Banka) on ackoint [*sic*] of the Imperri people residing there."[77] She wrote that she was "positively aware that the extent and limit between my territory and the Imperreh [*sic*] is in records in the hands of the British Government and can be referred in this case."[78] In an effort to settle the matter, District Commissioner Alldridge and Beh Sherbro travelled to the region on the eve of the declaration of the Protectorate.

Like the Shenge and Kagboro palaver in the previous case study, the two sides each presented their case by recounting historical evidence that was framed in the language of the protection of strangers. On the Jong side, Gaye's representative told a rather recent story from 1890 when several strangers arrived in Mattru to beg Queen Betsy Gaye for protection. The men, it was said, had travelled from Imperri to shield themselves from the Tongo players who were currently sweeping the Imperri seeking out human leopards. Although initially rejecting their request, the men were eventually permitted to settle in the towns of Banka, Mocharge, and

Kabati—three small villages about ten kilometers west of Mattru. Sessi Temmi noted in his testimony that these same towns had allegedly been "called out" and recognized as part of Gaye's district at her coronation as Sei Kama in 1888.[79] Seeking her patronage and protection, the men paid her "one head" of money to be placed under her "sceptre," a customary present from a stranger-tenant to a landlord. However, when a few people who had initially come to Gaye travelled back to Bogo, one of them (Kongtam) was burnt as a human leopard. Following this, Gaye called a large meeting of leaders from throughout the Jong to settle the matter and to formally ask the Mocharch, Kabati, and Banka people if they were "for her," to which they replied "yes." A "law book" was made to solidify the agreement by two Sierra Leone traders and another leader, Henry Tucker.[80]

The Imperri Speaker Largubah did not deny the previous events, but instead told a different story that stretched even farther back in time. His narrative began with the settlement of a stranger to Imperri named Sessi Gama.[81] At that time, the Sokong was a man named Kpanaboam. According to contemporary oral history, Kpanaboam was the younger brother of Solundo, the original founder of Imperri province who had settled in the region at the turn of the nineteenth century.[82] As per customary landlord-stranger agreements, Larugbah stated that Kpanaboam gave Sessi Gama a wife and an "island" called Mongray, asking his ally and brother-in-law Mr. Cleveland to "look after" Sessi Gama as long as he resided there.

The story clearly aimed to show that the settlement of Sessi Gama in Mongray was conducted entirely within Imperri networks. He had been a stranger under the protection of the Sokong, and thus outside the reach of Jong political power. Ultimately, Alldridge sided with the Imperri people, reasoning that if the men of those towns originally belonged to the Jong, why would they have to be placed under the "sceptre" of Gaye in 1890? And why would a "law book" need to be created affirming that the towns were under Gaye's jurisdiction if they had historically been so? Moreover, as these events occurred, Alldridge—knowing the Protectorate was imminent—stated that he believed that the border dispute should be "fixed" for the "benefit of the Crown."[83] Alldridge's confident declaration he could settle the border dispute was short-sighted. Less than two years after the creation of the Protectorate, Imperri and Jong leaders continued to wrestle over the ownership of Mocharch, Kabati, Banka, and several other towns located along their shared border. The Mongray people living in those contested spaces were not silent in the negotiations. Like the Sosant and other groups within the Protectorate, in 1901 they attempted to form a separate "Mongray Chiefdom" away from Jong and Imperri control. However, unlike their Mocobo neighbors, this request was considerably more difficult to justify. As Muslims, these men continued to be marked as "strangers" in the region, despite the fact that their ancestors founded towns in the region up to one hundred years ago. Despite this, Mongray leaders insisted that a separate chiefdom was justified on account that their unique history and religious identity constituted the right to self-determination. Mongray leaders tried to use the structure of indirect rule to formalize their historic claims to the Sherbro region in ways that were previously unavailable to them as strangers and Muslims.

Following the 1898 execution of the Sokong and his Speaker and the death of Betsy Gaye in 1901, Mongray leaders attempted to take advantage of the high level of political instability to present their claims again. Beginning in 1901, Sub-Chiefs from the Mongray sent petitions to the colonial Government asking for a "division" of their territory from Imperri. The Sokong's successor, Paramount Chief Reverend Daniel Flickinger Wilberforce, openly denounced their claims as "fictitious" and a deliberate "attempt by the Mongheri [*sic*] people to break away from his Chiefdom,"[84] subsequently threatening them to such an extent that many of the petitioners retracted their request out of fear.[85] Despite these intimidations, the Mongray leaders submitted another petition two years later. The 1903 primary signature on the petition—Chief Lucainey, alias Bangua[h]—proclaimed himself as the "Chief of Mongray" and their territory as the "Chiefdom of Mongray."[86] The petitioners argued that their towns should form their own district due to the fact that as "Mohammedans," their religion was "altogether opposite to that of the people of the Imperreh [*sic*]."[87] Petitioners capitalized on the renewed human leopard cases in the district, stating that their wish was to be "isolated" from Imperri to "keep from being dragged into their cases of Cannibalism."[88] The words of the petition were either prophetic or lies. Three years later, three of the men who signed the Mongray petition were accused of engaging in a human leopard murder.[89] In 1906, they were found guilty and executed.

These land disputes with Mongray occurred alongside a great deal of political turmoil in both chiefdoms. Between 1896 and 1913 the Imperri and Jong chiefdoms frequently changed leadership: three through death, one for misconduct, and five due to accusations of being connected to human leopard murders. Much to the surprise of many of his British and Krio supporters, Reverend Wilberforce was accused of participating in the same murder as the Mongray petitioners. Though Wilberforce was found not guilty during his trial, he was deposed from his position as Paramount Chief of Imperri. His replacement, Seh Kainjah, complained to the Government that his Sub-Chiefs, headmen, and people would not follow his orders and that they "did not like him as Paramount Chief."[90] Four years later, his replacement Alfred Goma (Gomer) Kertegbeh, who was reported to be a police court interpreter for the colonial Government, was appointed in 1910 as a favored candidate by the colonial Government, but also seems to have been descended from a founding family and was known to be a "leading Poro man."[91]

In Jong chiefdom, the political terrain was equally unstable. After Betsy Gaye's death in 1901, her daughter Priscilla became Paramount Chief. Following her death a few years later, Priscilla's daughter Alice became Paramount Chief. Alice's rule was as unpopular as her mothers, and she was deposed by her people on the grounds that she had "abus[ed] her Porroh [*sic*] oath by failing to administer justice impartially and receiving bribes," neglecting the "concerns of her Chiefdom in general." Additionally, she was accused of having "discard[ed] [her husband] in a fairly indiscriminate manner to the disgust of her people" by having sexual relations with a "slave boy" who was attempting to usurp control of the affairs of the Jong country." She was also said to be prone to extreme drunkenness.[92] Alice was deposed and deported from Sherbro in January 1910. Her brother, Bunting Williams, who had also been living in Freetown and working as a goldsmith, was elected Paramount Chief in her place.[93] Like his grandmother, mother, and sister before him, Williams inherited the title of Sei Kama when he was reportedly elected by the people.[94]

Although Mongray claims for their own chiefdom ended with the petitioners' executions in 1906, the frequent deposing of Paramount Chiefs in Imperri and Jong induced round after round of negotiations over the jurisdiction of Mongray. After Wilberforce's deposing, a portion of the Mongray country was "given back" to Priscilla Gaye's chiefdom.[95] Yet five years later, after the election of Williams and Kertegbeh, negotiations were reopened and the remainder of the towns were enfolded into the Jong. As the District Commissioner proclaimed, the "old boundary between Imperri and Jong has been formally restored, and consequently the Imperri Chiefdom is now much smaller."[96] Imperri Paramount Chief Kartegbeh reportedly took a "leading part in the proceedings connected with the restoration of the old boundary" and was granted several monetary concessions for his "loss," including a larger yearly stipend.[97] In this finalized agreement, which appears to still exist today, Bunting Williams gained permanent claim to the old Mongray territory and both sides of the Jong River. Kertegbeh's actions, however, appear to have been seen by his people as a flagrant misuse of his power and opportunity to hoard wealth for his own purposes. Like the Imperri Paramount Chiefs before him, he was accused of being a human leopard in a case in 1912 that centered on the town of Kabati.[98] After being arrested alongside several other Sherbro Paramount Chiefs, including Bunting Williams, he likely died in prison that year.

Frequent deposing due to accusations of human leopardism and other abuses of power suggest that Paramount Chiefs in the southern Protectorate engaged in extortion or other forms of extractive violence to financially compensate their loss of precolonial income.[99] The new constraints imposed by Protectorate rule made it essential for Paramount Chiefs to maximize the few monetary benefits from the colonial state like renumerations from hut tax, court fees, and obligatory labor from chiefdom residents. Because of this, expanding or contracting one's territory was clearly a tactical decision: a region that was rich in palm or transportation corridors, like the border of the Imperri/Jong was worth battling over, while less lucrative and depopulated spaces meant more land to manage and people to feed without additional compensation. For example, on the southern border of the Jong, the Gaye dynasty sought to expand their border into the Nongoba-Bullom Chiefdom where another group, the Byama people, sought to form their own chiefdom.When their request was denied, they petitioned to remain in the Jong chiefdom after Bunting Williams agreed to cede their land to the recently elected Charles William Tucker of Nongoba-Bullom Chiefdom.[100]

While the District Commissioner approved of the new borders, the people of those villages did not. In a seven-page handwritten petition submitted by seven "Sub-Chiefs" and nine "Headman," leaders expressed their deep dissatisfaction with Bunting and Tucker's land palaver. The petition contained a long history of the border conflict, describing the boundary markers between their land and the Nongoba-Bullom in intricate detail, which included trees, hills, rivers, and even a swamp. The leaders, which included Betsy Gaye's former son-in-law Adolphus Dick (married to Priscilla's sister), outlined how they had repeatedly implored Williams to assist them in clarifying "How is it that our lands are taken by Chief Tucker in that way?" but recounted that he provided no answer, saying they must work it out with Charles Tucker. The petition stated that the signatories did not believe that Williams had the "right of transferring our lands without our knowledge and consent," claiming that the result was "600 men, women, and children are turned away from these villages and farms belonging to Byamah and deprived of provision for food also the old and new crop in their farms and the palm trees from which they derive their living."[101] By 1913, Bunting Williams himself was deposed. The region was in a state of chaos, and the Government appointed Charles Tucker's first cousin Abraham Tucker as Paramount Chief of Jong in 1911.[102]

Conclusion

Conflict over the newly created Paramount Chieftaincies and borders of chiefdoms was a central feature of Protectorate politics in the first decade and a half of indirect rule. The deposing and electing of new Paramount Chiefs became critical moments for shoring up a descent lineage's right to rule and their territorial boundaries of their chiefdom. Many former treaty signatories were able to secure their families place as a "Ruling House" for future generations. Paramount Chiefs and other Protectorate residents integrated the customary pairing of settling land disputes and coronations into Protectorate policies, creating a series of ruptures. Debates over the status of strangers and their place in the new Protectorate framework wove old and new definitions of legitimate authority into the structure of indirect rule.

Conflict between leaders over land and leadership were emblematic of a fairly rapid shift from the flexible nature of precolonial governance to the more rigid institutions of indirect rule. Leaders sought to claim their right to title and territory based on historic narratives of settlement and occupancy, sometimes citing events that stretched back centuries. At stake was whether groups like the Caulkers or the Mongray had successfully transformed from "strangers" to founders. For the Sosants, the Caulkers were dismissed as mere "foreigners" who had been able to convince the British they were the ruling families because of their literacy. The Caulkers countered this position, claiming that their centuries-long settlement in the region and the development of Shenge as a successful port had secured their status as the sole ruling family in the region. In contrast, the Muslim Susu population along the Imperri and Jong border tried to use their distinctness as justification for a separate chiefdom. Eventually, however, the narratives presented by more established and seemingly "loyal" leaders were more compelling to the colonial state. Unfortunately, these same leaders required a level of protection from the colonial state to ensure they remained in power, resulting in new laws that did not accommodate older and more flexible expressions of legitimate authority. In this way, the paradox of protection established on the frontier continued into the Protectorate era, once again preventing the orderly reform of African political frameworks and growth of the economy desired by the British colonial state.

Debates that occurred during the election of new Paramount Chiefs were not the only forums where authority was negotiated. The creation of a new judicial system in the Protectorate provided African litigants with a new legal space to debate the meaning of rights and protections in the new Protectorate. Like political institutions, criminal legislation drew heavily from earlier protection schemes developed on the frontier and during the Insurrection of 1898. Like struggles over Paramount Chieftaincy and chiefdom borders, human leopard murder trials mobilized British protection language to justify British intervention in African customs and practices that appeared to challenge the "peace and security" of the region. African litigants, in turn, utilized human leopard trials as forums to debate and navigate the political and economic instability of indirect rule.

CHAPTER SIX

Litigants and Leopards

The Human Leopard Society in Protectorate Laws and Courts, 1901–1914

On December 9, 1908, Humpa Baiwa took the stand at the Moyamba Circuit Court. A farmer from Imperri, Baiwa was the first witness in what would become a three-week trial of five men accused of participating in a human leopard murder in the Imperri chiefdom. Over the first five days of the trial, Baiwa recalled a long and contradictory story about his role in the death of seven-year-old Mawoni. Baiwa testified that he and one of the defendants were approached by a Chief named Lamina who asked them to help him "catch Mawoni" in exchange for "money and a wife." After anointing the "borfima" with the blood of Mawoni, Lamina would use the powerful medicine for its intended purposes: to "get riches" and to "make a man strong and successful."[1]

When Lamina took the stand for the defense, he vehemently denied Baiwa's accusations. As the Chief of Victoria, he stated he had worked diligently alongside his fellow African leaders and the colonial Government to try and eliminate the Human Leopard Society. Believing Humpa Baiwa was an "old cannibal man," Lamina had him and ten other men arrested for being "mixed up in the Mawoni case." Following these events, Lamina testified that only after he sent Humpa Baiwa to the District Commissioner did Baiwa then accuse him of orchestrating the murder himself, stating that his alleged role in Mawoni's murder was "put into his head . . . I never sent Humpa Baiwa to do cannibal business.... If I wanted to do any cannibal business, I could easily send one of my own men."[2] Despite his protestations, Lamina was found guilty of murder and sentenced to death.

In the first decade and a half of indirect rule, over four hundred people in the southern Sierra Leone Protectorate were put on trial for charges connected to the Human Leopard Society. The criminalization of the Human Leopard Society and prosecution of men like Lamina in Protectorate courts represented an evolution of the paradox of protection: accused human leopards were subject to a level of judicial violence that profoundly destabilized the political and legal framework of indirect rule. The ritual murder of women, children, and slaves at the hands of some of the administration's appointed Paramount Chiefs came to represent the interminable failure of British control. In an effort to double down on defending the interests of the protecting power, colonial authorities passed legislation that gave the state a broad range of special powers, including the right to arrest, detain, and eventually deport anyone in an effort to "stamp out the cannibal society."[3] Despite protests from some Krio observers who saw these judicial procedures as too extreme, deportations, lifelong incarcerations, and executions like Lamina's were common outcomes of the over thirty cases held in Protectorate courts. Mirroring the fates of political prisoners of the past, some high-ranking defendants like Paramount Chiefs who were deemed a threat to the peace and security of the region were detained and deported regardless of being found not guilty.

This chapter argues that human leopard murder trials held in Protectorate courts between 1901 and 1913 were one of the primary centers of struggles over authority in the southern Sherbro region. Like war captains and Poro leaders before them, British officials regarded human leopards as a threat far beyond their alleged "cannibalism," defining them as a "criminal organization" that posed a serious threat to the political and economic order of indirect rule. To rectify this, courts and legislation were regarded as spaces of legal and cultural reform, keeping order as well as performing civilized justice for African and European observers. Like treaty articles, criminal laws in the Protectorate were structured to protect individuals and their property as well as preserve colonial access to power and resources. Criminal legislation and courts worked together to mobilize the language of protection to legitimate state use of juridical violence and punish behaviors that allegedly threatened the colonial order. Colonial laws empowered the Government to arrest, detain, and deport people at will, increasing the dependence of Paramount Chiefs on the colonial state to uphold their authority.

Like Protectorate subjects elsewhere in Africa, African litigants and witnesses used colonial courts as forums to negotiate the unprecedented political and economic instability of indirect rule.[4] In Sierra Leone, these judicial spaces emerged alongside struggles over land and legitimacy. As we saw in chapter three, accusations of human leopardism were frequently connected to antisocial behavior, including the perceived misuse of public resources through the utilization of bad medicines. Human leopardism as a strategy for seizing political control created a cycle of violence: the more tenuous a local leader felt their position was, the more they sought to bolster their authority and power by "feeding" the borfima by organizing a ritual murder.

Court transcripts reveal that African litigants and witnesses centered their testimony in human leopard cases on class structures and interpersonal relationships. Utilizing the protection of British jurisprudence, British courts constituted a new space for lower-ranking defendants to testify against higher-ranking defendants without the lethal or financial consequences they may have incurred in African courts. Low-status defendants and witnesses frequently describe how they were contracted by Paramount Chiefs or other powerful Big Men to "catch" and murder people for the purpose of cannibalism and feeding the borfima. Though many witnesses testified that they had been sworn to secrecy using various oaths and medicines, they openly told their case in colonial courtrooms, detailing the murders they participated in. For colonial officials, these testimonies confirmed an already established European narrative about the "political derangement" of the leadership in the region, prompting harsher punishments and legislation targeted at Paramount Chiefs and other important Big Men.

The topic of the Human Leopard Society during the colonial period has been examined by scholars from several angles over the past twenty years. Anthropologists have tended to connect the emergence of the society to capitalist extraction and struggles over land using a combination of fieldwork and published primary sources.[5] The major issue with this strategy is the authors' overreliance on contemporary oral accounts or written accounts that have been removed from archival context. At times, this method has led to the misinterpretation or the conflation of people, places, and events. Most historians have tended to focus on Britain's response to cannibalism and the Human Leopard Society as a reflection of colonial anxiety, paranoia, or the civilizing mission. Some of these studies have questioned whether human leopards or cannibalism even existed, attributing the policing of these actions to colonial desire to civilize the interior or even real leopard attacks due to deforestation. While fascinating, these studies tend to focus on a single court case, like the one involving prominent historical figures like Daniel Flickinger Wilberforce, or limit their study to cases of the Special Commissions Court of 1914.[6] While fascinating, this type of micro historical analysis tends to portray their case studies as isolated instances and not one of a series of continual human leopard cases that spanned from 1890 to 1914.

Instead, this chapter heavily relies on transcripts and summaries from the Mixed Court and Circuit Court Record Books held in the Sierra Leone Public Archives, as well as full transcripts of and colonial commentary on the cases located in the British National Archives. Within these volumes, I located thirteen cases of human leopard murder between 1901 and 1912 using a database I created. Five of these cases had full transcripts and the rest contained detailed daily summaries.[7] By focusing on the Mixed and Circuit Courts, this chapter reveals that human leopard murder trials were a more prevalent feature of Protectorate life than the current scholarship indicates. The murders, their investigation, and the trials themselves involved many people from different towns, backgrounds, and classes, including Krio and British administrators, police, and lawyers. My assertion is that the Human Leopard Society was a medicine society that sought to use the borfima to secure and protect one's power and authority during the tumultuous early years of indirect rule.[8]

That being said, this chapter is more of a meditation about the "truth" of what was said during the trials, but more so the ways these trials actively contributed to political and legal insecurity in the Protectorate. That being said, my reading of the archival materials has led me to believe that it was a real society that acted as the guardian of powerful protective medicines that initially emerged during the regional wars of the 1870s. Whether cannibalism occurred to secure members or to "anoint" the borfima is irrelevant, but the court transcripts I read clearly indicate communities undergoing a terrifying transition where, as the saying goes, desperate times called for desperate measures. Protectorate rule created, in the words of Paul Richards, "weak patrons," who were forced to fight amongst each other for the limited wealth that would secure their authority.[9] It appears likely that the borfima was part of a new kind of protection portfolio, a kind of supernatural arsenal in a world where raids and warfare were eliminated, that held the promise of countering what must have seemed like the indomitable imposition of colonial rule. Clearly, courts were one space to debate the moral legitimacy of this tool, especially as it disproportionally impacted everyday people by enfolding them in the murder of their own kinsmen for the benefit of their leaders. While some lower ranking participants might have participated in these murders with the hopes of acquiring power themselves, others used the proximity and protection of the colonial state to openly question those in power.

Courts and Legal Codes in the Early Protectorate: 1896–1904

Decades of legal engagement with local people in the southern hinterland shaped British and Krios' negative impressions of African law. As we saw in earlier in this book, treaty articles and other forms of diplomacy sought to reform African legal practices by preventing treaty signatories from dispensing justice like executing war captains on the battlefield or burning human leopards after a trial conducted by the Tongo. These stipulations amounted to the colonial administration's slow but persistent legal encroachment into African territory, culminating in the creation of the Protectorate in 1896.

Alongside the reordering of political structures, judicial reform was understood as the cornerstone of introducing civilization to African protectorates. While colonial officials regarded many aspects of African Courts as a mere curiosity, some practices were seen as antithetical to British notions of justice and liberty. Among these in the southern Sherbro was the practice of "buying the palaver," which gave the impression that African courts were "very open to bribery . . . [as] the man who gives the biggest present gets the verdict."[10] High court fees, observers believed, blocked everyday people from obtaining justice, as "the ordinary Chief gives decisions to the man who pays most, and there is no real justice."[11] In their role as a judge, one official claimed that a Paramount Chief's "authority is almost despotic," having "no knowledge of what justice is" and described those Chiefs as forcing people to obey by having them "flogged, or fined, or put them in logs (stocks)."[12]

Punishment like immolation of human leopards was characterized as not only an act of barbarism, but as extortion. In precolonial courts, when aggrieved persons initially brought a case to be judged, they were formally asked by the elders, "Will you cross the summons?" This would be done by presenting to the judge a "stake" (or "showing the palaver") where a certain amount of money or goods like palm wine, country cloth, tobacco, people, or other property was handed over.[13] The defendant then matched this amount, known as "answering the summons" or "betting."[14] When this was completed, the two parties would formally "bite the palaver," meaning that each had attested to the veracity of their position and their belief that they had "right on his side."[15] After this process was completed, each time the court opened, the palaver had to be "awakened" or "pulled down," meaning that each side had to pay a small court fee consisting of small amounts of cash, alcohol, tobacco, and so on.[16] If the trial was going long, cases were said to have got "rusty and required oiling and the plaintiff and defendant have to pull more copper."[17] In cases of human leopardism, the accused were able to avoid punishment by paying large fines, which were then redistributed to leaders and the community.

Cases that involved divination and ordealing were also often portrayed as a "rigged."[18] Colonial administrators criminalized African evidentiary practices and punishment for crimes with the Tongo Ordinance of 1892. This legislation marked a pivotal moment in the legal history of human leopard trials, as it transformed the British administration into the de facto human leopard detectors and punishers in the region. Despite numerous suggestions by African leaders to revive the Tongo after 1892, the administration's steadfast rejection of this particular form of African jurisprudence would lead to over two decades of investigating and trying human leopard–related crimes in British courts.

The declaration of the Protectorate facilitated a series of formal legislative regulations that sought to reform African legal practices along the lines of British ethics and interests. The region's status as a Protectorate and not a formal Colony allowed for the continuance of extra-legal precedents developed on the frontier that targeted any "subversive behavior" deemed repugnant or criminal. On the eve of the Protectorate, a series of human leopard murders in Imperri prompted the creation of the Human Leopard Ordinance (1895) that criminalized the possession of particular objects like leopard skins, "leopard knives," and the medicine associated with the human leopards: the borfima.[19] Identifying and criminalizing these "scheduled items" seemed to be a concrete way of targeting the society's members who were said to wear many of these items when they committed murder or were themselves the object thought to bestow power and wealth. The ordinance dictated that anyone found wearing or possessing these items without a "lawful purpose" was guilty of a felony and liable to fourteen years' imprisonment.[20]

Colonial lawmakers knew well enough that passing ordinances in the formal Colony was not enough to alter the behavior of their subjects in the Protectorate. Because of this, restricting the judicial power of African judges became a central feature of the Protectorate Ordinance of 1896. For Governor Cardew, installing European judges in Protectorate Courts was essential for limiting "the iniquities that often take place in courts of the native chiefs." Like other colonial officials, Cardew particularly cited betting and ordeals, along with unacceptable punishments like "death, mutilation, enslavement, or absolute forfeiture of all property, even including wives and children," as the primary reason for introducing a legal system along the lines of British common law.[21] The ordinance created a three court system: the District Commissioner's Court, the Mixed Court (also judged by the District Commissioner), and the Chief's Court. The first two were judged by the District Commissioner. Cases of serious crime like murder, rape, and human leopardism that only involved "Native" defendants were heard in the Mixed Court. In both courts, the judge was the District Commissioner, but he would be assisted by up to three Paramount Chiefs who acted as African Assessors.[22] Officially, assessors were placed in these courts to act as cultural interpreters for the District Commissioner and to uphold existing (and acceptable) African political and legal structures. Framed as yet another kind of tutelage, colonial officials believed that Paramount Chiefs' observation of colonial courts would gradually convince them of the superiority of British common law.

The implementation of courts in the first few years of the Protectorate was extremely haphazard. As with other aspects of Protectorate rule, local leaders pushed back against the imposition of colonial courts. The restriction of Paramount Chiefs to "customary courts," significantly decreased their income from fees acquired during the traditional betting and staking process and claiming of slaves and property after the conclusion of a witchcraft or human leopard trial. While the colonial state attempted to ameliorate these losses by their appointment of Assessors in British courts, Paramount Chiefs knew the District Commissioner had the power to veto their verdict. This likely made Mixed Courts (and later Circuit Courts) spaces where some African Assessors refrained from giving their true opinion; as several leaders in the Northern Ronietta District expressed in 1898, "What is the use of us going there if we are not to have a voice?" However, given the need to demonstrate loyalty amidst the persistent threat of deposition and deportation, many Assessors likely only participated in Mixed Courts as a way to avoid "show[ing] disrespect to the District Commissioners," when in reality they felt like "nonentities." In cases where the punishment for the crime may have seemed particularly harsh, some Paramount Chiefs worried that "they will be thought to have taken part in it" and further hated by their people.[23]

While these few fragments in the archive suggest how Paramount Chiefs felt about these newly imposed courts, it is even more difficult to know how African litigants perceived Mixed Courts' ability to settle their disputes in the first few years of Protectorate rule. Transcripts of early judicial proceedings in the Protectorate are extremely rare. The Sierra Leone Public Archives contains only a single volume of Mixed Court cases from the Ronietta District, which spans from May 27, 1901, to September 22, 1903, and contains only thirteen cases. While the volume is limited and incomplete, it contains five cases of regular homicide, three human leopard murders, three rape cases, and two cases of grievous bodily harm.

All three of the human leopard cases in the Mixed Court were held in 1901. The first was in June under District Commissioner Major D'Arcy Anderson with three African Assessors: Sophia Neale Caulker, Bangali Margai, and Pa Kam.[24] The three accused men were charged with the death of a boy named Farmah, the nephew of one of the defendants, Gbanna Lacka.[25] During the case, it was stated that Gbanna Lacka took Farmah and several of his brothers away from their mother because he was in a prior dispute with their father. During the trial, the boy's father testified that he had heard from another man that Gbanna Lacka had planned to "catch" the boy, meaning "to kill or hold for cannibalism." He also said that his son, who did not die instantly from his wounds, told him that Gbanna Lacka was the one who stabbed him. Gbanna Lacka denied the charges, instead accusing one of the witnesses of the murder, a man named Fogbawah who he called "a dealer in witchcraft." Throughout the trial, the African Assessors asked several questions to the witnesses and afterwards asked for permission to retire and consult with each other. They found Gbanna Lacka guilty of murder and he was sentenced to death. The other two men were sentenced to ten years in prison with hard labor.[26]

Several months later, two more cases of human leopard murder were held in the Mixed Court. Both addressed the murder of a boy named Cho who had been allegedly killed in May 1901. The first trial had two defendants, Saisai Tailah and Woojoo, the former of which was Cho's father.[27] Like many cases of human leopard murder in future Protectorate courtrooms, judicial procedure in this case contained several legally problematic elements, including the utilization of the witnesses from previous trials who had been granted immunity for their testimony. During the trial, Fogbawah returned to the stand, this time testifying that while he was at a "meeting of a cannibal society," he saw Saisai Taliah "[give] up his son." He described how Cho's body had been divided up and "given to the principle [*sic*] men of the society," a group that he explicitly stated did not include him. He stated that when he realized Cho had gone missing, he was shown the head and the legs of the boy to indicate that he was dead. Afterwards, he stated that an "enquiry" was held in which he gave "two shillings to show that he was satisfied with the result," but afterwards had to travel to Shenge with others to "pay fine" to Sophia Neale Caulker's Speaker George Domingo. Throughout the trial, Saisai Tailah asserted that he did not know who killed the boy, insisting that he was innocent and that "lies have been told against him." The other defendant, Woojoo, testified that he had no idea when he arrived in court that he was a defendant, as he thought he was there to be a witness. While the Assessors Madam Yoko, Sophia Neale Calker, and the District Commissioner unanimously found Saisai Tailah guilty and sentenced him to death, they differed in their assessment of Woojoo (Madam Yoko was the only one to find him guilty), and he was set free.[28]

The second case involving Cho's death involved a much more prominent defendant, Paramount Chief Sophia Caulker's Speaker George Domingo, who was charged with "planning and ordering the death of the boy Cho."[29] The case involved many of the same witnesses of the previous case, including Fogbawah and Saisai Talliah (who by this time had already been convicted). In this trial, Fogbawah added to his previous story, testifying that George Domingo, who he named the "chief of the society," had forced new members to pay two beads, two knives, some palm oil, and a chicken, as well as swear on medicine not to reveal anything about the murder. He also stated that it was Domingo who had told Saisai Talliah he needed to give up Cho, as he now "owed the cannibal society a debt." While a second witness confirmed much of Fogbawah's testimony, the witnesses for the defense told a much different story. The Paramount Chief of Bompeh, James Canreba Caulker, spoke in favor of the defendant, citing that he had actively been trying to "put down" the Human Leopard Society. Another witness, Madam Sophia Neale Caulker's Secretary Frank Dixon, stated that Fogbawah had previously been arrested twice by Sophia Neale Caulker for making "bad medicine to poison the life of Samuel Caulker" and for the attempted murder of another man in a nearby town. After having discredited the prosecution's main witness, several witnesses provided an alibi for Domingo, stating that he had been at a party in Shenge when the alleged meeting and crime took place.[30]

Taking the stand himself, Domingo openly declared Saisai Talliah the murderer. He explained Fogbawah's testimony by saying that it was in revenge for an "old grievance" between them. During the trial, Domingo emphasized all the efforts he had made trying to eliminate the threat of leopardism, stating that he had spent six weeks "working heart and soul to try to put an end to this terrible crime," including hiring a "medicine man" to administer an oath among the people that "everybody connected [with the human leopards] should die." He closed the case by speaking directly to the Assessor Chiefs Nancy Tucker, Bangali Margai, and Pa Keni: "notice who my witnesses are, Paramount Chiefs, Sub Chiefs and the Chief's Secretary, men of big position." Domingo was found not guilty by all three Assessors and the District Commissioner concurred.[31]

Though absent from newspaper coverage in Freetown, it seems likely that these three cases prompted the colonial Government to take additional action to address the limitations of British law in the Protectorate. Among these steps was the amendment of the Human Leopard Ordinance for 1901, which significantly expanded the rights for colonial officials or police to "arrest, enter, or examine any place" they suspected human leopards resided or their paraphernalia was hidden.[32] New kinds of punishments were introduced in this new legislation, including being subjected to a £50 fine or twelve months in prison for anyone who hindered those searches. Undoubtedly drawing from the experiences in the Mixed Court, much of the ordinance specifically targeted Paramount Chiefs, Sub-Chiefs, and Headmen with the assumption that they were either participants or permitted these murders. For instance, Article 10 of the ordinance stated that "Any Chief who directly or indirectly permits, encourages or abets, or is concerned in the celebration" and does not report it would be subject to a fine of £500 or twelve months' imprisonment. Colonial police and officials were further empowered to order the "arrest and detention" of any Chief or Sub-Chief "as it may be deemed expedient for the maintenance of peace and order and the suppression of the Human Leopard and Alligator Society." Finally, the ordinance empowered the Governor to "order the deportation of any such Chief or Sub-Chief," accused of participating in leopardism, paving the legislative road for another round of deportations like political prisoners in the past.

Judicial and Legislative Reform in the Protectorate

Indigenous communities were not the only African litigants in Protectorate Courts. Despite being targeted during the Insurrection of 1898, many Krios returned to the Protectorate and settled down primarily along the newly constructed railway line. Working as traders, missionaries, railway workers, and laborers, these "non-natives" (as they were legally designated) frequently settled their disputes in protectorate courts during the early years of indirect rule. Coming from a culture of intense litigiousness in Freetown, many were shocked by their experiences obtaining justice in protectorate spaces. Krios were generally appalled that they had to settle their cases through a District Commissioner who had no legal training or that they could not take cases that originated in the Protectorate into Colony courts (even if their business was in the formal Colony). Less than two years after the Protectorate was declared, these frustrations were articulated by the Sierra Leone Bar Association in a petition submitted to Governor Cardew outlining a series of grievances with the colonial legal system, including the "defective" administration of justice in the Protectorate. Their primary concern was the role of the District Commissioner as a judge in local courts, recommending that he be someone with a "fair knowledge of the law" if "he is to exercise judicial functions."[33] The unchecked power of the District Commissioner was seen as particularly problematic given the absence of an Appeals Court in the Protectorate and the fact that defendants were not permitted to have a lawyer.

The concerns in this 1898 petition, that were also echoed by David Chalmers in the Royal Commission Report on the Causes of the Insurrection, were not addressed until 1901. Under the Governor, Charles King-Harman, the Legislative Council in Freetown sought to consolidate and amend the laws and institutions that governed the Protectorate Ordinance. The revised legislation addressed many of the concerns presented by the Sierra Leone Bar three years previously, but only conceded to allowing appeals in cases that involved "non-natives" when sentences exceeded three months' imprisonment. While these changes were certainly agreeable to Krio members of the Legislative Council, other aspects of the Protectorate court system were not.[34] In his speech to the Council addressing the 1901 legislation, prominent Krio barrister Sir Samuel Lewis evoked the principles of legal order and protection upon which the Protectorate was built, reminding the Executive Council of the importance of clearly articulating the "obligations and duties of the Protecting power and the obligations and rights of the Protecting party."[35] Lewis continued to question the ability of the District Commissioner to judge cases in Mixed and District Commissioner's Court and the reason for banning counsel during criminal cases—rights he saw as essential for British subjects. During the first reading, he moved the ordinance be amended to include the right to representation, the introduction of a formal Appeals Court, and a reduction of the legal duties of District Commissioners.[36] Finally, he concluded by questioning the legality of deporting people from the Protectorate, including for cases of human leopardism, "without being given any opportunity of replying to the charges made against them or even being aware of the nature of these charges."[37]

Luckily for the Krio community, Governor King-Harman was more amenable to working with the citizens of Freetown than his predecessor Francis Cardew. Convinced by the Krio members of the Legislative Council and the Sierra Leone Bar, he wrote candidly to the Colonial Office that since his arrival in Sierra Leone, he had been "considerably staggered and even appalled at the crude and peculiar procedure and conclusions followed and arrived at by the District Commissioners when presiding in their respective Courts." Although he believed District Commissioners often had the best interests of the Protectorate people at heart, their "ignorance of the law and of legal procedure is a bar, and apparently an insuperable bar, to their securing the confidence of the people, either in the Protectorate or in the Colony as dispensers of justice." In December, he voiced his approval of the Sierra Leone Bar's motion that a district or "itinerant judge" be appointed. Furthermore, he recommended that the District Commissioner should not be permitted to judge cases that involved "severe or capital punishment" and that it would be better to "appoint a properly qualified and legally trained judge who would go on circuit in the several districts of the Protectorate and administer the law with authority and with capacity."[38]

Under King-Harman's leadership in 1902 and 1903, Krio barristers worked alongside the Legislative Committee drafting a new ordinance that would introduce "the principles of justice, equity, and good consciousness" to the Protectorate.[39] Patterned off early modern Assize Courts in Britain and the Circuit Court of Cape Colony, the Sierra Leone Circuit Court would travel throughout the Protectorate to the headquarters of the five districts. In establishing Circuit Courts, the Protectorate Courts Jurisdiction Ordinance of 1903 enacted a more formal criminal court than most Protectorates in British Africa.[40] Cases were to be heard by a European Judge through a combination of British common law and what the Attorney General referred to as "native institutions and idiosyncrasies," and would be assisted by two to three African Assessors.[41] Questioning and cross examination of defendants and witnesses was to be conducted by the judge, the Crown prosecutor, defense lawyers (if the defendants were represented), and the prisoners themselves. On the eve of their enactment, an article in the *Sierra Leone Weekly News* praised the judicial development, stating that "while the natives of the soil must be granted a 'free-hand' to develop on their own lines," they now have "the eye of one or another of His Majesty's Representatives so that amongst the untutored tribes, Justice must not be miscarried."[42]

While the Krio barristers of the Colony expressed high hopes for the Circuit Courts' ability to bring justice to the hinterland, the introduction of those courts in

1904 was largely regarded as experimental by British officials. Lawmakers appeared resigned that the Circuit Court would do little more than "introduce among the tribes of uncivilized natives in the Protectorate a Court of Law and assist in the evolution of Africans' primitive legal system as it had the British people themselves centuries before."[43] Statements like this reflect the pervasive idea that British courts were space to perform "justice" for the benefit of African observation and imitation as a means of reforming their own customary courts. However, like the stipulations of treaties, British lawmakers seemed oblivious to the potentially destabilizing impact of eliminating centuries of African court procedures and jurisprudence.

This was especially true in how Britons viewed the role of African Assessors. Indirect rule assumed a precolonial law system that was corrupt and dysfunctional. In reality, southern states in Sierra Leone were as litigious as their Krio counterparts, possessing a well-developed legal system complete with judges, lawyers, and even bailiffs that had been observed by Europeans since the 1600s.[44] Undoubtedly, this accounts for the remarks of the Attorney General after the inaugural year of the Circuit Court. He had been struck by the "zeal and intelligence" shown by the African Assessors during the trials. However, always noting the supremacy of British laws, he expressed his hope that Circuit Courts "may do some good in the Protectorate in the way of reforming the Native Courts as it affords to the Chiefs an opportunity of observing the procedure of English Courts which is certainly fairer to both sides . . . and does not offer the same opportunities for corruption and extortion." The Circuit Court, he praised, was a living demonstration of the separation of the judicial and executive power: it "revolutionizes the whole system of the Protectorate. Before . . . the District Commissioners were vested with supreme judicial and administrative power of punishment and enforcing their decision; now all their judicial jurisdiction except in the most trifling cases has been transferred to the Circuit Judge." While the Attorney General admitted that the introduction of Circuit Courts was perhaps too "premature" for Africans to comprehend, he believed them to be "an efficient tribunal and a safeguard of the liberties of the people."[45]

Human Leopard Murder Trials in the Circuit Courts: 1904–1913

In September 1904, the first case of human leopard murder was tried in the newly formed Circuit Court in Moyamba. The primary defendant was Beah Kindo, the Paramount Chief of Timdale Chiefdom, who was accused alongside the other defendants of murdering a boy named Joe Korteh for the purposes of making medicines for the Human Leopard Society. The newly appointed Judge Edward Turner Packard was accompanied by three African Assessors: Madam Yoko (Kpaa-Mende Chiefdom), Bangali Margai (Banta Chiefdom) and Beh Sherbro (Yoni Chiefdom). The first two, we will recall, had already been Assessors in human leopard cases in the Mixed Court in 1901. The prosecution was led by the District Commissioner George Page, a young man who had recently taken up the position and had no formal legal training. Now able to retain counsel, the defendants—all twenty-one of them—were represented by prominent Krio barrister, A. J. Shorunkeh-Sawyerr, a member of the Sierra Leone Bar Association and a participant in drafting the Protectorate Courts Ordinance.

Over the course of the trial, an astounding twenty-three witnesses were called to the stand. Five of the central witnesses called by the prosecution were men who admitted they had actively participated in the murder but had exchanged their testimony for immunity, including the Chief of the town where the murder took place, the victim's father, his (and the victim's) slave master, and a prominent "medicine man." On the first day, the prosecution's initial witness, Gbandah, testified that Beah Kindo had approached him one day under the shade of a camwood tree to "get" him a boy to make medicine, promising to make him "rich" if he complied. Gbandah and the other fourteen witnesses called by the prosecution recounted similar descriptions of Beah Kindo's visit to their town, the circumstances of the night of the murder, physical landmarks, objects used in the killing, and accounts of their arrest.

On the eighth day of the trial, the defense began their case. Despite representing all the defendants, Sawyerr largely focused his case on Beah Kindo, denying that he had planned the murder. Beah Kindo's eldest son, James Kindoh, provided an alibi, testifying that his father could not have been involved in the circumstances outlined by the prosecution as he was with him at the time of the murder. Like the case of *R. v. George Domingo* in 1901, a series of character witnesses for Beah Kindo also took the stand, including a number of his employees and other "respectable" members of society. After seventeen days of witness testimony, the verdict was read. As the lead Assessor, Madam Yoko, rejected much of Shorunkeh-Sawyerr's defense strategy, asserting that she doubted Kindo's eldest son had been with him for so many months if he was not ill. For her, Beah Kindo's disregard in reporting Joe's death to the colonial authorities implicated him of murder and leopardism in his chiefdom. The other two Assessors agreed with Madam Yoko's assertions, stating that while they believed the witnesses and some of the defendants did physically plan and execute the murder of Joe Konteh, there had to be a more powerful "principal man" to lead a Human Leopard Society. Beah Kindo and fifteen of the other defendants were found guilty and were sentenced to death.

Between 1904 and 1913, the Circuit Court heard upwards of thirty cases of human leopard murder like *R. v. Beah Kindo and Others*, sixteen of which were in the first two years. This constituted approximately 8 percent of all criminal cases heard during those years.[46] When comparing them with other cases, however, one can immediately see that they were distinct from the other criminal trials held in Circuit Courts. Unlike assault, rape, arson, or homicide, human leopard cases lacked an equivalency in British common law, making them highly susceptible to the excessive use of judicial discretion as a means of reinforcing British hegemony. They were also unusual in their form: cases of human leopard murder were typically much longer than regular homicide trials, with one lasting an incredible thirty days. Furthermore, unlike other trials in the Circuit Court which typically had one to three defendants, cases of human leopard murder frequently tried upwards of twenty-five defendants during a single trial, despite being accused of different aspects of the crime which ranged from aiding and abetting, kidnapping, murder, or possessing medicines connected associated with leopardism.

While each human leopard murder trial had its own unique set of circumstances, the cases surprisingly follow much the same format.[47] Cases involved the murder of young people, many of whom were enslaved. Upon their taking the stand, witnesses gave their account of the circumstances of the murder and their role in those events. Following this, they were typically cross-examined by the judge, lawyers, and the other defendants. When other defendants were conducting the questioning, the exchanges seemed to mirror the typical format of local palavers where a series of questions would be asked, followed by the person's ability to clarify mistakes or misunderstandings. Unfortunately for the historian, however, the transcripts rarely contain the questions being asked of the witness. This type of transcription often makes for a choppy and confusing narrative that often forces the reader to imagine the questions the witnesses are responding to. After the prosecution and defense finished presenting their cases, the opinion of the African Assessors was typically recorded in full alongside the judge's verdict and sentencing.

During these trials, the courtroom was filled with a broad swath of Sierra Leone's African population who participated as lawyers, defendants, assessors, witnesses, translators, bailiffs, and audience members from a wide spectrum of social statuses. When comparing available Circuit Court transcripts between 1904 and 1913, defendants can broadly be identified as belonging to two oppositional categories, each of which had very different roles in relation to the trials and the alleged murder itself. The first were what we might label "high-status defendants," like Paramount Chiefs or Sub-Chiefs of important towns.[48] High status defendants also frequently included a man who was identified as a "medicine man" or "murray man" who was accused of either physically committing the murder or who led the "processing" of the body afterwards. The second category were what we might call "lower-status defendants." This often included the father or owner of the victim (if they were enslaved) and other lower-status men in the town like farmers or messengers who were allegedly contracted by the higher-ranking defendant to procure the child, participate in the murder, or deliver parts of the body to them. This category of defendant frequently identified themselves as "members of the cannibal society" in court and were usually the first to "confess" their crimes to the District Commissioner, police, or other colonial administrators.

Criminal courts in the Protectorate constituted a new forum for debating the nature of protection and individual rights among and between these different groups. In the absence of "hard evidence" for these murders, human leopard cases typically devolved into a sort of he said/he said, pitting the lower-status defendants and witnesses—many of whom had traded their testimony for immunity—against the high-ranking defendants. Most cases opened with what one might call the prosecution's "key witness." This tended to be a man who was related to the victim in some way. Like Gbandah in the Beah Kindo case mentioned previously, the key witness would spend a considerable time recounting the details of how he was recruited by one of the higher-ranking defendants (Paramount or Sub-Chief) to find a child to "catch." Following this testimony (which often went on for a couple days), similarly ranking men would often take the stand to reiterate the key witness's story, describing how they helped "catch" and kill the victim. While many of these witnesses had legal immunity, others were defendants. These disparities made for a peculiar trial, as some defendants' testimonies amounted to self-recrimination, while others (who often played an even larger role in the murder) left the courtroom as free men.

When analyzing the transcripts of these trials, the relationships between the defendants and witnesses were clearly of central concern to the Africans who took the stand. Particularly when cross-examining each other, much emphasis was placed on how they knew each other, how long they knew each other, when they met, and if they were related. Transcripts include statements such as "Amarra is my father. I don't know if Amarra is your brother" and "Pie is no relation of mine. Pie is your servant."[49] While not always fully legible to the historian, it is clear that articulating these social relationships was not a means of explaining whether the person actually committed the crime, but whether they should be considered culpable. In every transcript, low-ranking witnesses described these relationships as a way to emphasize how they had been coerced or threatened into participating in the murder or the consumption of the victim: as one witness stated, "If a paramount chief told you to do a thing you have to do it. So you cannot do a thing if the chief tells you not to do it."[50] To emphasize their lower-ranking status, many grown men identified themselves to the court as a "small boy" or "slave."[51] For example, when the key witness Gbandah was asked why he agreed to Beah Kindo's terms, he stated, "I have got no power, I am a slave. I have got no country."[52]

This power difference was further highlighted by particular witnesses' descriptions of how high-ranking defendants used their position in the country to compel others to do their bidding. For instance, Gbandah emphasized how Beah Kindo had assured him that he was a "big man of the country. Whatever I press down (conceal) no body can find out."[53] Likewise, in *R. v. Humpa Saloo*, the key witness, an enslaved man named Kai Challeh, told the court that one of the primary high-ranking defendants Peah Yumbo had told him to "Give this child. I am a big man in this country, if anything, I will be responsible for it."[54] To further emphasize these class differences, some witnesses describe how the "Big Men" received particularly powerful parts of the victim's body to indicate their rank within the Human Leopard Society.[55] In all these examples, we see how Africans' participation in human leopard trials diverged significantly from British evidence-based judicial norms and intentions.

Within these tangled and multi-layered testimonies, it is difficult to reconcile the often-significant divergence in the narratives of low-status and high-status defendants. On one side were men who confessed to the crime by implicating Paramount and other important Chiefs through highly elaborate stories that shared many common details. On the other were the high-ranking men themselves, who steadfastly denied the charges, frequently insisting that they had been working to eliminate the human leopards by administering oaths, engaging in particular ceremonies, or arresting known "old cannibals" when they arrived in town. In reading the transcripts, one cannot help but wonder who to believe: the testimony of the low-ranking witnesses, which would indicate a series of high-ranking men trying to cover up their role in planning these murders, or the stories of high-ranking Chiefs, who insisted that they were "framed" in the context of personal and political vendettas? Put another way, were high-status men attempting to use borfima to secure wealth and status, as described by Humpa Baiwa at the beginning of this chapter? Were they recruiting lower-ranking men as pawns to do their "dirty work" to strengthen their rule in the midst of political insecurity? Or was there something else going on that was kept silent in the courts?

In paying close attention to the rank and status of witnesses and defendants in the court, we do see a connection between the circumstances of the human leopard murders and broader allegations of extortion and the misuse of power that were commonly associated with "cannibalism." The murder and "consumption" of the low-status minor was indicative of the immoral extraction of wealth and labor without a sufficient redistribution of wealth to the community. Human leopard murder cases are rife with allusions to debt. Reminiscent of Sama or panyarring, if a new victim was not provided to more high ranking members of the Human Leopard Society at a specified time, the debt could be violently "reclaimed" in the form of the new member's child or slave.[56] The perverse payment of this "debt" being the murder or consumption of young (productive and/or reproductive) labor twisted the typical bonds of protective reciprocity between elites and their dependents. Like a real leopard in the bush, the human leopard "consumed" his victim for pure self-satisfaction and greed, taboo actions that lay outside the boundaries of human morality.

While many low-ranking defendants justified their participation in the Human Leopard Society as forced obligation, they also used the courts to discredit the high-status defendant by describing the ways they reneged on their fiscal promises, either of cash payment, a wife, or "employment from the Government" in exchange for acquiring the victim.[57] We might also consider that this included a denial of full participation in the borfima ceremony afterwards, indicated by the fact they were not given a "share" of the body.[58] Moreover, in several cases, witnesses described how they had been, or were currently in, financial debt to at least one of the high-ranking defendants prior to the murder.

Stories of extortion were often centered on the parents of the victim. In one case, the father of the victim recalled how he was compelled to go to the Chief's Court and/or pay a certain amount of money to the Chief to indicate that they had been "satisfied" with the investigation of their child's death, even though it was clear they were not.[59] It is possible, then, that their decision to "confess" their crimes to a British authority figure (police officer, Paramount Chief, or District Commissioner) after having already settled the matter in the customary courts indicates a sort of "jurisdictional jockeying" in an effort to gain a more favorable resolution of their child's death (either in terms of fines or something else), even if this included revealing their participation in it.[60] This may explain why low-ranking litigants did not initially tell colonial authorities about a Paramount or Sub-Chiefs role in the murder until they were assured protection from police and administrators. Within this context, we might suggest that human leopard trials allowed for low-ranking defendants to "voice their truth" and expose what they saw as political or moral injustice, even if they themselves admitted to participation in the murder. Circuit Court cases, therefore, became a new type of forum where everyday people could speak out against their leaders, be protected from violence, and find resolution.[61]

At the same time, evidence of long-standing disputes or debts between low- and high-ranking ones might also suggest the possibility of false accusations. In one trial, the key witness described how he had been previously fined by the high-ranking defendant for fourteen bushels of palm kernels, while another stated he had been "fined once for making a complaint against the chief to his face."[62] Likewise, in *R. v. Lavari and Others*, the key witness was collecting debts on behalf of his high-ranking uncle from several of the other defendants in the town when the murder took place. When one of the debtees could not pay his debts in full, his son was murdered. While this case lacked some of the features of later human leopard murder trials, it is clear that some members of the family regarded the murdered boy as repayment for the debt, as the mother of the victim accused the debt collector of "kill[ing] my son and now you are going to eat it."[63] In the Beah Kindo case, the key witness, Gbandah, testified that he was surprised by Beah Kindo's request to assist him in finding a victim, as his village and the Paramount Chief had an antagonistic relationship in the past, having been previously fined by Beah Kindo for not joining the Human Leopard Society.

When high-ranking defendants took the stand, their testimony tended to confirm these personal and political vendettas. Not surprisingly, many used these feuds to counter the accusations against them. This type of defense can be seen in cases ranging from 1901 (*R. v. George Domingo*) to 1912 (*R. v. Bunting Williams and Others*). In many of these cases, the men who accused the high-ranking defendants were from regions that were engaged in the land and leadership disputes we saw in the previous chapter. The defense council brought in witnesses like other Paramount Chiefs, missionaries, and traders that spoke to the reputation of their client. In the case with which this chapter began, *R. v. Lamina and Others* (1908), Lamina himself testified that he had collected money to "finish the cannibal troubles . . . so that the Government would be pleased," and had subsequently arrested many of the witnesses, including Humpa Baiwa. While Lamina included this as part of his defense, the collection of these funds had likely placed several Sub-Chiefs and Headmen in debt and caused further grievances against him. Unfortunately, Lamina tied his own noose by confessing to delivering "human fat" to Reverend Wilberforce several years earlier, which he had testified to previously in *R. v. Sanusi Gboto* in 1905.[64] He was further implicated by possessing several objects that had been seized from his home, including an alligator skin box containing medicine and papers with Arabic text. Likewise, in *R. v. Peah Yumbo*, the Paramount Chief of Timdale recalled in detail how he had forced a series of communities to send as much as £10 and to swear an oath on "Alfiateh" flour that if they "follow and agree with the cannibal people I am going to die of this medicine."[65]

While we will never know who was telling the truth in those courtrooms, it does appear British judicial officials and African litigants often seemed to be operating at cross-purposes. British lawyers and judges continually tried to ascertain the circumstances of the murder and the hard evidence that demonstrated guilt. Within this colonial mind frame, protection for the public was restored when the accused were found guilty and removed from society through either death or incarceration. On the other side, African litigants and witnesses were less interested in how the crime was committed or even who physically committed the murder, but rather why it was done and who was "responsible," which was not always the person who held the knife. As one African Assessor noted at the end of one trial in 1904, "We don't know English law, we will tell you the native. It is different. The Cannibal Society is in our country, many of them. We try and catch them and warn them and now they stop. By the native custom, it would have finished but the Government try and find it out."[66] Comments like these demonstrate that the key to eradicating human leopards was not by trying them individually in court, but by eliminating the core societal or even supernatural imbalance that their existence perpetuated. Throughout this period, allusions to the existence of the Tongo and their service continued, but the criminalization of this organization prevented African leaders from utilizing their services. Following the paradox of protection, British courts were unable to "stamp out" the human leopards due to the self-imposed limits of their own laws and the criminalization of African ones.

The "Principal Men": Targeting Paramount Chiefs in Legislation and Courts, 1909–1913

In African protectorates throughout the British Empire, Paramount Chiefs were seen as the cornerstone of indirect rule. Their role as colonial intermediaries charged them with two contradictory duties: protect their people and protect the interests of the colonial state. When either of these tasks were unsatisfactorily met, British intervention was justified in the name of preserving peace: the more serious the infraction, the more violence was condoned in the name of restoring order. The narratives that emerged in Protectorate Circuit Courts that Paramount Chiefs lead or participated in human leopard murders reified the long-standing stereotype of Sherbro leaders as duplicitous and secretive. The ongoing exposure of this covert and "cannibalistic" behavior in Protectorate courts by the British Government's most important intermediaries produced a visible chink in the colonial armor. The extra-legal measures that were implemented to repair it, however, only succeeded in further tearing apart the political fabric.

Upon reflection of his first year as Circuit Court Judge in 1904, Arthur Hudson remarked that while he found the amount of "serious crime" to be satisfactorily light, the crimes perpetuated by secret societies in the Ronietta District were "most difficult to deal with." The "hidden crime" of human leopard murder, he expressed, required "great vigilance and . . . prompt punishment of the guilty" even if this meant limiting the due process of defendants and accepting less than satisfactory witnesses who themselves had participated in the crimes. Courts, he stated, played a vital role in "stamping out these and similar crimes," but to do so required that the focus was placed on high-ranking Chiefs. Following Hudson's report, Governor Probyn reiterated this position to the Colonial Office in London, stating that "It may be almost taken as axiom that no event can take place in any village, without the Chiefs and Headman being fully conversant of everything: further it is almost impossible for the natives of any village to take the initiative in any matters, certainly, not of such a serious import as a human leopard murder, without direct encouragement from their Chiefs and Headman."[67] From the creation of Circuit Courts in 1904, legislation and policing connected to the Human Leopard Society increasingly targeted Paramount Chiefs and other central Big Men.

As the decade progressed, however, the obvious ineffectiveness of British law prompted the colonial Government to consider additional policies for eliminating the Human Leopard Society. In 1907, this included making good on a 1904 threat to "occupy" the Imperri with troops because of the Paramount Chief's inability to eliminate the Human Leopard Society. Another strategy, suggested by the Attorney General, was to legislate and "exercise arbitrary powers over the inhabitants" in a manner that resembled the Insurgents Temporary Detention Ordinance of 1898 during the Insurrection.[68] Within this suggestion, the Attorney General seemed to liken his strategy to the Tongo itself, outlining how years before, Madam Yoko had warned him that the Tongo "was the only really effective way of dealing with the human leopards" as "she did not think that a trial by English law and procedure would 'catch' them as it was a secret society."[69] Despite Governors' assertions that "the English system of trial are very perfect," many like Governor Probyn were "forced to admit that it is not wholly applicable to Leopard murder cases."[70] Various methods were attempted, including the use of "native spies" as used in the investigation into criminal societies in other British colonies like India.[71]

As cases continued to increase, the proposed solutions became more extreme. In 1908, District Commissioner Page's recommendations echoed military expeditions on the frontier. He recommended that "in every case of human leopardism, the people of the town should be deported, the town should be burnt down, and no town should be allowed to rise again on its site." Amazingly, Page's suggestions drew heavily from the Tongo, stating that "In olden times human leopards were shewn no mercy as we all know, they were frequently searched out by the Tongo men; when caught they were burnt, their property sequestered and the whole of their relations driven out of the country." Within his dispatch, he described how he had once used this as inspiration in the Northern Sherbro District, stating that after a human leopard murder trial in Banika (*R. v. Lavari and Others*), he had "half the town pulled down" in "accordance with native custom, but I ought to have been more resolute and have had the whole place pulled down then perhaps we should not so soon have had another murder there. You may get convictions wholesale, as I have done, but so long as the population of Timdale and Imperri have their old traditions so deeply ingrained in them so long will these murders continue. The only remedy appears to me to be removal from their old pernicious surroundings."[72]

This evolution of human leopard policies was reflected in shifts in court sentencing and punishment. Initially, most defendants who were found guilty of human leopard murder were sentenced to death and then publicly executed in the Protectorate in a manner that harkened back to the hanging of war captains on the frontier.[73] As the decade progressed, the punishments for guilty defendants became more varied: the majority of high-status defendants—who were never accused of directly committing the murder—were most frequently given the maximum sentence of death, while many of the low-status defendants—and the protected witnesses—were either sentenced to life in prison or found not guilty.[74] By 1909, however, the execution of so many high-ranking men became a concern to colonial officials. Deportation was thought to be a better tool to limit the political instability caused by the execution and deposing of so many Paramount Chiefs, particularly in Imperri and Timdale Chiefdoms.[75] As we saw in the previous chapter, three successive Imperri Paramount Chiefs—Daniel Flickinger Wilberforce, Seh Kainjah, and Alfred Goma Kartegbeh—were deposed after being accused of participating in human leopard murders. This same pattern occurred in the neighboring chiefdom of Timdale. Both Beah Kindo and his replacement Peah Yumbo were charged and executed for human leopardism. In 1909, his replacement, Beah Kindo's son James Kindoh who had testified as the primary alibi in his father's trial, was reportedly unanimously elected by his people.

The trial and execution of so many Paramount Chiefs and other Big Men reflects the continuation of the paradox of protection. As the number of trials, executions, and deportations escalated, the structure of indirect rule became increasingly destabilized, diminishing the judicial and executive authority of its most important intermediaries. A significant source of tension was the gap between the legislation that defined and criminalized "human leopards" and how these crimes were tried in court. Up until 1912, the Human Leopard Ordinance did not define being a human leopard or even cannibalism as a crime per se; instead, it was a crime to possess particular paraphernalia connected to the society, by planning or committing an actual murder, or not reporting one. When the court trials centered on these individual crimes, one can see why human leopards persisted: no matter how many trials occurred in British courts, the deeper causes of leopardism (illegitimate or weakened authority due to indirect rule) continued to exist and "eat" (misuse resources) their young victims (who represented the productive future of the entire community).

From 1895 onwards, the Human Leopard Ordinance was continually amended. While initial versions focused on banning scheduled items and empowering the Government with unlimited rights of search and arrest, subsequent articles focused more on punishment like deportation. After the Circuit Court trial *R. v. Peah Yumbo*, the Human Leopard Ordinance was amended to strip Protectorate peoples of the freedom of association, declaring the "human leopards" as "unlawful societies." This made it a crime to belong to or participate in operations or meetings and expanded the power of the police and colonial officials to search homes and detain people.

By 1909, the "tribal Administration" in both Imperri and Timdale was "suspended." Both chiefdoms were occupied by a substantial number of colonial troops as their respective Paramount Chiefs had been deposed. Desperate for solutions to end the "terror" of human leopards, colonial authorities passed legislation that created a "Court of Special Commissioners" to deal with the overwhelming number of pending human leopard murder cases. To empower this new court, the Human Leopard Ordinance was further revised in 1912. This law replicated many of the articles and procedures of the past, empowering the Governor to "order the arrest and detention in custody of *any person* . . . he may consider desirable in the interests of justice."[76]

The legislation was a prime example of the long-standing contradictions in British protection schemes. In his remarks on the new legislation, the Attorney General stressed how the Human Leopard Society was now headed by some of Protectorate's leading Chiefs, explaining that while "20 years ago its operations were confined to, not the big men of the Protectorate, but the lessor people . . . it seems as years have gone by, this state of things have changed, either from natural inclination or from force of circumstances, and the Society has become too strong for the Chiefs, with the result that the Paramount Chiefs themselves have been drawn into the Society and are now the leaders in it."[77] The "intimidation practiced by the influential chiefs" over their people, he argued, had led to significant issues with obtaining evidence and producing witnesses. Because of this, the ordinance was amended to allow the immediate arrest and detainment of any "Chief of the District." This power, the Attorney General admitted, "seems drastic, but still the circumstances of these murders are so exceptional that drastic powers are required." The ordinance added several more banned objects connected to the society, including a kukoi (whistle) that was used to call human leopards to the bush, and an iron needle used for "branding members of this unlawful society."[78]

While the European members of the Legislative Council passed this bill unanimously at the first reading, the unofficial Krio members questioned its validity. Barristers J. J. Thomas and A. J. Shorunkeh-Sawyerr—who had been the defense lawyer in *R. v. Beah Kindo* and several other human leopard murder cases—warned the Government against passing bills with such "extraordinary measures," stating that they felt "in the dark" about the reasons that these extreme amendments were being made. In particular, Shorunkeh-Sawyerr questioned the retrospective nature of the bill that made it a crime to join the Human Leopard Society *before* the bill's enactment. He argued that if a person joined an organization in the past but the group had committed no crimes while they had been a member, they should not be subject to arrest and potential deportation: "Last week I was not a criminal, but by an act of legislation of a retrospective nature, this week I am made a criminal. I must say that is not a principle of English Law." Or, what if the men were members only because they had been "entrapped into membership"? Another Krio member agreed with Shorunkeh-Sawyerr's remarks, stating that while he understood how such emergency measures might be implemented in other cases where an organization was "conspiring or plotting against His Majesty's Government," he could not see how this was the case here. Of the power of search, he asked the Legislative Council: "Where is this going to end? If after searching nothing of the kind is found, what then? Who would like to be searched like that just because we want to put down crime?" Finally, he reiterated the concerns that barristers in the Sierra Leone Bar Association had expressed for years concerning the ability of the Government to deport anyone, especially those who had not been formally convicted of a crime. While the Governor acknowledged these comments, he rejected the points made by the unofficial members, stating that "drastic steps" were necessary to prevent the spread of the Human Leopard Society to the parts of the Protectorate adjacent to the Colony, or even to Freetown itself.[79]

After the bill was passed, upwards of four hundred people, including a number of Paramount and Sub-Chiefs, were arrested with an unprecedented "show of force" throughout the Ronietta District. Just as in the Circuit Courts, some of the arrested became "informers" and 118 of the total men arrested were committed for trial.[80] The four main trials in the Special Commissions Court for human leopard murder (and several smaller trials for the possession of borfima) commenced in late 1912. The judge, Sir William Brandford Griffith, was the former Chief Justice of the Gold Coast. Griffith was assisted by a "judges panel" which consisted of high-ranking colonial officials, including Police Magistrate Kenneth J. Beatty who would later publish an account of the trials, and two African Assessors. While historians have often focused on the Special Commissions Court as distinct, the trials largely replicated the structure of Circuit Court trials from the past decade.[81] They all hinged on lower-ranking witnesses who claimed they had been coerced into participating in the murder of their relation or slave by elderly or high-ranking

FIGURE 12. Human Leopard murder prisoners awaiting trial in Imperri Chiefdom.
FROM KENNETH BEATTY, *THE HUMAN LEOPARDS OF SIERRA LEONE* (1914).

men.[82] Cases centered on the acquisition of a victim to "feed" the borfima, which "had the purpose of making a man rich and powerful and made his face 'dreadful' to others, i.e. it made him an object of respect."[83]

The format and narrative of the trials were not the only recognizable aspects of the Special Commission Court. Several familiar defendants and witnesses from Circuit Court cases emerged in 1912. In *R. v Bunting Williams*, two of the high-ranking defendants, Mori Fodi and Amarra, were the same men who petitioned for a separate Mongray Chiefdom that we saw in the previous chapter. Two years after the land was transferred from the Imperri to the Jong Chiefdom, Bunting Williams was accused of participating in the death of Mori Fodi's niece. The events of the case occurred in Kabati, one of the primary places in the original petition from Mongray leaders in 1901. The main witness, Kong Yangba, described how Amarra had killed the girl with a "firi," a horsetail with cloth wrapped around the handle, an object that was later found in Bunting Williams' home.[84] Two of the other cases were centered in Imperri Chiefdom, implicating its Paramount Chief Alfred Goma "Gomer" Kertegbeh. Amazingly, the former Paramount Chief Daniel Wilberforce, who had been found not guilty of human leopard murder but was deposed nonetheless in 1906, was charged with another case of "cannibal murder" that had allegedly taken place in 1909.

There are several ways to interpret these cases and their high-profile defendants. On one hand, it is possible that the high level of volatility and political competition within and between Jong and Imperri Chiefdom instigated an intense scramble for powerful supernatural resources to ensure political and legal success. On the other hand, by 1912 accusing someone of human leopardism may have developed into a political strategy by the accused person's competitors, as it almost certainly ensured deportation, if not death.[85] In one of the more blatant accusations of "framing," Bunting Williams testified that it was well known that the town of Kabati had recently been transferred to his chiefdom from Imperri and he had imposed laws to "put a stop to cannibalism," including fining and deposing a prominent Chief. He stated that Kong Yangba in particular "had a special ill feeling toward him" and had "only mentioned his name in connection with this matter after compulsion on the part of the District Commissioner."[86] Like many defense strategies in the past, Williams and Kertegbeh attempted to demonstrate throughout the trial how they had taken a number of steps to prevent the Human Leopard Society, prompting the question of whether this policing may have been additional motivation for the "real" human leopards to accuse him. The deciding factor in the case, however, was the discovery of the firi and other "supernatural" items in Bunting Williams' home; the items had been discovered during a search made permissible through the Human Leopard Ordinance. Though he systematically denied they were connected to the Human Leopard Society, the writing was on the wall. The colonial Government held fast to the notion that Paramount Chiefs were responsible for the murders, even if they themselves did not wield the claws.

While the large numbers of arrests prior to the Special Commissions Court cases amounted to the legal equivalent of a shock and awe campaign, the outcome of the cases were a more targeted shot aimed at the region's leadership. Of the thirty-four people brought to trial, nine were convicted of murder, ten were convicted of a lessor offence, and fifteen were acquitted. Seven of the nine men found guilty were executed, and the other two were commuted to life in prison. Of the fifteen acquitted, eleven were deported to Southern Nigeria.[87] Within this group, four Paramount Chiefs who had all been found not guilty in their trials, but were deemed to be such a threat to the "security" of the Protectorate, were deported: Bunting Williams (Jong), Alfred Goma Kertegbeh (Imperri), Fama Yonni (Yoni, Sherbro Island), and Francis Farwundu (Mano Sa-Krim). Kertegbeh's Speaker Mallingi, who was said to have "gained an ascendency over the people of the Chiefdom unequaled by even the Chief himself," was found guilty of possessing the "Mother Borfima" and was sentenced with fourteen years imprisonment.[88] Despite the legal counsel of four Krio lawyers (half of the total number of lawyers in the Colony), Reverend Wilberforce was also unable to evade the second round of accusations. Additional amendments of the Human Leopard Ordinance permitted the "expulsion" of Wilberforce to Liberia, removing him permanently from his birthplace. Some sixty-six other men who were found guilty were "expelled" from the Northern Sherbro District to other places in the Protectorate, presumably due to the substantial burden they would have placed on prisons in Lagos and other West African Colonies.[89]

In his summary remarks on the Special Commissions Court to the Colonial Office, Governor Merewether wrote that "while it was permissible to believe that the action taken by the Government has had the effect of checking the activities of the Human Leopard Society . . . it would be by no means prudent to assert that this criminal organization has been broken up. Many persons of whose connection with the Society there is little or no doubt are still at large and probably there are a few others who have hitherto not come under the notice of authorities." Falling back on the extreme stereotypes of Africans, he noted that so long as peoples in the Protectorate held the "blind belief" of the efficacy of borfima as well as the "tendency on the part of some natives to cannibalism pure and simple," they will "contribute to the survival of this baneful organization."[90] In an attempt to legislatively put the final nail in the coffin of leopardism, Merewether made the Human Leopard Ordinance a permanent feature of Protectorate lawbooks. It would remain so until independence in 1961.

Conclusion

What remains embedded in these overlapping rumors, memos, court transcripts, and punishments is a sustained struggle between and among British and African actors over authority amid the early years of indirect rule. Criminal courts constituted a new space to define and debate political legitimacy, what constituted a crime, and how people who transgressed the law ought to be punished—one of the most significant indicators of sovereign power. The colonial administration capitalized on the absence of the formal rights of Indigenous residents to institute a series of extraordinary measures to arrest, detain, try, and deport those connected with human leopardism to protect the colonial state's interests. As the decade progressed, this included those who were merely suspected of being connected to the Human Leopard Society, drawing an unbroken line from the practices established on the frontier to the operation of the judicial system in the Protectorate. Within the structure of indirect rule, the monopoly on violence by the colonial state secured their place as the ruling power. The execution and exile of Paramount Chiefs and other important men reflected the paradox of protection that had become woven into the structure of indirect rule.

Human leopard trials became forums for Africans to reconcile new types of relationships that emerged alongside unprecedented level of political and economic upheaval. Trial transcripts allow us a rare glimpse into how African notions of justice collided with British ones, as defendants used their time on the witness stand to debate culpability in a crime based on rank and class using the language of debt, obligation, and consumption. From our twenty-first-century vantage point, it is difficult to understand why these men said what they said, often describing their own participation in murder or cannibalism. However, as historian Arlette Farge has poignantly written, these testimonies are but "a few transcribed phrases . . . that we can neither count nor classify, but were one day spoken and assembled into discourse—no matter how thin it may be—on which a fate was wagered."[91] On what "fate" those litigants gambled on, we will never know. No matter which details of the cases were "true," the human leopard murder trials reflected a deeply unsettling political and social crisis that resulted from the evolution of British protection schemes designed to secure wealth and authority. The varied strategies that many leaders utilized to secure their place in this new system, including accusations of compelling those lower in status to sacrifice and "eat" their own family, were indicative of this immoral extortion.

Conclusion

This book has aimed to show how African and British contestation over what constituted protection, and who had the authority to bestow it, was central in shaping both the physical and conceptual boundaries of indirect rule. The arrival of Krio traders and British administrators to the southern Sierra Leone region at mid-century contributed to existent tensions among local communities brought about by the abolition of the slave trade and the development of agricultural commerce. Along with other African strangers, the arrival of Krio traders introduced competing notions of sovereignty and jurisdiction that would alter local ideas of subjecthood and territoriality. African engagement with British protection schemes represented innovative strategies to secure their physical and political protection in a time of unprecedented warfare and political unrest. Over five decades, negotiations over protection between Africans and Britons reflected changing conditions in both colonial policy and African internal politics. British attempts to enact protection schemes to secure economic control over the hinterland produced a series of indelible contradictions that ultimately weakened the power of the very African intermediaries they needed to secure them. The constraints on African leaders in treaty stipulations were eventually integrated into the framework of indirect rule and enforced through violence. These actions initiated a paradox of protection that limited Africans from engaging in Indigenous pathways to protection and prevented African coalitions and network building outside the patronage of the colonial state.

When researching and writing this book, I was inspired by a variety of new works that drew meaningful connections between the precolonial and colonial period.[1] My objective in tracing the long history of protection from informal to formal rule was to counter three prevalent assumptions that students and scholars of colonialism still maintain. The first is the continued impression that the legal and political framework of African protectorates was the product of colonial handbooks or colonial "invention." The majority of scholarly works on indirect rule in Africa still contain very little information on how the legality of frontier spaces, especially in regard to African precolonial jurisprudence and judicial systems, contributed to the political and juridical framework of Protectorates. Instead, most works continue to attribute the framework of indirect rule to Lord Lugard's *The Dual Mandate in British Tropical Africa*, generally considered the colonial manual for creating and ruling Protectorates. Most follow Lugard with a discussion on the relationship between indirect rule and the "invention of tradition": the idea that Britons drew from their collective imagination of what African societies were ("tribes" with Chiefs who lived in discrete chiefdoms) and then created a model of governance. In doing so, these works often fail to trace this process of transformation from the imperial frontier to the colonial period. My hope is that this book begins to remedy this oversight by revealing the integral role that African law and politics had in shaping frontier relations and that "indirect rule" was just one part of a much longer transformation of the legal culture of this little corner of West Africa.

My second aim is to counter the impression that imperial frontiers were merely zones of 'gunboat diplomacy,' inevitably lead to formal colonization. Similarly, treaties were not the first step in a well-thought-out plan. British administrators drafted highly improvisational articles aimed at solving on-the-spot problems without considering the long-term consequences. In contrast, the long-game was often being played by Africans signatories, many of whom attempted to use British treaties to secure leverage in their own internal (and often long-standing) disputes over land and legitimacy. Time and time again, we see how imperial treaties were meaningful and legible agreements that reflected African agency and their need to secure physical and political protection.

Thirdly, this study sheds important light on how non-centralized states navigated the transition from early imperialism to formal colonial rule. Unlike more centralized states, the opportunity for so many leaders in southern Sierra Leone to make claims for British protection as "rightful owners of the land" fostered a volatile and highly competitive landscape. Untangling who and what type of leaders formed alliances with the colonial state allows for a richer understanding of the foundation of colonial policies that would eventually govern the Protectorate. The turbulence of the first fifteen years of Protectorate rule reflects the reality that the creation of Paramount Chiefs and chiefdoms was not a return to the distant precolonial past, but a more complex process that was contingent on African leaders' previous alliances with the British state. Many of the descendants of the families who were able to secure their lineage's right to leadership and land in the early years of the Protectorate maintain that status as Founding Families today. Because of this, understanding how these political structures were established at the turn of the century allows us to better understand the operation of rural politics in post-colonial Sierra Leone.

My choice to ground this study through the lens of protection resulted from the search for a concept that had resonance for both African and British actors over a long period of time. At mid-century, promises of protection were particularly salient in southern Sierra Leone. The rise of internal warfare impacted the security of both Indigenous and Krio people living in the Sherbro hinterland. Perhaps more importantly than the annexation of British Sherbro in 1861, the farthest reach of Krio settlement constituted an informal imperial frontier that marked the limits of colonial law. When raided or kidnapped, Krio calls for protection as British subjects compelled British and African leaders to negotiate complex legal questions about the nature of political sovereignty. Vulnerable African leaders whose rule was challenged by both Indigenous and Krio newcomers attempted to form coalitions with the colonial state in an effort to gain political and physical protection in exchange for the safety of British subjects and secured trade routes. In this way, treaties of peace and commerce signed in Sherbro by this new group of "aligned leaders" were viewed as potential opportunities to shield themselves from their competitors and tap into new economic and legal networks to bolster their political authority.

Coastal and riverine leaders in the Sherbro who placed themselves under British protection frequently used their status as "rightful owners of the land" to convince the colonial state that they possessed legitimate authority over land and labor. The distinction between founder and stranger became an elevated feature of internal politics when newcomer war captains or Big Men threatened the authority of their original landlords or employers. Physical and supernatural conflict within and between different communities and coalitions signaled the (re)formation of new kinds of political and spatial networks that aimed to consolidate political and territorial jurisdiction. The emergence of both war captains and human leopards signaled internal shifts in power and authority that partly resulted from the emergent capitalist economy. Both attempted to use violence and fear, as well as the promise of protection, to disrupt the authority of more established leaders. War captains engaged in raids as acts of retaliation between warring coalitions, but the raids were also used to legally collect debts between people. Likewise, while the execution of human leopards by the Tongo may have been viewed by the British as acts of barbarism, they also represented rational measures by community leaders to restore the political, economic, and spiritual order.

Diplomacy with the British was only one of a number of Indigenous protection strategies deployed by African leaders. The hiring of mercenaries, the fortification of towns, and the increased circulation of protective objects all addressed the unprecedented times these communities were experiencing. Throughout this book, I showed how the paradox of protection gained particular traction when British economic interests like securing traders and transportation routes clashed with African security measures like panyarring, placing poro embargos on produce, and using witch detectives or supernatural medicines or amulets that ran contrary to rational liberalism and the capitalist economy. Thus, while treaty stipulations initially sought to compel local leaders to protect British subjects, they gradually introduced an informal criminal code that utilized a detailed a set of extra-legal punishments like incarceration, deportation, and execution when Africans failed to adhere to treaty stipulations or engaged in "repugnant" legal practices.

Local leaders' own conceptions of land ownership and tenancy, along with innumerable assurances from the colonial state that they had no interests in interfering in their "country customs," initially gave nothing to suggest that their sovereignty was threatened. However, as we saw in chapter two, military expeditions in the mid-1870s shifted colonial engagement on the frontier from protecting British interests to actively defending them. Frequent British engagement in military campaigns along the rivers reframed the frontier from an economic sphere to an active battlefield, a designation that legally legitimated the detention of "political prisoners" and devastating shock and awe campaigns. Over time, British racial and legal logic reframed African warfare in the hinterland as a kind of insurgency against the colonial state. This justified the use of extreme violence and extra-legal strategies that "rested on the assumption that exceptional circumstances required exceptional treatment."[2] British military expeditions in the name of punishing those who broke treaty agreements blurred the legal distinction between the sovereignty of African nations and the occupation of British troops in foreign territory in wartime. As the century progressed, British punitive measures and "small wars" transformed the nature of patronage in the region from one of interconnected coalitions—in which the British were only one of several members—to vertical power relations that favored British interests.[3]

Indirect rule did not solve the paradox of protection. Rather than impose the stability and order they desired, the governmental and legal structure of the Protectorate elevated the level of political and economic disorder. Indirect rule further constrained an even more limited set of African Paramount Chiefs to assert meaningful judicial and executive power. For me, the clear statements of disbelief and anguish in the petitions from leaders in those early months of Protectorate rule have been among the most moving and poignant sources I have read while writing this book. The events of 1898 so clearly reflect the betrayal felt by so many of the administration's most long-standing allies—not only because of the establishment of formal rule, but perhaps most especially because of the refusal to negotiate its terms. When viewed in the context of the previous four decades, the pushback by southern leaders under Poro leadership after 1896 must be reframed as part of a much larger struggle between strangers and autochthon leaders. Violence directed at Krios and colonial officials recall earlier raids like the one in Gundema in 1869 that had been organized by the Poro to eliminate strangers who were unlawfully occupying their and their ancestor's land. After the Insurrection of 1898, the execution and deportation of the most senior Kings and Poro men acted as a bridge between extra-legal British protection schemes on the frontier and legislation in the Protectorate, evidenced by the continued use of deposing and deportation for everyone from insurgents to human leopards. As self-appointed peacemakers, mediators, leopard detectives, judges, and King makers (and destroyers), the colonial state now assumed the former legal and judicial role of the Poro but was never able to exercise its spiritual authority.

In tracing these continuities, the final three chapters of this book reveal how Britain's designation of vast rural spaces in Africa as "protectorates" was not only an economic strategy to control resources in the "scramble for Africa," but a legal one as well. The "native" status of Indigenous people in Protectorates dispossessed them of any legal rights on the false premise that they retained their "internal sovereignty," making violence without due process part of everyday legal culture.[4]

Creating a Protectorate allowed for the continuance of many of the extra-legal practices that had developed on the frontier or had been previously legitimated through *ad hominum* legislation. Put another way, Protectorates existed with an ever-present haze of the "state of exception" or martial law hanging over it, a tactic that allowed the colonial Government to enact racially based violence that would never be condoned in the metropole or even the formal Colony. These laws further constrained Paramount Chiefs from being effective community leaders by criminalizing expressions of legitimate authority that were perceived to counter British interests and dismantling the collaborative framework of precolonial governance. Laws that limited African leaders' ability to forge coalitions as they had in the past compelled them to defer to state-sanctioned protection alongside alternative (and often "criminal") means to secure their political position.

Assuming the position of Paramount Chief meant placing oneself in a precarious position in the first decade and a half of colonial rule. Colonial attempts to "restore" leadership to those who could demonstrate ancestral connections to the land exacerbated tensions between more established leaders, competing families, and the newcomers who had settled throughout the nineteenth century. The existence of a more flexible system of investiture allowed for succession through primogeniture resulted in intense struggles over leadership at each period of interregnum. Efforts to establish rightful authority over the land widened the social and political gap between those who could claimed ancestral lineage and those who could not. Leaders and their competitors drew from a wide variety of sources to make claims as rightful founders, including British treaties and correspondence, and utilized colonial laws and forums as a means of removing leaders they claimed were unqualified or illegitimate to rule. Charges that Paramount Chiefs engaged in extortion, illegitimacy, and human leopardism alert us to new contradictions in colonial policy that simultaneously promised to protect African institutions while limiting their ability to meaningfully project power.

The final chapter of this book situates the emergence of human leopard murders in the twentieth century within the longer history of protection in this region. For Protectorate residents, the introduction of circuit courts constituted a forum to debate new kinds of social and political dynamics that emerged with the consolidation of Protectorate rule. A close examination of human leopard murder trials in Protectorate courts reveal that the factual circumstances of the murder were not always the most immediate concerns to African litigants and witnesses. Instead, their testimonies frequently centered on examining relationships of social and economic debt, some new and some old, but ties that were nevertheless rooted within a longer history of protection and authority. British characterization of these murders as part of a larger criminal conspiracy grounded in supernatural barbarism recalls earlier descriptions of other kinds of "bandits" and "insurgents" whose activities ran counter to British economic and political control. Descriptions of covert cannibalism in courts that were organized by the very intermediaries they sought to bolster compelled the British to double-down on their commitment to protection in an effort to justify colonization.

Viewed together, war captains, Tongo players, Poro "insurgents," and human leopards represent a single thread that runs through the legal history of protection in southern Sierra Leone. As colonial aims shifted alongside global legal ideas, the varied strategies of African leaders to secure their own political and physical safety impacted how British protection schemes were conceptualized and enacted. While some alliances of mutual aid between Africans and Britons were productive for local leaders in consolidating political and territorial control, clashes in how protection was understood frequently led to unprecedented physical and juridical violence. While British administrators feverishly attempted to portray a style of rule centered on orderly justice, the paradox of protection ensured that Protectorate people and their leaders remained as vulnerable, or even more so, as they had been decades before.

Notes

INTRODUCTION

1. While much has been written about the establishment of Freetown in 1787 until the 1840s, considerably less has been written on its population in the second half of the century. Recent works include: Bronwen Everill, *Abolition and Empire in Sierra Leone and Liberia* (Springer, 2012); Paul E. Lovejoy and Suzanne Schwarz, *Sierra Leone in the Eighteenth and Nineteenth Centuries* (Africa World Press, 2015); Padraic X. Scanlan, *Freedom's Debtors: British Antislavery in Sierra Leone in the Age of Revolution* (Yale University Press, 2017); Ruma Chopra, *Almost Home: Maroons between Slavery and Freedom in Jamaica, Nova Scotia, and Sierra Leone* (Yale University Press 2018); Richard Peter Anderson, *Abolition in Sierra Leone: Re-Building Lives and Identities in Nineteenth-Century West Africa* (Cambridge University Press, 2020).
2. Christina Twomey, "Protecting Slaves and Aborigines," *Pacific Historical Review* 87, no. 1 (February 1, 2018): 10–29.
3. Christina Twomey and Katherine Ellinghaus, "Protection: Global Genealogies, Local Practices," *Pacific Historical Review* 87, no. 1 (2018): 4.
4. Saliha Belmessous, *Empire by Treaty: Negotiating European Expansion, 1600–1900* (Oxford University Press, 2014).
5. Richard Roberts, *Conflicts of Colonialism: The Rule of Law, French Soudan, and Faama Mademba Seye* (Cambridge University Press, 2022).

6. Richard D. Waller, "Witchcraft and Colonial Law in Kenya," *Past & Present*, no. 180 (2003): 256.
7. On this transition, generally see Robin Law, *From Slave Trade to "Legitimate" Commerce: The Commercial Transition in Nineteenth-Century West Africa* (Cambridge University Press, 2002). On the abolition of slavery in rural Sierra Leone, see John Grace, *Domestic Slavery in West Africa: With Particular Reference to the Sierra Leone Protectorate, 1896–1927* (Barnes & Noble, 1975); Philip Misevich, *Abolition and the Transformation of Atlantic Commerce in Southern Sierra Leone, 1790s to 1860s* (Africa World Press, 2019); Sarah Delius, "The Same in All but Name? The Intersections of Marriage and Slavery in Sierra Leone, 1890–1930," *Slavery & Abolition* 43, no. 2 (2022): 320–345.
8. Lauren Benton, Adam Clucow, and Bain Attwood, *Protection and Empire: A Global History* (Cambridge University Press, 2018), 1.
9. Benton, Clucow, and Attwood, *Protection*, 1.
10. Nasser Hussain, *The Jurisprudence of Emergency: Colonialism and the Rule of Law* (University of Michigan Press, 2019); Lyndall Ryan, "Martial Law in the British Empire," *Violence, Colonialism and Empire in the Modern World*, ed. Philip Dwyer and Amanda Nettlebeck (Palgrave Macmillan, 2018), 93–109; Michael Lobban, *Imperial Incarceration: Detention Without Trial in the Making of British Colonial Africa* (Cambridge University Press, 2021); Richard N. Price, "The Psychology of Colonial Violence," in *Violence, Colonialism and Empire in the Modern World*, ed. Philip Dwyer and Amanda Nettlebeck (Palgrave Macmillan, 2018), 25–52; Elizabeth Kolsky, "The Colonial Rule of Law and the Legal Regime of Exception: Frontier 'Fanaticism' and State Violence in British India," *American Historical Review* 120, no. 4 (2015): 1218–1246; Christopher Szabla, "Civilising Violence: International Law and Colonial War in the British Empire, 1850–1900," *Journal of the History of International Law/Revue d'histoire Du Droit International* 25, no. 1 (2023): 70–104.
11. Benton, Clucow, and Attwood, *Protection*, 2.
12. Rosalind Shaw, *Memories of the Slave Trade: Ritual and the Historical Imagination in Sierra Leone* (University of Chicago Press, 2020), 29.
13. David J. Siddle, "War-Towns in Sierra Leone: A Study in Social Change," *Africa* 38, no. 1 (1968): 50.
14. Shaw, *Memories of the Slave Trade*, 32.
15. Sean Kelley, "The Dirty Business of Panyarring and Palaver: Slave Trading on the Upper Guinea Coast in the Eighteenth Century," in *Slavery, Abolition and the Transition to Colonialism in Sierra Leone*, ed. Paul Lovejoy and Suzanne Schwarz (Africa World Press, 2014), 89–108.

16. Philip J. Stern, "'A Politie of Civill & Military Power': Political Thought and the Late Seventeenth-Century Foundations of the East India Company-State," *Journal of British Studies* 47, no. 2 (2008): 253–283.
17. Allen M. Howard, "Re-Marking on the Past: Spatial Structures and Dynamics in the Sierra Leone-Guinea Plain, 1860–1920s," in *The Spatial Factor in African History*, ed. Allen Marvin Howard and Richard Matthew Shain (Brill, 2005). Also see John Davidson, *Trade and Politics in the Sherbro Hinterland, 1849–1890*, University of Wisconsin–Madison dissertation, 1969, 109–112.
18. Howard, "Re-Marking on the Past," 295.
19. Howard, "Re-Marking on the Past," 295.
20. Anthropologist Paul Richards accounts for this need for "cultural convergence" as the result of the relatively small geographic space that forest communities in Sierra Leone along the coast had to share to access to Atlantic commerce. Unlike the lower Guinea forest belt in Congo, communities in Sierra Leone had less space to "split and go their separate ways" when conflicts arose and therefore developed a unique set of cultural practices and institutions that emphasized the collaboration of newcomers and autochthon leaders. Paul Richards, *Fighting for the Rainforest: War, Youth, and Resources in Sierra Leone* (Heinemann/James Currey, 1996), 78–79.
21. Allan Howard refers to these polities in Sierra Leone as "mini-states." Howard, "Re-Marking on the Past"; also see Allen M. Howard, "Nodes, Networks, Landscapes, and Regions: Reading the Social History of Tropical Africa 1700s–1920," in *The Spatial Factor in African History*, ed. Allen Marvin Howard and Richard Matthew Shain (Brill, 2005), 21–140.
22. Understanding how precolonial political formations (centralized versus decentralized) impacted development in contemporary Africa has been a popular topic of social scientists of late, especially in regard to Sierra Leone. See Daron Acemoglu, Tristan Reed, and James A. Robinson, "Chiefs: Economic Development and Elite Control of Civil Society in Sierra Leone," *Journal of Political Economy* 122, no. 2 (2014): 319–368; Daron Acemoglu, Isaías N. Chaves, Philip Osafo-Kwaako, and James A. Robinson, "Indirect Rule and State Weakness in Africa: Sierra Leone in Comparative Perspective," in *African Successes, Volume IV: Sustainable Growth* (University of Chicago Press, 2014), 343–370.
23. Siddle, "War-Towns in Sierra Leone," 47; Christopher R. DeCorse, "Fortified Towns of the Koinadugu Plateau: Northern Sierra Leone in the Pre-Atlantic and Atlantic Worlds," *Power and Landscape in Atlantic West Africa: Archaeological Perspectives*, ed. J. Cameron Monroe and Akinwumi Ogundiran (Cambridge University Press, 2012), 278–308. For an interesting contemporary study of these war towns, see Paul Basu, "Reanimating Cultural

Heritage: Digital Curatorship, Knowledge Networks, and Social Transformation in Sierra Leone," in *The International Handbooks of Museum Studies: Museum Transformations*, (John Wiley and Sons, n.d.).

24. Alusine Jalloh and David E. Skinner, *Islam and Trade in Sierra Leone* (Africa World Press, 1997). For the use of protective amulets in precolonial Ghana, see David Owusu-Ansah, "Islamic Influence in a Forest Kingdom: The Role of Protective Amulets in Early 19th Century Asante," *Transafrican Journal of History* 12 (1983): 100–133. For the use of "mystical weapons" in the twentieth century, see Stephen Ellis, "Mystical Weapons: Some Evidence From the Liberian War," *Journal of Religion in Africa* 31, no. 2 (2001): 222–236; Nathalie Wlodarczyk, *Magic and warfare: Appearance and reality in contemporary African conflict and beyond.* (Palgrave Macmillan, 2009).
25. For a fascinating look on how these objects circulated in the Atlantic world, see Matthew Francis Rarey, *Insignificant Things: Amulets and the Art of Survival in the Early Black Atlantic* (Duke University Press, 2023).
26. Stephen Ellis, *The Mask of Anarchy: The Destruction of Liberia and the Religious Dimension of an African Civil War* (New York University Press, 1999), 230.
27. Daniel F. Wilberforce, *Sherbro and the Sherbros: Or, A Native African's Account of His Country and People* (United Brethren Publishing House, 1886), 24–25. Readers familiar with the civil war in Sierra Leone and Liberia will no doubt find this 1880s observation strikingly similar to tactics used by combatants in the 1990s. See Stephen Ellis, *The Mask of Anarchy: The Destruction of Liberia and the Religious Dimension of an African Civil War.*
28. Kenneth Little, *Mende of Sierra Leone* (Routledge, 2013), 274–275. Howard, *Islam and Trade*, 34.
29. Katrina Keefer, "Poro on Trial: The 1913 Special Commission Court Case of Rex v. Fino, Bofio and Kalfalla," *African Studies Review* 61, no. 3 (2018): 56–78
30. Lauren Benton and Lisa Ford, *Rage for Order: The British Empire and the Origins of International Law, 1800–1850* (Harvard University Press, 2016).
31. This wider coastal group was known as the "Sapes" by European traders and included the Bullom, Baga, Nalou, Gola, Krim, and Kissi.
32. John Newton, *Thoughts upon the African Slave Trade* (Printed for J. Buckland, in Pater-Noster-Row; and J. Johnson, in St. Paul's Church-yard, 1788), 25.
33. Newton, *Thoughts*, 25–26.
34. Jane I. Guyer and Samuel M. Eno Belinga, "Wealth in People as Wealth in Knowledge: Accumulation and Composition in Equatorial Africa," *Journal of African History* 36, no. 1 (1995): 91–120.

35. Carol MacCormack, "Wono: Institutionalized Dependency in Sherbro Descent Groups (Sierra Leone)." In *Slavery in Africa: Historical and Anthropological Perspectives*, ed. S. Miers and I Kopytoff, 1977, 192.
36. On the important role of the marriage of one's daughter or niece between community leaders in solidifying their coalition ("bilateral kinship system"), see Richards, *Fighting for the Rainforest*, 80.
37. Carol P. MacCormack, "Dying as Transformation to Ancestorhood: The Sherbro Coast of Sierra Leone," *Sterben Und Tod Eine Kulturvergleichende Analyse*, 1986, 117–126.
38. V. R. Dorjahn and Christopher Fyfe, "Landlord and Stranger: Change in Tenancy Relations in Sierra Leone," *The Journal of African History* 3, no. 3 (1962): 391–397; Bruce L. Mouser, "Accommodation and Assimilation in the Landlord-Stranger Relationship," in *West African Culture Dynamics: Archaeological and Historical Perspectives* (De Gruyter, 1980), 495–514; Anaïs Ménard, *Integrating Strangers: Sherbro Identity and The Politics of Reciprocity along the Sierra Leonean Coast* (Berghahn Books, 2023).
39. There is much debate about the role of women in Poro. For the best description of this see Lynda Day, *Gender and Power in Sierra Leone: Women Chiefs of the Last Two Centuries* (Palgrave Macmillan, 2012), 17. For a counter-opinion, see Arthur Abraham, *Mende Government and Politics Under Colonial Rule: A Historical Study of Political Change in Sierra Leone, 1890–1937* (Oxford University Press, 1979), 253–258.
40. Thomas Joshua Alldridge, *The Sherbro and Its Hinterland.* (Macmillan and Company, 1901), 126. Kenneth Little, *Mende of Sierra Leone* (Routledge, 2013), 243.
41. Richard M. Fulton, "The Political Structures and Functions of Poro in Kpelle Society," *American Anthropologist* 74, no. 5 (1972): 1218–1233; Kenneth Little, "The Political Function of the Poro, Part I," *Africa* 35, no. 4 (October 1965): 349–365; Kenneth Little, "The Political Function of the Poro, Part II," *Africa* 36, no. 1 (January 1966): 62–72; James L. Gibbs, Jr., "Poro Values and Courtroom Procedures in a Kpelle Chiefdom," *Southwestern Journal of Anthropology* 18, no. 4 (1962): 341–350; Richard P. Fahey, "The Poro as a System of Judicial Administration in Northwestern Liberia: Its Intraclan and Interclan Functions," *The Journal of Legal Pluralism and Unofficial Law* 3, no. 4 (1971): 1–25.
42. Hoffer notes that leaders would try and escape this role and had to be "held down" for seven days to pursued him to be the leader. Carol Pulley Hoffer, *Acquisition and Exercise of Political Power by a Woman Paramount Chief of the Sherbro People* (Bryn Mawr College, 1971), 213–214.
43. See Beryl L. Bellman, *The Language of Secrecy: Symbols & Metaphors in Poro Ritual* (Rutgers University Press, 1984); Mary H. Nooter, "Secrecy: African Art That Conceals

and Reveals," *African Arts* 26, no. 1 (1993): 55–102; E. Ojo Arewa and Everett E. Hale, "Poro Communications (West Africa). A Spiritual Channel Where Men Are the Means of Transmission," *Anthropos* (1975): 78–96. For more recent accounts of the use of secrecy see Mariane C. Ferme, *The Underneath of Things: Violence, History, and the Everyday in Sierra Leone* (University of California Press, 2001); Peter Albrecht, "Secrets, Strangers, and Order-Making in Rural Sierra Leone," *Journal of Contemporary African Studies* 34, no. 4 (2016): 519–537.

44. Hoffer, *Acquisition and Exercise*, 213–214.
45. In families who had many dependents, a descent group could be further divided into minimal and maximal rams. Those in the latter category were people who could trace their lineage directly from the founder of the lineage through their father's line—in some cases making them stronger candidates for leadership. Genealogically shallower groups competed against each other to become leaders. Hoffer, *Acquisition and Exercise*, 138–143.
46. References to the "petty Kingdom" of Sherbro began as early as the late 1600s. In a recent article, anthropologist Paul Richards refers to places like Imperri as "village republics," but it is unclear whether he is describing the Mende states north of the Sherbro state or the other polities within the broader Sherbro hinterland. Paul Richards, "Public Authority and Its Demons: The Sherbro Leopard Murders in Sierra Leone," *Africa* 91, no. 2 (2021): 226–248.
47. In some cases, important towns were also ruled through a titled position, such as the *Do Fama* of Mattru. It is unclear if this was the result of conflict between the titular leader of the Jong (Sei Kama) and Mattru, or if this region historically constituted a separate political state. Abraham, *Mende Government and Politics*, 33 and 35.
48. Other titular leaders included the Ta Bompey of Nongoba, Sei Bureh of Tormah-Bum, and So Fa of Cha. Abraham, *Mende Government and Politics*, 35.
49. Dalton (1796) Quoted in Abraham, *Mende Government and Politics*, 35.
50. Thomas Joshua Alldridge, *A Transformed Colony, Sierra Leone, as It Was, and as It Is: Its Progress, Peoples, Native Customs and Undeveloped Wealth* (J. B. Lippincott, 1910), 268–269.
51. Walter Hawthorne, "States and Statelessness," in *The Oxford Handbook of Modern African History*. (Oxford University Press, 2013), 77–78.
52. Kenneth Little, "The Political Function of the Poro, Part I," *Africa* 35, no. 4 (October 1965): 349–365; Kenneth Little, "The Political Function of the Poro, Part II," *Africa* 36, no. 1 (January 1966): 62–72.
53. Robert Clarke, *Sierra Leone: A Description of the Manners and Customs of the Liberated*

Africans; with Observations upon the Natural History of the Colony, and a Notice of the Native Tribes, vol. 1 (J. Ridgway, 1843), 68; Nemata Amelia Blyden, *West Indians in West Africa, 1808–1880: The African Diaspora in Reverse* (University of Rochester Press, 2000).

54. Christopher Fyfe, *A History of Sierra Leone* (Oxford University Press, 1962); Leo Spitzer, *Sierra Leone Creole Reactions to Westernization, 1870–1925* (University of Wisconsin–Madison, 1969); Akintola Wyse, *The Krio of Sierra Leone: An Interpretive History* (C. Hurst & Co., 1989); Gibril R. Cole, *The Krio of West Africa: Islam, Culture, Creolization, and Colonialism in the Nineteenth Century* (Ohio University Press, 2013). On debates over Krio identity, see David Skinner and Barbara E. Harrell-Bond, "Misunderstandings Arising from the Use of the Term 'Creole' in the Literature on Sierra Leone," *Africa: Journal of the International African Institute* 47, no. 3 (1977): 305–320; Akintola J. G. Wyse, "On Misunderstandings Arising from the Use of the Term 'Creole' in the Literature on Sierra Leone: A Rejoinder," *Africa* 49, no. 4 (1979): 408–417; Mac Dixon-Fyle and Gibril Raschid Cole, *New Perspectives on the Sierra Leone Krio*, vol. 204 (Peter Lang, 2006).
55. It is also possible that many of the people who identified as "Creoles" were born outside of the formal Colony and adopted this identity (and perhaps even legal status) through customs, manners, dress, religion, etc. Skinner and Harrell-Bond, "Misunderstandings Arising from the Use of the Term 'Creole' in the Literature on Sierra Leone," 306–307. Skinner and Harell-Bond point out that the image of a cohesive group was crafted by the literate African population who also used the terms "Sierra Leonean," "native," "educated native," or "British subject" while some also used more specific terms based on their heritage like "Ebo" or "Aku." Also see Menard, *Integrating Strangers* on Sherbro adoption of Krio identities.
56. E. Frances White, *Sierra Leone's Settler Women Traders: Women on the Afro-European Frontier* (University of Michigan Press, 1987). Martin Lynn, "Technology, Trade, and 'A Race of Native Capitalists': The Krio Diaspora of West Africa and the Steamship. 1852–95," *The Journal of African History* 33, no. 3 (1992): 421–440.
57. For more on the development of the Krio community, see Mac Dixon-Fyle and Gibril Raschid Cole, eds., introduction to *New Perspectives on the Sierra Leone Krio*, vol. 204 (Peter Lang, 2006).
58. See especially Spitzer, *Sierra Leone Creole Reactions to Westernization, 1870–1925.*
59. "Headwaters" refers to the place where the river is no longer navigable.
60. See Benedikt Korf, Tobias Hagmann, and Martin Doevenspeck, "Geographies of Violence and Sovereignty: The African Frontier Revisited," in *Violence on the Margins: States, Conflict, and Borderlands* (Springer, 2013), 29–54.

CHAPTER ONE. COALITIONS AND CONFLICTS: PHYSICAL AND LEGAL JURISDICTION ON THE SHERBRO COAST, 1840–1870

1. This group of migrants to Freetown in 1800 was known as the Maroons. For more on their unique history, see Mavis Christine Campbell and George Ross, *Back to Africa: George Ross and the Maroons: From Nova Scotia to Sierra Leone* (Africa World Press, 1993); Ruma Chopra, *Almost Home: Maroons between Slavery and Freedom in Jamaica, Nova Scotia, and Sierra Leone* (Yale University Press, 2018).
2. J. H. Kopytoff, *A Preface to Modern Nigeria: The Sierra Leonians in Yoruba, 1830–1890* (University of Wisconsin Press, 1965); Martin Lynn, "Technology, trade and a 'race of native capitalists': The Krio diaspora of West African and the steamship, 1852–95," *The Journal of African History* 33, no. 3 (1992): 421–440.
3. Allen M. Howard, "Re-Marking on the Past: Spatial Structures and Dynamics in the Sierra Leone-Guinea Plain, 1860–1920s," in *The Spatial Factor in African History*, ed. Allen Marvin Howard and Richard Matthew Shain (Brill, 2005), 292.
4. Saliha Belmessous, *Empire by Treaty: Negotiating European Expansion, 1600–1900* (Oxford University Press, 2014); Saliha Belmessous, *Native Claims: Indigenous Law against Empire, 1500–1920*. Oxford University Press, 2012.
5. Saadia Touval, "Treaties, Borders, and the Partition of Africa," *The Journal of African History* 7, no. 2 (1966): 279–293; John Mugambwa, "Treaties or Scraps of Paper? A Second Look at the Legal Character of the Nineteenth Century British/African Colonial Agreements," *Comparative and International Law Journal of Southern Africa* 20, no. 1 (1987): 79–93; Reşat Kasaba, "Treaties and Friendships: British Imperialism, the Ottoman Empire, and China in the Nineteenth Century," *Journal of World History* 4, no. 2 (Fall 1993): 215–241; Steven M. Harris, "Manufacturing International Law: Pre-Printed Treaties in the 'Scramble for Africa,'" *Journal of the History of International Law* 23, no. 3 (May 2020): 439–465; Matthew Craven, "What Happened to Unequal Treaties? The Continuities of Informal Empire," *Nordic Journal of International Law* 74 (2005): 335–382; Anietie A. Inyang and Manasseh Edidem Bassey, "Imperial Treaties and the Origins of British Colonial Rule in Southern Nigeria, 1860–1890," *Mediterranean Journal of Social Sciences* 5, no. 20 (September 2014): 1946–53; Belmessous, *Empire by Treaty*.
6. Antony Anghie, "Finding the Peripheries: Sovereignty and Colonialism in Nineteenth-Century International Law," *Harvard International Law Journal* 40, no. 1 (Winter 1999): 1–71.
7. Imodale Caulker-Burnett, *The Caulkers of Sierra Leone: The Story of a Ruling Family and Their Times* (Xlibris Corporation, 2010), 40–41; Carol Pulley Hoffer, *Acquisition and Exercise of Political Power by a Woman Paramount Chief of the Sherbro People* (Bryn

Mawr College, 1971), 104. Somewhat in opposition to this story, the Sosant family (also sometimes referred to as the Sosant-Dick, Sousanth, or Sosandick family) assert original claims to the land through the erection of an ancestral shrine in Tasso located in Mokane. They claimed the Ya Cumba people had been their "slaves" and had been sent to the coast from their inland headquarters in Mocharch (later Mocobo) to cook (evaporate) salt for them. Centuries later, both sides asserted the other was historically their "clients," though in reality, they and the Caulkers, would frequently intermarry with each other. Hoffer, *Acquisition and Exercise*, 98–103; James A. Robinson and Tristan Reed, *The Chiefdoms of Sierra Leone*, 96–97. Also see Caulker-Burnett, *The Caulkers of Sierra Leone*, 47–48.

8. V. R. Dorjahn and Christopher Fyfe, "Landlord and Stranger: Change in Tenancy Relations in Sierra Leone," *The Journal of African History* 3, no. 3 (1962): 391–397; Bruce L. Mouser, "Trade, Coasters, and Conflict in the Rio Pongo from 1790 to 1808," *The Journal of African History* 14, no. 1 (1973): 45–64; Bruce L. Mouser, "Accommodation and Assimilation in the Landlord-Stranger Relationship," in *West African Culture Dynamics: Archaeological and Historical Perspectives* (De Gruyter, 1980), 495–514.
9. John Davidson, *Trade and Politics in the Sherbro Hinterland, 1849–1890*, University of Wisconsin–Madison dissertation, 1969, 100.
10. Caulker-Burnett, *The Caulkers of Sierra Leone*, 41–42.
11. Over time, the name "Corker" eventually became "Caulker." See Caulker-Burnett, *The Caulkers of Sierra Leone*, 141.
12. Anaïs Ménard, *Integrating Strangers: Sherbro Identity and The Politics of Reciprocity along the Sierra Leonean Coast* (Berghahn Books, 2023), 10–11; Carol P. MacCormack, "Wono: Institutionalized Dependency in Sherbro Descent Groups (Sierra Leone),' *Slavery in Africa*, 1977, 198.
13. Caulker-Burnett, *The Caulkers of Sierra Leone*, 50.
14. This is the narrative according to the Caulker Family. Caulker-Burnett, *The Caulkers of Sierra Leone*, 46.
15. Hoffer, *Acquisition and Exercise*, 108–109. Also see Matthew H. Hill, "Where to Begin? The Place of the Hunter Founder in Mende Histories," *Anthropos* (1984): 653–656.
16. Carol MacCormack, "Control of Land, Labor, and Capital in Rural Southern Sierra Leone," in *Women and Work in Africa* (Westview Press Boulder, 1982), 49.
17. Allen M. Howard, "Nineteenth-Century Coastal Slave Trading and the British Abolition Campaign in Sierra Leone," *Slavery and Abolition* 27, no. 1 (April 2006): 23–49; Philip Misevich, *Abolition and the Transformation of Atlantic Commerce in Southern Sierra Leone, 1790s to 1860s* (Africa World Press, 2019).

18. On the ethnic breakdown of slaves captured in the Sherbro region see Philip Misevich, "The Mende and Sherbro Diaspora in Nineteenth-Century Southern Sierra Leone," *The Rise and Demise of Slavery and the Slave Trade in the Atlantic World*, 2016, 247–265.
19. Caulker-Burnett, *The Caulkers of Sierra Leone*, 141. The division occurred sometime between 1810 and 1832. The name Shenge means "salt" and Bompeh means "a portion or section of the whole vast land." Canreba's father was Thomas Kon Tham.
20. Caulker-Burnett, *The Caulkers of Sierra Leone*, 97.
21. Thomas Stephen's accusations that Canreba's mother's status as a slave also fueled Canreba's hatred of him and perpetuated the war between the two of them in his lifetime. Caulker-Burnett, *The Caulkers of Sierra Leone*, 99.
22. Arthur Abraham, *An Introduction to the Precolonial History of the Mende* (Edwin Mellon Press, 2003), Chapter 5.
23. Arthur Abraham, *Mende Government and Politics Under Colonial Rule: A Historical Study of Political Change in Sierra Leone, 1890–1937* (Oxford University Press, 1979), 1–4.
24. Abraham, *Precolonial History of the Mende*, 137–138. On the Wunde, see W. Addison, "The Wunde Society: Protectorate of Sierra Leone, British West Africa," *Man* (1936): 207–209.
25. Canreba's son Richard Canreba Caulker gave Gbenjeh a wife named Yoko (who would eventually become the leader of the Kpaa-Mende). Gbenjeh, in turn, gave Richard his daughter as a wife. Gbenjeh's daughter was Yogbo (later called Bora). Gbenjeh died in 1873. His nephew Gbanyah assumed his position as leader of the Kpaa-Mende and took Yoko as his wife. It was then Gbanyah and Yoko (who arrived with her brother Lamboi) who would establish Senehun as the new capital of the Kpaa-Mende. Abraham, *Precolonial History of the Mende*, 145.
26. The Banta are regarded as having supernatural powers which includes having the ability to transform into elephants when they die. It was said that when a hunter killed an elephant, he spoke Banta before his death. Abraham, *Precolonial History of the Mende*, 139–140.
27. As the Kpaa-Mende engaged further in their conquest, displaced people moved southwards along the Jong and the Banta established a capital in Gbangbatoke. Eventually when Mende would settle in the Bompeh, they would ignore the Sherbro leaders and be loyal to the already established Mende leaders. For a list of Mende towns in Sherbro territory, see Abraham, *Precolonial History of the Mende*, 146.
28. James Sherman, "Correspondence, Intelligence, &. Sierra Leone," *The Harbinger: The Countess of Huntingdon's New Magazine*. March 1852, 91.
29. This would not be the last Caulker said to do this. Canreba's son, Richard Canreba Caulker was also rumored to had supernatural abilities. Caulker-Burnett, *The Caulkers of*

Sierra Leone, 105–106.

30. Caulker-Burnett, *The Caulkers of Sierra Leone*, 97–99.
31. Sherman, *The Harbinger*, 92.
32. One description recounted that he had an "Arab priest" with him at his country residence of Barmantee. *The Harbinger*, 91.
33. Several Caulkers signed the 1825 "Turners Treaty."
34. Sherman, *The Harbinger*, 91.
35. Caulker-Burnett, *The Caulkers of Sierra Leone*, 105.
36. Treaty with the Chiefs of Sherbro (1849). *Hertslet's Commercial Treaties* (1856). Volume 9, 41–44.
37. Treaty with the Chiefs of Sherbro (1849). *Hertslet's Commercial Treaties* (1856). Volume 9, 42. Section VI. Three years later, they signed another series of treaties that outlined the succession for the next generation of leaders of the Bompeh and Plantain/Shenge chiefdoms.
38. It is possible that he also believed Christianity to be another useful source of spiritual protection. Krio missionaries told Canreba that the bible they gave him as a gift was "God's own book" and that "if he kept such a book no *gree gree*, fetish, charm or any other bad thing would happen to him." In a world that already possessed an extensive occult economy, the settlement of Krio missionaries may have also been viewed as access to both supernatural as well as economic capital. He gave Krio and other missionaries permission to establish a mission station and school and sent his son to England for an education. *The Harbinger*, 91.
39. Belmessous, *Empire by Treaty*, 4–5. Also see Inge Van Hulle, *Britain and International Law in West Africa: The Practice of Empire* (Oxford University Press, 2020).
40. Thomas Theophilus' son was James Canreba Caulker who became Chief of Shenge in 1899 after the death of Thomas Neale Caulker and John Canreba who became Chief in 1901. His nephew was Richard Canreba Caulker.
41. Caulker-Burnett, *The Caulkers of Sierra Leone*. For further history on the Ribbi, see Robinson and Reed, *Chiefdoms*, 101–102. It seems "Pa Keni" may have also been a titular position, as another one was "crowned" by a man named Canray Mahoi in 1893.
42. Although Thomas Theophilus had been educated in Freetown at the Government school, it appears he did retain a high-ranking position in the Poro.
43. Enclosure: Deposition of Nancy Nicol to Colonial Government. August 20, 1860. BNA/CO 267/267/9755. The first resided at Hamburg Factory in the Ribbi River.
44. Pa Cainy and Lahai Bundoo to Governor. August 20, 1860. BNA/CO 267/267/9755.
45. Governor to Colonial Office. Enclosure: Sierra Leone Memorial presented to the

Governor. August 20, 1860. BNA/CO 267/267/9755.

46. Governor to Colonial Office. Enclosure: Sierra Leone Memorial presented to the Governor. August 20, 1860. BNA/CO 267/267/9755.
47. Governor to Colonial Office. Enclosure: Sierra Leone Memorial presented to the Governor. August 20, 1860. BNA/CO 267/267/9755.
48. Alan Lester and Fae Dussart, "Trajectories of Protection: Protectorates of Aborigines in Early 19th Century Australia and Aotearoa New Zealand," *New Zealand Geographer* 64, no. 3 (2008): 205–220; Shaunnagh Dorsett, "Metropolitan Theorising: Legal Frameworks, Protectorates and Models for Māori Governance 1837–1838," *Law & History* 3, no. 3 (2016): 1–18; Lauren Benton, Adam Clucow, and Bain Attwood, *Protection and Empire: A Global History* (Cambridge University Press, 2018); Lauren Benton and Adam Clulow, "Protection Shopping Among Empires: Suspended Sovereignty in the Cocos-Keeling Islands," *Past & Present*, 2021, 1–40; Van Hulle, *Britain and International Law*.
49. Akintola Wyse, *The Krio of Sierra Leone: An Interpretive History* (C. Hurst & Co., 1989); Leo Spitzer, *Sierra Leone Creole Reactions to Westernization, 1870–1925* (University of Wisconsin–Madison, 1969). For newer works on the Krio, see Gibril R. Cole, *The Krio of West Africa: Islam, Culture, Creolization, and Colonialism in the Nineteenth Century* (Ohio University Press, 2013); Mac Dixon-Fyle and Gibril Raschid Cole, *New Perspectives on the Sierra Leone Krio* (Peter Lang, 2006); Festus Cole, "Anglo-Krio Relations: A Study of a Disadvantaged Community in a Colonial Setting, 1895–1922," *The Journal of Imperial and Commonwealth History* 50, no. 4 (2022): 607–638.
50. Van Hulle, *Britain and International Law*, 121.
51. Pa Cainy and Lahai Bundoo to Governor. August 20, 1860. BNA/CO 267/267/9755.
52. For more on ransoming in West African, see Nathan Carpenter, "Ransom as Political Strategy: Captivity beyond Commercial Transaction on the Upper Guinea Coast in the Late Nineteenth and Early Twentieth Centuries," *Journal of West African History* 4, no. 2 (2018): 1–18; Olatunji Ojo and Jennifer Lofkrantz, "West African Responses to Illegal Enslavement and Failed Ransom Negotiations," *Journal of African History* 52 (2012).
53. Caulker-Burnett, *The Caulkers of Sierra Leone*, 97–98. At one point during supposed peace talks, Thomas Stephen was almost assassinated by members of the Poro, only to be saved by a man whose daughter had been married to Thomas Stephen's father.
54. Jonga a.k.a. Thomas Nightengale. His bugler was William Domingo, grandfather of the author of The Caulker Manuscripts (George Domingo). The manuscripts are reprinted in Caulker-Burnett, *The Caulkers of Sierra Leone*.
55. Caulker-Burnett, *The Caulkers of Sierra Leone*, 101. Thomas Stephen's son, George Stephen II, became leader. He went to school in England for seven years around mid-century and

spent time in French Guinea. His death was in 1871.

56. In 1841 Thomas Stephen Caulker signed the treaty alongside Canreba that promised to refrain from engaging in the slave trade and was also given a stipend to compensate for his losses. He allowed missionaries from the United Brethren of Christ in America to settle in his town of Shenge where twenty-three of his children were educated. Fyfe, *A History of Sierra Leone* (Oxford University Press, 1962), 285.
57. Fyfe, *A History of Sierra Leone*, 286.
58. For example, in 1858, an incident occurred when a French trader claimed to have been "insulted" by the Chief of Bendu, Thomas Stephen Caulker. In retaliation, the French bombarded the Sherbro coast. Perhaps fearing for his own safety, Caulker wrote Governor Hill at Freetown and offered to cede Bendu to him in exchange for protection against the French. This relatively minor incident transformed into one of more convincing and most-used arguments for the cession of Bendu, although it seems as though in reality at in this decade, French imperial ambitions in the region were fairly minimal.
59. Treaty of 1861. November 14, 1861. BNA/CO 267/271/1050.
60. Treaty of 1861. November 14, 1861. BNA/CO 267/271/1050.
61. Suzanne Schwarz, "Land and Settlement: Temne Responses to British Abolitionist Intervention in Sierra Leone in the Late Eighteenth and Early Nineteenth Centuries," *African Economic History* 49, no. 1 (2021): 222–248.
62. In 1849, the Plantain Islands were also ceded.
63. Lawson to Governor. January 28, 1873. SLPA/GI LB. 13.
64. Many of these leaders were relatively important men, judging from their titles and the prominence of the towns they hailed from.
65. This appears to be the most complete list of leaders, perhaps suggesting why British jurisdiction of Sherbro Island appears to have never been questioned after 1861 and why the new capital was placed in Bonthe.
66. Thus, while the Foreign Jurisdiction Act of 1849 explicitly stated that African leaders must refrain from punishing British subjects who committed crimes in their territory, it was unclear just what territory was British and who exactly was a British subject. Fyfe, *History of Sierra Leone*, 255.
67. 1883 [C. 3765]. Correspondence on the Disturbances in the Neighbourhood of British Sherbro in April and May 1883 Presented to Parliament. Pinkett to Earl of Derby. April 19, 1883. 1–2.
68. Arthur Abraham refers to two kinds of "states" in the region: Territorial (Sherbro, Lubu, Gallinas, Bumpeh, and Kpaa-Mende) and Hegemonies (Ticonkoh, Kpanguma, Gaura, and Luawa). The former were defined by more fixed borders, while the later represented

the limits of individual named leaders to project power. Abraham, *Mende Government and Politics*, 33–35. For an example of a map, see Sherbro and Mendi from "A Cyclopedia of Missions" by Rev. Harvey Newcomb, Charles Scribner, New York, 1856.

69. Lauren Benton, *A Search for Sovereignty: Law and Geography in European Empires, 1400–1900* (Cambridge University Press, 2009).
70. Governor to CO. April 29, 1870. BNA/CO 267/305/5242.
71. Beah Boom to Commandant Walshe. March 1, 1870. BNA/CO 267/305/5342. Bundooka's name also provides clues of his raising and kidnapping. The Bunduka people were a subset of Fula traders whose homeland was in Fuuta Toro in Senegal. They had settled in the region and were traditionally aligned with the Temne people in the region since the late eighteenth century. Fyfe, *History of Sierra Leone*, 67–66; Alusine Jalloh, *African Entrepreneurship* (Ohio University Press, 1999), 4.
72. In the Treaty of 1861, a "So Kam, Chief of Imperay" is listed as a signatory. It is difficult to know if this person was the "Sokong" or if he was the leader who died in 1870. Fyfe, *History of Sierra Leone*, 370–371.
73. Lolme settled in the Sherbro region in Mano the 1860s to work for a British man (possibly a missionary) in the timber trade.
74. Enclosure: Deposition of Bundoh. BNA/CO 267/305/5241. This practice is confirmed by Davidson, *Trade and Politics*, 185. The leader was Fah Hegi of Gangamah.
75. Testimony of Edward Green Conolly. BNA/CO 267/305/5241. Conolly testified that when he returned to Gundema he found two of Bundooka's brothers dead; both had been disemboweled, one had his private parts and left hand cut off, and both had slashed necks almost to the point of decapitation. Governor to CO. April 29, 1870. BNA/CO 267/305/5242. For more on "ritual" murder for the production of medicines in Sierra Leone generally, see Rosalind Shaw, "The Politician and the Diviner: Divination and the Consumption of Power in Sierra Leone," *Journal of Religion in Africa* 26, no. 1 (1996): 30–55.
76. "Information Regarding the Different Districts and Tribes: Despatch from Administrator." November 6, 1886. BNA/CO 267/25/1549.
77. Governor to CO. April 29, 1870. BNA/CO 267/305/5242.
78. Attachment Walshe to Governor. March 13, 1870. BNA/CO 267/305/5241.
79. The signature on the Treaty of 1861 is "Beeah Boom [*sic*]"; no town is listed. His name is listed after the "So Kong," providing a clue that it may be the same man.
80. The death of the Sokong in 1870 contributed to the political divisiveness of the region.
81. Suzanne Schwartz describes this type of violence in conflicts over land during struggles between local Temne leaders and British colonial administrators during the founding of

Freetown. Schwarz, "Land and Settlement."

82. Attachment Walshe to Governor. March 13, 1870. BNA/CO 267/305/5241. Governor to CO. April 16, 1870. BNA/CO 267/305/5241.
83. Within this information, the Commandant of Sherbro went up the river with a detachment of police and to detain Ansummana Lolme and Mormodoo Groma, whom he believed were the ringleaders. He also wrote the Governor to tell him that if he could find sufficient evidence to justify it, he would detain and punish Beah Boom, who he labelled a "notoriously turbulent Chief" in the area.
84. Rowe to Lawson. October 24, 1873. SLPA/GI LB. 106.
85. Governor to Colonial Office. June 7, 1870. BNA/CO 267/306/6868.
86. His actions may have even been a suggestion from his boss Ansumana Lolme, who was known to "play" with the borders himself to avoid the reach of colonial law. After another crime occurred implemented Lolme in 1873, a memo written by Lawson explicitly stated that Lolme's constant change of address was way for him to avoid facing any charges for his crimes. The Government Interpreter Thomas George Lawson wrote that although it was well known to all that Lolme's town was "Mano" (a town well within British territory), his true headquarters was a town called Pettifoo, which was outside British jurisdiction. Because of this connection, it is possible that Lolme was responsible for the raids on Mano in 1859, and then claimed the town as his. Rowe to Lawson. October 24, 1873. SLPA/GI LB, 106.
87. Governor to Colonial Office. June 7, 1870. BNA/CO 267/306/6868. My emphasis.
88. Governor to Colonial Office. June 7, 1870. BNA/CO 267/306/6868.
89. Governor to Colonial Office. June 7, 1870. BNA/CO 267/306/6868.
90. Minutes of the Executive Council. May 20, 1870. BNA/CO 267/306/8281.
91. Meeting of the Executive Council. November 8, 1870. BNA/CO 267/307/12453.
92. Fyfe, *A History of Sierra Leone*, 371.
93. The end of the Atlantic slave trade led to the creation of a new internal slave trade route that, instead of running east to west, travelled south to north to the groundnut growing regions of Upper Guinea. Slave merchants altered their routes to escape British anti-slavery detection along the coast, primarily targeting children from the Sherbro region. Local leaders became increasingly dependent on Muslim merchants for access to foreign goods and frequently became indebted to them without means to repay them. See Misevich, *Abolition and the Transformation of Atlantic Commerce in Southern Sierra Leone, 1790s to 1860s*, chapter 4, 158–159; Winston McGowan, "The Establishment of Long-Distance Trade between Sierra Leone and Its Hinterland, 1787–1821," *Journal of African History* 31, no. 1 (1990): 25–41.

94. Perhaps this is why in 1846, Canreba captured and placed several Susu traders in chains, threatening to expel them from the Sherbro territory. This story is told in Misevich, *Abolition and the Transformation of Atlantic Commerce in Southern Sierra Leone, 1790s to 1860s*, 182.

CHAPTER TWO. TREATIES AND TRIBULATIONS: POLICING AND PUNITIVE MEASURES ON THE SIERRA LEONE FRONTIER, 1870–1885

1. 1875 [C.1343] Papers relating to Her Majesty's possessions in West Africa. Sierra Leone and Gold Coast Colony, including Lago. Statement of Mrs. Jane Taylor to the Acting Commandant. June 8, 1875. 43–44.
2. Edward Keene, "The Treaty-Making Revolution of the Nineteenth Century," *The International History Review* 34, no. 3 (September 2012): 475–500.
3. Saadia Touval, "Treaties, Borders, and the Partition of Africa," *The Journal of African History* 7, no. 2 (1966): 279–293; John Mugambwa, "Treaties or Scraps of Paper? A Second Look at the Legal Character of the Nineteenth Century British/African Colonial Agreements," *Comparative and International Law Journal of Southern Africa* 20, no. 1 (1987): 79–93; Reşat Kasaba, "Treaties and Friendships: British Imperialism, the Ottoman Empire, and China in the Nineteenth Century," *Journal of World History* 4, no. 2 (Fall 1993): 215–241; Steven M. Harris, "Manufacturing International Law: Pre-Printed Treaties in the 'Scramble for Africa,'" *Journal of the History of International Law* 23, no. 3 (May 2020): 439–465; Matthew Craven, "What Happened to Unequal Treaties? The Continuities of Informal Empire," *Nordic Journal of International Law* 74 (2005): 335–382; Anietie A. Inyang and Manasseh Edidem Bassey, "Imperial Treaties and the Origins of British Colonial Rule in Southern Nigeria, 1860–1890," *Mediterranean Journal of Social Sciences* 5, no. 20 (September 2014): 1946–1953; Saliha Belmessous, *Empire by Treaty: Negotiating European Expansion, 1600–1900* (Oxford University Press, 2014); Elizabeth Kolsky, "The Colonial Rule of Law and the Legal Regime of Exception: Frontier 'Fanaticism' and State Violence in British India," *American Historical Review* 120, no. 4 (2015): 1218–1246.
4. Belmessous, *Empire by Treaty*, 6. Also see how palavers were used in negotiations in negotiations over the establishment of the Sierra Leone Colony. Suzanne Schwarz, "Land and Settlement: Temne Responses to British Abolitionist Intervention in Sierra Leone in the Late Eighteenth and Early Nineteenth Centuries," *African Economic History* 49, no. 1 (2021): 222–248. For the use of palavers elsewhere see Shumway, Rebecca. "Palavers and Treaty-Making in the British Acquisition of the Gold Coast Colony (West Africa)." *Empire*

by Treaty. Negotiating European Expansion, 1600–1900 ed. Saliha Belmessous (2014): 161–185.

5. Lyndall Ryan, "Martial Law in the British Empire," *Violence, Colonialism and Empire in the Modern World* (Palgrave Macmillan, 2018), 93–109; Richard N. Price, "The Psychology of Colonial Violence," *Violence, Colonialism and Empire in the Modern World*, ed. Philip Dwyer and Amanda Nettlebeck (Palgrave Macmillan, 2018), 25–52; Nasser Hussain, *The Jurisprudence of Emergency: Colonialism and the Rule of Law* (University of Michigan Press, 2019); Christopher Szabla, "Civilising Violence: International Law and Colonial War in the British Empire, 1850–1900," *Journal of the History of International Law/Revue d'histoire Du Droit International* 25, no. 1 (2023): 70–104.
6. It is possible that the decline of the timber trade was the result of the ongoing wars between Thomas Stephen Caulker and Canreba. Imodale Caulker-Burnett *The Caulkers of Sierra Leone: The Story of a Ruling Family and Their Times* (Xlibris Corporation, 2010), 184. In his 1875 report, Commandant Darnell Davis notes that the total imports of palm produce and rice in 1871 was £140,055. This is the reason for the "approximate" in this sentence. The numbers from 1854 come from Martin Lynn, *Commerce and Economic Change in West Africa: The Palm Oil Trade in the Nineteenth Century* (Cambridge University Press, 2002), 25; and 1876 [C.1343] papers Relating to Her Majesty's possessions in West Africa. Darnell Davis, "Notes upon the State of British Sherbro," March 1, 1875, 17.
7. 1876 [C. 1402] Papers relating to Her Majesty's possessions in West Africa. Sierra Leone and Gold Coast Colony, including Lagos. Governor Rowe to Carnavon. September 11, 1875. 17.
8. Journey of Mr. Edwards and Loggie to Sherbro, Kittam, Boom, Gallinas, Sulymah, and Mannoh Districts. November 9, 1878. BNA/CO 267/335/15190.
9. Lynda Day argues that this was also a particularly challenging time for female leaders among the Mende who relied on their ritual power as a basis of legitimate authority. Lynda Day, *Gender and Power in Sierra Leone: Women Chiefs of the Last Two Centuries* (Palgrave Macmillan, 2012), Chapter 3.
10. Capturing women and children was especially lucrative as they could be sold in the emergent internal slave trade to regions far north of Sierra Leone or could be utilized to process palm produce in the Sherbro itself.
11. Day, *Gender and Power*; Arthur Abraham, *Mende Government and Politics Under Colonial Rule: A Historical Study of Political Change in Sierra Leone, 1890–1937* (Oxford University Press, 1979).
12. Sherbro District Report. George Page. July 23, 1907. CO 267/495/28246; Sean Kelley, "The

Dirty Business of Panyarring and Palaver: Slave Trading on the Upper Guinea Coast in the Eighteenth Century," in *Slavery, Abolition and the Transition to Colonialism in Sierra Leone*, ed. Paul Lovejoy and Suzanne Schwarz (Africa World Press, 2014), 89–108.

13. Olatunji Ojo and Jennifer Lofkrantz, "West African Responses to Illegal Enslavement And Failed Ransom Negotiations," *Journal of African History* 52 (2012); Nathan Carpenter, "Ransom as Political Strategy: Captivity beyond Commercial Transaction on the Upper Guinea Coast in the Late Nineteenth and Early Twentieth Centuries," *Journal of West African History* 4, no. 2 (2018): 1–18; Kelley, Lovejoy, and Schwarz, "The Dirty Business of Panyarring and Palaver."
14. John Davidson, *Trade and Politics in the Sherbro Hinterland, 1849–1890*, University of Wisconsin–Madison dissertation, 1969, 104. In some accounts, he is described as a "slave." "Information Regarding the Different Districts and Tribes: Despatch from Administrator." November 6, 1886. BNA/ CO 267/25/150.
15. Commandant to Governor. July 12, 1882. SLPA/SHER LB. 5.
16. Lawson to Governor. February 14, 1873. SLPA/GI LB. 18. Also see Nicolas Darnell Davis, *Chiefs and their Wars in West Africa*. For private circulation, 1876 for a description of this conflict and colonial attempts to settle it.
17. Davidson, *Trade and Politics*, 181.
18. George Thompson, *Thompson in Africa: Or, An Account of the Missionary Labors, Sufferings, Travels, and Observations, of George Thompson, in Western Africa, at the Mendi Mission* (Published by the author, 1854), 93.
19. Davidson, *Trade and Politics*, 189. Also see Winston McGowan, "The Establishment of Long-Distance Trade between Sierra Leone and Its Hinterland, 1787–1821," *The Journal of African History* 31, no. 1 (1990): 25–41; David E. Skinner, "Mande Settlement and the Development of Islamic Institutions in Sierra Leone," *The International Journal of African Historical Studies* 11, no. 1 (1978): 32–62.
20. War soon spread to the Upper Boom River, known as the Lubu country, which was already embroiled in conflict. Their dispute was a power struggle between two high officers in the Lubu, the "Prime Minister" and the "Head Speaker." The Lubu crisis blended with the Mongray crisis, as Tom Cabbie Smith aligned himself with one side and Lahai Serifoo with the other.
21. For more on this crisis, see Rowe to Colonial Office. December 28, 1876. BNA/CO 267/380/15310. Also, see Davidson, *Trade and Politics*, 192–193 and Abraham, *Mende Government and Politics*, 52–53.
22. Lawson to Governor. October 29, 1873. SLPA/GI LB.
23. *Hertslet's Commercial Treaties* (1880). Volume 14. Treaty with the Boom Country (Small

Boom, Bagroo etc) Peace. Commerce. Bonthe. February 1874, 19.

24. "Our Sherbro Policy," *The Independent*, February 24, 1876.
25. Walter Rodney, *History of the Upper Guinea Coast: 1545–1800* (NYU Press, 1982), 68.
26. Daniel F. Wilberforce, *Sherbro and the Sherbros: Or, A Native African's Account of His Country and People* (United Brethren Publishing House, 1886), 26; Abraham, *Precolonial History of the Mende*, 69.
27. Directly prior to the Insurrection of 1896, observers remarked that after Poro elders agreed to wage war against colonial rule, their messengers circulated a burnt palm leaf to all the communities in the Sherbro and Mende region as a signal of war, along with a collection of rocks that represented the number of days until all communities simultaneously rebelled.
28. Davis, *Chiefs and their Wars*.
29. Consequently, Freetown and Sherbro became less popular as ports of entry for goods and smuggling increased along the coats.
30. In 1873, exports dropped to £119,489 compared to 140,055 in 1871. This included rice as well as palm products.
31. Davidson, *Trade and Politics*, 196.
32. Davidson, *Trade and Politics*, 187.
33. Chiefs of the Big Boom to Commandant Loggie. February 14, 1878. BNA/CO 267/334/7027.
34. 1875. [C.1343] Papers relating to Her Majesty's possessions in West Africa. Sierra Leone and Gold Coast Colony, including Lagos. R. J. Collier to Davis. July 17, 1875. 7. This amount, at least £3,400 which was due to be paid at the customs house in July alone, was substantial for what was a rapidly diminishing revenue. 1876 [C.1402] Papers relating to Her Majesty's possessions in West Africa. Sierra Leone and Gold Coast Colony, including Lagos. July 20, 1875. Davis to Rowe. 9. The total surplus revenue for the past three years was £8,556. 1876 [C.1343] Papers relating to Her Majesty's possessions in West Africa. Sierra Leone and Gold Coast Colony, including Lagos. Carnavon to Rowe. September 24, 1875. 15.
35. "Sherbro," *The Independent*, November 25, 1875.
36. "Sherbro Again," *The Independent*, September 23, 1875; "Sherbro Again," *The Independent*, June 24, 1875.
37. In the Boom River, treaty signatory SaiSai Hanimo told the Governor that the Boom leaders were "all waiting to see what step your Excellency will take to assist them. In fact, I assure your Excellency that all our friendly chiefs and their men are ready to see Cannagbour [*sic*] and his men all perish at once in Mr. Bongo's small town

[Leemeejeemah], so that it might forever remain to teach the Bompeh to learn and respect all letters or any of Her Majesty's representative." J. A. Williams to Governor. February 19, 1878. BNA/CO 267/334/7027.

38. Walker to Rowe. March 14, 1878. BNA/CO 267/336/4717. The dispatch also mentions that "the fact that we pay duty in Sherbro on produce purchased in that River as well as on Goods sold therein." The Colonial Office replied flatly that treaties did guarantee traders the right to assistance when outside jurisdiction.
39. "Sherbro Again," *The Independent*, June 24, 1875.
40. Chiefs of the Big Boom to Commandant Loggie. February 14, 1878. BNA/CO 267/334/7027. The Tecongoh or Ticonko was a small neighboring community in the Upper Boom River region of Temne people who aligned with the Bompeh Mendes in this conflict.
41. 1875 [C.1343] Papers relating to Her Majesty's possessions in West Africa. Budge to the Mongray Chiefs. June 12, 1875. 46–47.
42. 1875 [C.1343] Papers relating to Her Majesty's possessions in West Africa. T. A. Wall to Mr. Budge (Acting Commandant of Sherbro). June 17, 1875. 48–52.
43. 1875 [C.1343] Papers relating to Her Majesty's possessions in West Africa. Sierra Leone and Gold Coast Colony, including Lagos. Budge to the Mongray Chiefs. June 12, 1875. 48.
44. 1876 [C.1402] Papers relating to Her Majesty's possessions. Yanga Fanna (Matacong, Gbanna Boom's father), Ka Teybe (Gundamah), Beah Bome (Gbambiah), Fanna Digono (Tontook) to Commandant. July 5, 1875. 5.
45. Rowe fought in the Ashanti Wars in 1873 and had extensive experience as a magistrate, military doctor, and army captain in Lagos, the Gold Coast, and Gambia since 1866 and had been bestowed with several awards for his role in conflicts there. "Sir Samuel Rowe." Oxford *Dictionary of National Biography*.
46. 1876 [C.1402] Papers relating to Her Majesty's possessions in West Africa. Davis to Rowe. July 20, 1875. 9.
47. 1876 [C.1402] Papers relating to Her Majesty's possessions. Davis to Rowe. July 20, 1875. 9.; Rowe to CO. October 9, 1875. 25.
48. To do this, he described entering towns "feign[ing] great rage" and threatening to tear down their stockade." If they responded positively, he took it as an opportunity to demonstrate his sympathy and generosity, particularly to women. However, when faced with hostility, Rowe described firing rockets at the "war-fences" while the townspeople fled in a "panic." 1876 [C.1402] Papers relating to Her Majesty's possessions. Rowe to CO. January 28, 1876. 57–58.
49. Abraham, *Precolonial History of the Mende*, 149. Abraham outlines the events and

aftermath of the Bompeh Expedition or "Keninigbo War" from pages 148 to 150, including how it facilitated the rise of Madam Yoko after the death of Gbanyah in 1878. Lynda Day recounts her version of events and Yoko's rise in *Gender and Power in Sierra Leone*, 87–9 and 103–105.

50. 1876 [C.1402] Papers relating to Her Majesty's possessions. Rowe to CO. January 28, 1876. 57–58.
51. *Hertslet's Commercial Treaties* (1880). Volume 14. Agreement with the Chiefs of Sherbro and Mendi People (Bompey, Ribbee, Mahmoo, Dodo). Peace. Sennehoo, December 21, 1875, 32. Agreement with the Chiefs of Sherbro and Mendi People (Tasso, Bendo-Thumba, Thumba, Mannoh, Bompehtook, Cockboo). Peace. Shaingay, December 30, 1875. 34.
52. Rowe told the Colonial Office that this phrasing was meant to capture a feeling much like an "act of discourtesy exhibited towards a Chief of their own who had filled a position similar to that of Her Majesty in these treaties." Rowe to CO. May 13, 1876. BNA/CO 267/329/6908.
53. Rowe to CO. May 13, 1876. BNA/CO 267/329/6908. Appendix: Agreement signed May 8, 1876.
54. The eight leaders who were Mende came from towns throughout the region. This included Gbanyah, the leader of the Kpaa-Mende, and several Mende warriors, who were known allies with the Sherbro signatories.
55. The lines demarcating the different provinces and state roughly match similar but not perfect reflections of boundaries later in the century. This indicates that in 1876 the borders of the titular provinces in the south were still fluid and in the process of territorial consolidation.
56. Interestingly, four years after the Whobay trial, there still appears to be the "invisible line" that Commandant Walshe referred to in his testimony.
57. This region would be integrated into colonial territory in 1890 and would then revert to becoming part of the Protectorate in 1899.
58. Prior to the 1876 meeting, Vangang had been caught trying to intercept messengers spreading the news about the meeting. Lawson to Governor. June 24, 1881. SLPA/GI 1881.
59. Fahjongobah was delivered up by William E. Tucker, a prominent leader and descendent of an Anglo-African family in the lower Boom River region.
60. On political prisoners throughout the British Empire, see Michael Lobban, *Imperial Incarceration: Detention Without Trial in the Making of British Colonial Africa* (Cambridge University Press, 2021). Also see Trina Leah Hogg, "From Bandits to Political Prisoners: Detention and Deportation on the Sierra Leone Frontier," in *Africans in Exile: Mobility,*

Law, and Identity (Indiana University Press, 2018).

61. Lauren Benton, *They Called It Peace: Worlds of Imperial Violence* (Princeton University Press, 2024).
62. Benton, *They Called It Peace*; Hussain, *The Jurisprudence of Emergency*.
63. Havelock to CO. May 19, 1881. BNA/CO 267/344/18442.
64. Havelock to CO. August 27, 1881. BNA/CO 267/344/16535.
65. Governor to CO. August 25, 1881. BNA/CO 267/345/10534.
66. Colonial Office to George Stephen Caulker. April 22, 1881. BNA/CO 267/347/9294.
67. Chiefs of Shenge to Governor. October 17, 1878. BNA/CO 267 344/9812.
68. Thomas Neale Caulker would remain leader until his murder during the 1898 Insurrection.
69. For more on these and other accounts of political prisoners, see Hogg, "From Bandits to Political Prisoners."
70. Abraham, *Mende Government and Politics*, 3.
71. By 1890 Betsy Gaye herself asserted she had the right to "exercise authority" there. By 1902, Gaye's daughter Priscilla was living in and ruling the town as Paramount Chief. Parkes to Commandant of Sherbro. July 8, 1890. SLPA/ABOR LB. Governor King-Harman to CO. February 23, 1903. CO 267/467/8954. Beh Kelleh and Betsy Gaye would continue to be in conflict with each other for the next two decades until Kelleh's death in a Freetown prison as a political prisoner in 1899. SLPA/ABOR MP 1890.
72. Affairs of Sierra Leone; further correspondence. African No. 175. Rowe to Beach. April 23, 1879. Letter No. 100 with various attachments. BNA/ CO 879/15/6.
73. 1884 [C.3420] Correspondence Respecting the Proceedings at the Jong River in May 1882. Governor Havelock to Colonial Office. June 5, 1882. 3–5.
74. *Hertslet's Commercial Treaties* (1880), Volume 14. Treaty with the Boom Country (Small Boom, Bagroo, etc.) Peace. Commerce. Bonthe. February 1874. 19. He was ordered to withdraw all his warboys in the 1875 Treaty of Senehoo. *Hertslet's Commercial Treaties* (1880), 30. The following year, he was accused of kidnapping a British subject. In that correspondence, he was listed as "Chief of Mongray." October 19, 1876, SLPA/SHER LB 1876.
75. 1884 [C.3420] Correspondence Respecting the Proceedings at the Jong River in May 1882. Traders of the Jong to Governor Havelock. May 12, 1882. 10.
76. 1884 [C.3420] Correspondence Respecting the Proceedings at the Jong River in May 1882. Traders of the Jong to Governor Havelock. May 12, 1883. 10.
77. 1884 [C.3420] Correspondence Respecting the Proceedings at the Jong River in May 1882. Traders in the River Jong to Governor Havelock. May 12, 1882. The King's name is

Humpa Gbaingay. In this correspondence, Lawson assured the Governor that Gbaingay "commands no property . . . he must have some right to the Kingship of the country otherwise he would have not been crowned. The natives are very particular in this." Thomas George Lawson to Governor. April 6, 1880. SLPA/GI LB 1880. 75.

78. 1884 [C.3420] Correspondence Respecting the Proceedings at the Jong River in May 1882. Betsy [*sic*] Gaye to Mssrs. Cleveland, Farmah and Lahy Serifoo. February 27, 1882.

79. Gaye's mother was likely the women known as Ma Rigbah in 1882. It is likely Betsy Gaye's African name was Boye Biggy. This daughter is described in some detail by the Commandant of Sherbro in debates over Tom Cabbie Smith's will after his death. The switch to the name "Betsy Gaye" suggests that she may have received some education at a missionary school, perhaps at Kawmendi or Mano. February 22, 1877, SLPA/SHER LB. In two treaties signed in 1872, a woman named "Regbafri" signed and was listed as the "Principal Lady of Manho." It is unknown whether these are the same woman, or whether one was the mother of Ma Rigba. This new archival evidence contrasts with Christopher Fyfe's assertion that Gaye owed her position as Queen of the Jong "less to hereditary right that from her known influence with the Colony Government." Christopher Fyfe, *A History of Sierra Leone* (Oxford University Press, 1962), 440. Abraham reiterates Fyfe's position about Gaye (and all other female "Queens") in Abraham, *Mende Government and Politics*, 251–253.

80. It is unclear what role Beh Kelleh played in these events.

81. 1884 [C. 3420] Sierra Leone. Correspondence respecting the proceedings at the Jong River in May 1882. "Report from a highly intelligent and educated native." September 4, 1882. 4. The anonymous author here could have been S. B. A. MacFoy, a prominent Krio merchant.

82. 1884 [C. 3420] Sierra Leone. Correspondence respecting the proceedings at the Jong River in May 1882. "Report from a highly intelligent and educated native." September 4, 1882. 4.

83. 1884 [C. 3420] 1884 Sierra Leone. Correspondence respecting the proceedings at the Jong River in May 1882. "Report from a highly intelligent and educated native." September 4, 1882. 4.

84. 1884 [C. 3420] 1884 Sierra Leone. Correspondence respecting the proceedings at the Jong River in May 1882. Colonial Office to Charles Hopwood. March 5, 1883. 16. Bey Kelleh, Dooli Semoo (the speaker of Mongray and Lahai Serifoo) and Bocarry Soosoo escaped.

85. 1884 [C.3420] Correspondence Respecting the Proceedings at the Jong River in May 1882. Havelock to CO. July 28, 1882. 17. Their "weakness" therefore forced them to join the Bompeh in the larger war that was happening in the region. As we recall, the article in

The Times stated that Lahsurrhu had occupied Cleveland's former town of Mattru. Letter authors Betsy Gaye, Humper Femah, Humper Congo, and Farmah and Steven Cleveland.

86. Report by T. G. Lawson. August 1, 1882. BNA/CO 267/349/19034.
87. 1884 [C.3420] Correspondence Respecting the Proceedings at the Jong River in May 1882. CO to Havelock. September 8, 1882. 18.
88. 1884 [C.3420] Correspondence Respecting the Proceedings at the Jong River in May 1882. CO to Havelock. September 8, 1882. 110.
89. Death of Lahai Serifoo. May 26, 1884. SLPA/SHER MP. No. 54.
90. 1884 [C.3420] Correspondence Respecting the Proceedings at the Jong River in May 1882. CO to Havelock. September 8, 1882.
91. Lauren Benton and Lisa Ford, *Rage for Order: The British Empire and the Origins of International Law, 1800–1850* (Harvard University Press, 2016), 85–116.

CHAPTER THREE. AFRICAN COURTS AND TONGO TRIALS: THE JURISDICTION OF HUMAN LEOPARD MURDER CASES, 1882–1892

1. Rosalind Shaw, "Cannibal Transformations: Colonialism and Commodification in the Sierra Leone Hinterland," in *Magical Interpretations, Material Realities*, ed. Henrietta L. Moore and Todd Sanders (Routledge, 2003), 56, 63, 64. However, Shaw notes that the most significant difference between witches and human leopards was that the killing of people to produce or activate "bad medicines" was not the same as the "invisible" actions that witches engaged in. She states that the human leopards rendered visible the usually "invisible cannibalism of witches."
2. Carol MacCormack, "Human Leopards and Crocodiles: Political Meanings of Categorical Ambiguities," in *The Ethnography of Cannibalism* (Society for Psychological Anthropology, 1983), 56–58. Paul Richards states that the specific term for "leopard cannibalism" or "leopardism" is *koli hinda*. Paul Richards, "Public Authority and Its Demons: The Sherbro Leopard Murders in Sierra Leone," *Africa* 91, no. 2 (2021): 226–248. The word for "cannibal" is *koli-moi*. Arthur Abraham, "Cannibalism and African Historiography," *Présence Africaine*, no. 1 (1978): 222.
3. MacCormack, "Human Leopards and Crocodiles," 55. There are many examples of this in the archives.
4. Colin W. Newbury, "Credit in Early Nineteenth Century West African Trade," *The Journal of African History* 13, no. 1 (1972): 81–95.
5. Shaw's work suggests that human leopard murders also recalled the memory of slave raids during the transatlantic slave trade. Also see, Testimony of Ba Sin in Bonthe. July 22,

1890. Report of the Queen's Advocate and Supporting Documents. August 26, 1890. CO 267/384/18004.

6. Paul Richards, "Chimpanzees as Political Animals," *Natural Enemies: People-Wildlife Conflicts in Anthropological Perspective* (Routledge, 2000), 78.
7. Rosalind Shaw, "The Production of Witchcraft: Memory, Modernity, and the Slave Trade in Sierra Leone," *American Ethnologist* 24, no. 4 (1997): 858; Luise White, *Speaking with Vampires: Rumor and History in Colonial Africa* (University of California Press, 2000)
8. In later accounts, there was much disagreement over who "summoned" the Tongo, though (much to the shock of the colonial Government) many stated that it was Reverend Wilberforce who paid their fee. Others said it was Banna Bunjay, Cannagboh, and even MacFoy. The fee was said to be thirty-six British pounds, a considerable amount of money in 1890. Report of Commandant Bennett. Report of the Queen's Advocate and Supporting Documents. August 26, 1890. BNA/CO 267/384/18004. The town was also said to have been founded by a man named Koli, the Mende word for leopard.
9. Andrea Major, *Sovereignty and Social Reform in India: British Colonialism and the Campaign against Sati, 1830–1860*, (Routledge, 2010). Inge Van Hulle, "British Humanitarianism, International Law and Human Sacrifice in West Africa," in *International Law in the Long Nineteenth Century (1776–1914)* (Brill, 2019), 105–125.
10. Stacey Hynd, "Killing the Condemned: The Practice and Process of Capital Punishment in British Africa, 1900–1950s." *Journal of African History* 49, no. 3 (2008): 403–418.
11. Exceptions that focus on the precolonial period are Leslie Allin, "Bodily Disintegrations: Forensic Exposure and the Human Leopard Society in Sierra Leone," in *Penetrating Critiques* (University of Toronto Press, 2020), 155–193; Richards, "Public Authority and Its Demons." Studies that focus on the colonial period include Katrina Keefer, "Poro on Trial: The 1913 Special Commission Court Case of *Rex v. Fino, Bofio and Kalfalla*," *African Studies Review* 61, no. 3 (2018): 56–78; Christine Whyte, "'The Strangest Problem': Daniel Wilberforce, the Human Leopards Panic and the Special Court in Sierra Leone," in *Anxieties, Fear and Panic in Colonial Settings* (Springer, 2016), 345–368; Gareth Griffiths, "The Other Mr. Wilberforce: Role Conflict and Colonial Governance in Sierra Leone 1878–1913," *African Identities* 7, no. 4 (2009): 435–449; Katrina HB Keefer, *Cannibalism Myths, Empire, and Identity in Colonial Sierra Leone* (Lexington Books, 2024). For an account of human leopards in Nigeria, see David Pratten, *Man-Leopard Murders: History and Society in Colonial Nigeria* (Edinburgh University Press, 2007).
12. Paul Richards, *Fighting for the Rainforest: War, Youth, and Resources in Sierra Leone* (Heinemann/James Currey, 1996); Richards, "Chimpanzees as Political," 78–103; Shaw, "Cannibal Transformations"; Stephanie Zehnle, "Liminal Youth between Town and Bush:

Humans, Leopards and Initiation in West African History," *Animal History in the Modern City*, 2019, 161; Allin, "Bodily Disintegrations," 155–193; Richards, "Public Authority and Its Demons."

13. Shaw, "The Production of Witchcraft," 864–866.
14. David Skinner. "Thomas George Lawson: Colonial Servant in Sierra Leone, 1846–1889." *West African Colonial Civil Servants in the Nineteenth Century: African Participation in British Colonial Expansion in West Africa.* (University of Leiden, 1985).
15. Lawson to Governor. July 12, 1883. SLPA/GI LB. 211–213.
16. Letter from John Parker on Behalf of the Mendi Chiefs to Lawson. January 2, 1883. SLPA/ABOR MP 3b.
17. Captain Lawson to Captain Jackson. May 9, 1883. SLPA/ABOR MP 24.
18. Statement of Mende Chiefs taken by Lawson. Attachment. June 18, 1883. SLPA/ABOR MP 38.
19. Lynda Day, *Gender and Power in Sierra Leone*: *Women Chiefs of the Last Two Centuries* (Palgrave Macmillan, 2012), 87–91.
20. Both Shaw and Richards suggest that the encroachment of people into the habitats of these animals during the spread of legitimate commerce is also significant. In some cases, this has prompted scholars to consider whether these "murders" were actually the result of real leopards who were being ebbed out of their habitat. Shaw, "Cannibal Transformations"; Richards, "Chimpanzees as Political."; Keefer, *Cannibalism Myths,* Chapter 2.
21. As anthropologist Rosalind Shaw has written, "stories and accusations of cannibalism have long been (and still are) a dynamic part of inherited cultural images that configure visions of extractive relationships." Shaw, "Cannibal Transformations," 51.
22. In many descriptions of hiring the Tongo, it is described that a "Poro was formed or that the Poro went into the bush with the Tongo," suggesting that the human leopards were a conflict between established ancestral leaders. MacCormack, "Human Leopards and Crocodiles."
23. For primary source descriptions, see Thomas Winterbottom, *Account of the Native Africans in the Neighbourhood of Sierra Leone: To Which Is Added, an Account of the Present State of Medicine among Them*, vol. 1 (Cambridge University Press, 1803); Thomas Joshua Alldridge, *The Sherbro and Its Hinterland* (Macmillan and Company, 1901). Also see Sarah Louise Davies, "The Sasswood Ordeal of the West Atlantic Tribes of Sierra Leone and Liberia: An Ethnohistoriographic Survey," 1973; Katrina Keefer, "Poro, Witchcraft and Red Water in Early Colonial Sierra Leone: G. R. Nylander's Ethnography and Systems of Authority on the Bullom Shore," *Canadian Journal of African Studies/*

Revue Canadienne Des Études Africaines, 2020, 1–17.

24. The lower court was also possibly divided. Sub-Chiefs did not handle serious cases and passed these disputes upwards to high-ranking leaders (Kings). Testimony of Dr. Hood, *Chalmers Commission* II, 2.
25. In his recent article on the human leopards in Sherbro, Paul Richards states that during his recent field work, people continued to tell him that "cannibalism is something for chiefs, whereas witchcraft is found everywhere and affects everybody." Richards, "Public Authority and Its Demons," 233–234.
26. Testimony of Ba Sin in Bonthe. July 22, 1890. Report of the Queen's Advocate and Supporting Documents. August 26, 1890. CO 267/384/18004.
27. Banna Boom to Commandant. August 15, 1884. SLPA/SHER LB. That same month, a number of Krio traders had been accused of assaulting a woman in the same town. Commandant to Governor. August 25, 1884. SLPA/SHER LB.
28. Statement of Sei Hannah on behalf of Banna Sokaka to Commandant. August 19, 1884. SLPA/SHER MP. My emphasis.
29. Statement of Sei Hannah on behalf of Banna Sokaka to Commandant. August 19, 1884. SLPA/SHER MP.
30. While Kpaa-Mende was clearly understood as outside of British jurisdiction, the second case in Bengeh was more questionable. If the burning had occurred in Bagroo, it would have been considered British territory. Imperri had aways represented a grey area of British jurisdiction, despite the fact that numerous Imperri leaders had signed the Treaty of 1861. This was discussed and debated frequently, most especially with the rise of the human leopards. Lawson to Governor. July 7, 1885. SLPA/GI LB. 24.
31. Lawson to Mende Chiefs, May 11, 1883, SLPA/GI LB.
32. This included Madam Yoko, who would rise to become the leader of the Kpaa-Mende and Paramount Chief after 1896.
33. Statement of Sei Hannah on behalf of Banna Sokaka to Commandant. August 19, 1884. SLPA/SHER MP.
34. Letters from Mende Chiefs to Lawson. Various. July and October 1883. ABOR MP 48A and 48B. It is likely some of these leaders witnessed—or knew of—the public hanging in 1876 of John Calker, Vanna, and Kinigbo. Also see July 30, 1883. SLPA/GI LB 235.
35. Lawson to Governor. July 30, 1883. SLPA/GI LB. 234.
36. Mende leaders to Lawson. June 18, 1883. SLPA/ABOR LB. 38–40; Statement of Sei Hannah on behalf of Banna Sokaka to Commandant. August 19, 1884. SLPA/SHER MP.
37. "Report of Human Alligators," September 15, 1886, *Early Dawn*; "Cannibalism," October 30, 1886, *Early Dawn*. "On Cannibalism," December 13, 1886. *Early Dawn*; "Cannibalism

Again," May 15, 1888, *Early Dawn*; "Dear Editor—It Is Rumored about Here, since Last Month That There Are Some Cannibels [*sic*] through the Broad Road from . . . to Dodo and Kibbim, and since Last Month to This, I Am Sorry to Tell, That We Have . . . Six Months, Caught by Cannibals," September 30, 1889, *Early Dawn.*

38. "Cannibalism," September 30, 1889. *Early Dawn.*
39. "General News," November 15, 1884, *Sierra Leone Weekly News*. Logic suggests that this case was the Bengeh case as it was located on the boundary of African and British territory. The others were reported in the *Early Dawn*. "Cannibalism Again" May 15, 1888. *Early Dawn.*
40. "Cannibalism Again," May 15, 1888. *Early Dawn.*
41. Gbannah Will Caulker to Governor. December 7, 1889. SLPA/ABOR MP. Reprinted in Kalous, *Cannibals and Tongo Players of Sierra Leone*, 51. Unable to locate in the SLPA.
42. Parkes to Neal Caulker. January 5, 1890. 172. SLPA/ABOR LB.
43. Parkes to Chiefs of "Manoh Bagroo": Peah Sare and Bannah Will. June 20, 1890. SLPA/ABOR LB.
44. Maccaulay frequently corresponded with the colonial Government and assisted with peace negotiations and treaties.
45. T. J. Alldridge to Governor. March 6, 1895. SLPA: General Minute Papers. Also cited in Kalous, *Cannibals and Tongo Players of Sierra Leone*, 40.
46. T. J. Alldridge, March 6, 1895. SLPA: GEN MP cited in Kalous, *Cannibals and Tongo Players of Sierra Leone*, 40.
47. This is why colonial officials sometimes interpreted these wars as "tribal" as the Bompeh and Imperri leaders could be either Sherbro or Mende.
48. Cannagboh settled in Imperri in the late 1880s.
49. Richards states that most of the cases came from Imperri after 1890. However, his confinement to published source materials (especially Kalous) obscured the fact that while the cases that appear to have centered on Imperri, this also included people and places from neighboring titular provinces. In fact, almost as many cases centered on Timdale as Imperri in the colonial period.
50. H. P. Fitzgerald Marriott, "The Secret Societies of West Africa," *Journal of the Anthropological Institute of Great Britain and Ireland* (1899): 21–27.
51. Alldridge to Colonial Secretary. September 13, 1894, SLPA: General Minute Papers, cited in Kalous, *Cannibals and Tongo Players of Sierra Leone*, 36–37. Alldridge also describes this in his book, *Sherbro and its Hinterland.*
52. The likelihood that the origins of leopardism was in Kpaa-Mende is further strengthened by accounts that the Tongo also originated there. Daniel Flickinger Wilberforce, "The

True Verdict," 11, UB Foreign Missions 2280–3-3:16. I thank Katrina Keefer for sharing this source with me.

53. Beatty, *Human Leopards*, 74.
54. Some of these Krio traders include Mr. Fleury, Mr. Kitell, and Mr. S. B. A. MacFoy.
55. Governor to CO. Enclosure: Complaint of Ka Tegbeh. May 27, 1890. BNA/CO 267/382/11722.
56. In 1885, Wilberforce went back to America briefly and published his experiences in a fifty-page pamphlet called *Sherbro and the Sherbros: Or, A Native African's Account of His Country and People*. A few years later, he returned, settling near his uncle Beah Boom's town.
57. Paul Richards states that Banna Bunjay was Beah Boom's son, but I have not seen any documentation in the archives confirming this.
58. Gbannah Bunjay and the Imperreh. January 13, 1890. SLPA/ABOR MP. 27.
59. Big meeting of Chiefs Beah Will, Cannagboh, Wilberforce and Banna Bunjay with J. C. E. Parkes. February,1890. SLPA/ABOR MP. 99.
60. Chief Bassin of Bogo. April 17, 1890. SLPA/ABOR MP. Beah Boom died in 1888.
61. Parkes to COM. April 14, 1890. SLNA/ABOR LB.
62. Commandant Mosely to Parkes. "Suppression of Cannibalism in Bargroo" (Attachment) January 13, 1890. SLPA/ABOR MP. 37.
63. Big meeting of Chiefs Beah Will, Cannagboh, Wilberforce and Banna Bunjay with J. C. E. Parkes. February,1890. SLPA/ABOR MP. 99.
64. Report of the Queen's Advocate and Supporting Documents. August 26, 1890. CO 267/384/18004.
65. Colonial Office Notes. Governor Hay to Colonial Office. June 20, 1890. BNA/CO 267/383/13045.
66. Governor Hay to Colonial Office. June 20, 1890. BNA/CO 267/383/13045.
67. Governor Hay to Colonial Office. June 20, 1890. BNA/CO 267/383/13045. Emphasis in the original.
68. The "political prisoners" taken to Bonthe were Kategbah, Farmah Larugbah, and Jurangbatay.
69. Report of the Queen's Advocate and Supporting Documents. August 26, 1890. BNA/ CO 267/384/18004.
70. Report of the Queen's Advocate and Supporting Documents. August 26, 1890. BNA/ CO 267/384/18004.
71. Testimony of Ba Sin in Bonthe. July 22, 1890. Report of the Queen's Advocate and Supporting Documents. August 26, 1890. BNA/ CO 267/384/18004. This was highly ironic

as Ba Sin would be found guilty of being a human leopard two years later by a different Tongo leader and burned along with his father and other family members.

72. Report of the Queen's Advocate and Supporting Documents. August 26, 1890. BNA/ CO 267/384/18004.
73. Bennett's Findings. Report of the Queen's Advocate and Supporting Documents. August 26, 1890. BNA/CO 267/384/18004.
74. They concluded that the death of Bunjay resulted from the rumor that he was about to hand the place over to S. B. A. MacFoy, which, as we know from earlier dispatches, was only somewhat true, as he had raided his son's land for cattle only months before his death.
75. Brett to Governor. August 26, 1890. BNA/ CO 267/384/18004.
76. Report of the Queen's Advocate and Supporting Documents. August 26, 1890. BNA/CO 267/384/18004.
77. Report of the Queen's Advocate and Supporting Documents. August 26, 1890. BNA/CO 267/384/18004.
78. Report of the Queen's Advocate and Supporting Documents. August 26, 1890. BNA/CO 267/384/18004.
79. A copy of the Proclamation of Annexation was published in "Visit of His Excellency to the Imperreh Country," November 8, 1890, *Sierra Leone Weekly News*.
80. Governor Hay's remarks. Report of the Queen's Advocate and Supporting Documents. August 26, 1890. BNA/CO 267/384/18004. My emphasis.
81. Report of the Queen's Advocate and Supporting Documents. August 26, 1890. BNA/CO 267/384/18004.
82. Hay to Colonial Office. November 1, 1890. BNA/CO 267/385/22812; "Visit of His Excellency to the Imperreh Country," November 8, 1890, *Sierra Leone Weekly News*. The newspaper reported that Hay's journey "through the Imperreh [*sic*] country received a most warm welcome from the chiefs and people who manifested their joy on learning that they now belong to the Queen and that protection is assured them from the Man Leopards and unscrupulous Traders."
83. Report of the Queen's Advocate and Supporting Documents. August 26, 1890. BNA/CO 267/384/18004.
84. Antony Anghie, "Finding the Peripheries: Sovereignty and Colonialism in Nineteenth-Century International Law," *Harvard International Law Journal* 40, no. 1 (Winter 1999): 1–71.
85. Governor Hay to the Colonial Office. Enclosure: Commandant Garrett's Report. November 7, 1888. BNA/CO 267/372/23715.

86. Governor Hay to Colonial Office. February 29, 1889. BNA/CO 267/376/6840.
87. Governor Hay To Kehtegbeh and the Other Chiefs of the Imperreh. October 28, 1890. SLPA/ABOR LB.
88. *Sierra Leone Times*. March 26, 1892. Reprinted in Leo Spitzer, *Sierra Leone Creole Reactions to Westernization, 1870–1925* (University of Wisconsin–Madison, 1969), 79.
89. "Sherbroland," September 30, 1891, *Early Dawn*.
90. "Extraordinary Stories from West Africa: Black 'Jack the Rippers.'" *Liverpool Weekly Courier*, February 28, 1891. Reprinted in the *Sierra Leone Weekly News*, April 4, 1891.
91. Richard D. Waller, "Witchcraft and Colonial Law in Kenya," *Past & Present*, no. 180 (2003): 241–275; Alan R. Booth, "'European Courts Protect Women and Witches': Colonial Law Courts as Redistributors of Power in Swaziland 1920–1950," *Journal of Southern African Studies* 18, no. 2 (1992): 253–275; Katherine Luongo, *Witchcraft and Colonial Rule in Kenya, 1900–1955* (Cambridge University Press, 2011).
92. Nine Chiefs of the Imperri to Governor Hay. October 27, 1890. BNA/CO 267/385/22803. The authors of the above letter were Kartegbeh, Bah [*sic*] Sin, Fonny Vanjahwa [*sic*], Tuah Yeamie, Gbonny, Fahmah Lallugba, Bahwhen Candoh, Bannah Bome, Moonoofeh.
93. Governor Hay to "Kehtegbeh [*sic*] and the Other Chiefs of the Imperreh." October 28, 1890. SLPA/ABOR LB 1890.
94. This trial is described by Thomas Joshua Aldridge in his 1901 book The *Sherbro and Its Hinterland* (though he states an incorrect date). Here, he describes a different divination process used by the Tongo involving the retrieval of iron circles from a cauldron of hot oil. Aldridge, *The Sherbro and Its Hinterland*, 157–159.
95. Governor Fleming to Colonial Office. Enclosure: Commandant Huggins to Governor. June 22, 1892. August 30, 1892. BNA/CO 267/395/18850.
96. The letter was written by Gbannah Boom, Kartegbeh, Foney Vanjahwah (headman of Gbambaiah), Buarki Buaki (headman of Kekkeh), Bah Mormoh (Tosoh), Borbor (Imperri town), Pah Vorgay (Ganggahmah) and Mori (?) Tengeh of Mori (?). Bahoon Kondon, Ba Sin.
97. Deposition of Beah Tassoh of Chahman (Imperri). Governor Fleming to Colonial Office. Enclosure: Commandant Huggins to Governor. June 22, 1892. August 30, 1892. BNA/CO 267/395/18850.
98. Governor Fleming to Colonial Office; Enclosures: Commandant Huggins to Governor and Deposition of William Stonewall Jackson, a blacksmith at Bandasuma; August 30, 1892. BNA/CO 267/395/18850.
99. Governor Fleming to Colonial Office. Enclosure: Colonel Ellis' Report, August 30, 1892. BNA/CO 267/395/18850.

100. Governor Fleming to Colonial Office. Enclosure: Colonel Ellis' Report, August 30, 1892. BNA/CO 267/395/18850. Governor Fleming to Colonial Office. Enclosure: Commandant Huggins to Governor. June 22, 1892. August 30, 1892. BNA/ CO 267/395/18850.
101. Sub-Inspector Sawyer to the Inspector General of Police Sierra Leone. SLPA: General Minute Papers 1892. Unable to find in the SLPA, Cited in Kalous, *Cannibals and Tongo Players of Sierra Leone*, 206.
102. Fleming to Colonial Office. April 10, 1893. BNA/ CO 267/401/6953.
103. Fleming to Colonial Office. April 10, 1893. BNA/ CO 267/401/6953.
104. "The Imperi District," November 1892, *Sierra Leone Times*.
105. Fleming to Colonial Office. April 16, 1893. BNA/ CO 267/401/7047.
106. "The Tongo Ordinance," October 1, 1893, *Sierra Leone Times*.
107. Beatty, *Human Leopards*.
108. Fleming to Colonial Office. April 10, 1893. BNA/ CO 267/401/6953.

CHAPTER FOUR. THESE LAWS ARE TOO STRONG FOR US: PETITIONS, POROS, AND PUUGWEI (THE WHITE MAN'S WAR), 1896–1898

1. In his book *A Transformed Colony*, Thomas Joshua Alldridge states that the coronation was in 1896, however this is an error on his part. According to several documents in the Sierra Leone Public Archives, it was actually in April or May of 1895.
2. Alldridge, *A Transformed Colony*, 269.
3. Alldridge, *A Transformed Colony*, 270.
4. Comment by Meade. Francis Fleming to Colonial Office. April 10, 1893. BNA/CO 267/401/6953.
5. Comment by Meade. Francis Fleming to Colonial Office. April 10, 1893. BNA/CO 267/401/6953.
6. Surprisingly little has been written on the "Hut Tax War" in Sierra Leone. See Arthur Abraham, "Nyagua, the British, and the Hut Tax War," *The International Journal of African Historical Studies* 5, no. 1 (1972): 94–98; Arthur Abraham, "Bai Bureh, The British, and the Hut Tax War," *The International Journal of African Historical Studies* 7, no. 1 (1974): 99–106; Takehiko Ochiai, "In a Grove? Sierra Leone's 1898 Hut Tax War Reconsidered," *Asian Journal of African Studies* 41 (2017): 53–86; Michelle Gordon, *Extreme Violence and the 'British Way*, 2020, Chapter 3. For primary sources see Thomas Joshua Alldridge, *The Sherbro and Its Hinterland* (Macmillan and Company, 1901), Chapter XXVII; Charles Braithwaite Wallis, *The Advance of Our West African Empire* (T. Fisher Unwin, 1903).
7. Leo Spitzer, *Sierra Leone Creole Reactions to Westernization, 1870–1925* (University of

Wisconsin–Madison, 1969), 90. Christopher Fyfe, "European and Creole Influence in the Hinterland of Sierra Leone before 1896," *Sierra Leone Studies* 6 (1956): 113–123; E. Frances. White, *Sierra Leone's Settler Women Traders: Women on the Afro-European Frontier.* (University of Michigan Press, 1987).

8. Jan Nederveen Pieterse, *White on Black: Images of Africa and Blacks in Western Popular Culture* (Yale University Press, 1992), Chapter 5.
9. This included "treaty, capitulation, grant, usage, sufferance and other lawful means Her Majesty the Queen has jurisdiction within diverse foreign countries." Foreign Jurisdiction Act of 1890.
10. Antony Anghie, "Finding the Peripheries: Sovereignty and Colonialism in Nineteenth-Century International Law," *Harvard International Law Journal* 40, no. 1 (Winter 1999): 1–71.
11. "The Protectorate Ordinance, 1896," *Sierra Leone Weekly News*, September 12, 1896.
12. "Circular Letter from Native Affairs Department Explaining Protectorate Ordinance," October 21, 1896, *Chalmers' Commission*, Appendix II, Volume II, 568.
13. "Circular Letter from Native Affairs Department Explaining Protectorate Ordinance," October 21, 1896, *Chalmers' Commission*, Appendix II, Volume II, 568.
14. "Circular Letter from Native Affairs Department Explaining Protectorate Ordinance," October 21, 1896, *Chalmers' Commission*, Appendix II, Volume II, 568. For more on the Hut Tax War and taxes, see Laura Channing, "Taxing Chiefs: The Design and Introduction of Direct Taxation in the Sierra Leone Protectorate, 1896–1914," *The Journal of Imperial and Commonwealth History* 48, no. 3 (2020): 395–424.
15. "Chiefs of Sulima and Gallinas to Sir S. Lewis C.," December 1896, *Chalmers' Commission*, Appendix II, 573; Madam Yoko to Secretary Native Affairs, as to Protectorate Ordinance" (1896), *Chalmers' Commission*, 571.
16. "Chiefs of Sulima and Gallinas to Sir S. Lewis C.," December 1896, *Chalmers' Commission*, Appendix II, 573.
17. Mr. Moses Zacchaeus Macaulay, deposition. *Chalmers' Commission*, Volume II, 171.
18. As Thomas J Alldridge remarked in 1894, "When debating the conditions of a treaty, their questions often showed that they thoroughly understood the nature of the obligations that they were about to take upon themselves . . . [since then] they have frequently reminded me of those obligations and have told me what they promised to do and what they had not promised to do." Thomas Joshua Alldridge, "Wanderings in the Sierra Leone Hinterland" *The Geographic Journal* (1894), 131.
19. "Chiefs at Morfuay [*sic*] to Secretary Native Affairs, expressing inability to pay the Hut Tax," October 1896, *Chalmers' Commission*, Appendix II, 569–570.

20. "Chiefs of Sulima and Gallinas to Sir S. Lewis," December 18, 1896, *Chalmers' Commission,* Volume II, 573–574.
21. Chief Gberri, deposition. *Chalmers' Commission*, Volume II, 53.
22. Karene Chiefs, deposition. *Chalmers' Commission*, Volume II, 66.
23. "Madam Yoko to Secretary Native Affairs, as to Protectorate Ordinance," November 3, 1896, *Chalmers' Commission*, Appendix II, 571.
24. "Madam Yoko to Secretary Native Affairs, as to Protectorate Ordinance," November 3, 1896, *Chalmers' Commission*, Appendix II, 572.
25. Mr. Domingo, deposition. *Chalmers' Commission*, Volume II, 475–479.
26. According to colonial records, Beh Sherbro requested a stipend in 1878, which he received until 1896. In 1895, Beh Sherbro was accused of ordering a Frontier Force to arrest a local man for cutting down some local palm trees and then to subsequently hold his own "court of inquiry." For this he was severely reprimanded. Alldridge to Colonial Secretary. June 27, 1895. SLPA/SHER LB.
27. Historian and descendent of the Tucker family, Peter Tucker, refers to him as the "Poro Supremo." Peter L. Tucker, *The Tuckers of Sierra Leone 1665–1914* (Self-published, 1997), 102.
28. Mr. Ebenezer Albert Lewis, deposition. *Chalmers' Commission*, Volume II, 485. It is likely this lawyer was Samuel Lewis, as the remark came from his brother, a trader in Mano-Bagru. Also see Parkes to Governor Cardew. May 3, 1897. NA Confidential LB. Parkes said that there was a rumor that the leaders of Imperri and Bandajuma had given Banna Lewis (Beh Sherbro) five hundred pounds to fund his trip to Freetown to protest the Protectorate Ordinance, but Parkes believed that none of the subscriptions had been used in the intended way that threat he would like permission to let the Chiefs of Bandajuma and Imperri know this.
29. Parkes to Governor Cardew. May 3, 1897. SLPA/NA LB. 1889–1898.
30. Parkes to Beh Sherbro. February 2, 1897. SLPA/NA LB. 1889–1898.
31. Aldolphus Dick, deposition. *Chalmers' Commission*, Volume II, 427.
32. Francis Farwoonda, deposition. *Chalmers' Commission*, Volume II, 335.
33. Queen Betsy Gaye to J. C. E. Parkes. February 10, 1897. SLPA/NA LB.
34. Francis Farwoonda, deposition. *Chalmers' Commission*, Volume II, 336. Peter Tucker states in his book that Beh Sherbro was detained directly after the meeting, but doesn't provide evidence or a citation to support this claim. Tucker, *The Tuckers of Sierra Leone*, 103.
35. Cardew to Colonial Office. December 31, 1896. BNA/CO 267/427/1966.
36. Cardew to Colonial Office. December 31, 1896. BNA/CO 267/427/1966.

37. District Commissioner of Sherbro to Governor, November 10, 1997, SLPA/SHER LB 1897.
38. Domestic slavery was not abolished, but slaves could redeem themselves and family members for £4 for an adult and £2 for a child. Despite this avenue, other laws made it considerably difficult for slaves to seek freedom and redeem themselves. See Sara Delius, "The Same in All but Name? The Intersections of Marriage and Slavery in Sierra Leone, 1890–1930," *Slavery & Abolition* 43, no. 2 (2022): 325. For an older source see John Grace, *Domestic Slavery in West Africa: With Particular Reference to the Sierra Leone Protectorate, 1896–1927* (Barnes & Noble, 1975).
39. For more on the palm trade, see Martin Lynn, *Commerce and Economic Change in West Africa: The Palm Oil Trade in the Nineteenth Century* (Cambridge University Press, 2002).
40. Delius, "The Same in All but Name," 335–337.
41. See Lynda Day, *Gender and Power in Sierra Leone: Women Chiefs of the Last Two Centuries* (Palgrave Macmillan, 2012), Chapters 3 and 4.
42. Alldridge to Colonial Secretary. June 18, 1896. SLPA/SHER LB.
43. Spitzer, *The Creoles of Sierra Leone*, Chapter 3.
44. Parkes to the Colonial Secretary. September 4, 1897. SLPA/NA LB.
45. Peter L. Tucker, *The Tuckers of Sierra Leone.*
46. District Commissioner of Sherbro to Governor. November 10, 1997. SLPA/Sherbro Letterbook, 1897.
47. Kenneth Little, The *Mende of Sierra Leone* (Published in 1967, reprinted by Routledge, 2013), 184–185. For more on the relationship between Poro and conservation, see Aiah R. Lebbie and Raymond P. Guries, "Ethnobotanical Value and Conservation of Sacred Groves of the Kpaa Mende in Sierra Leone," *Economic Botany*, 1995, 297–308. Also see Mariane C. Ferme, *The Underneath of Things: Violence, History, and the Everyday in Sierra Leone* (University of California Press, 2001), 36.
48. "A Letter from 'A Voice from the Boom,'" *The Watchman*, October 30, 1879; "Journey of Mr. Edwards and Loggie to Sherbro, Kittam, Boom, Gallinas, Sulymah and Mannoh Districts," November 9, 1878. BNA/CO 267/335/15190.
49. If we recall from chapter two, it was one of the primary grievances of traders in the election of the Sei Kama in Mattru in 1882, which lead to the attack on Commandant Laborde's ship and Lahsurrhu's arrest.
50. Lawson to John Parker. October 28, 1881. SLPA/GI LB. 644–645.
51. Mr. Moses Zacchaeus Macaulay J.P, deposition. *Chalmers' Commission*, Volume II, 168.
52. Alldridge to Colonial Secretary, n.d. (between February and April) 1897 SLPA/SHER LB.
53. Mr. Moses Zacchaeus Macaulay J.P, deposition. *Chalmers' Commission*, Volume II, 168–169.

54. Wilbraham to Col. Sec. June 30,1897 and Wilbraham to Col. Secretary. July 26, 1897. SLPA/SHER LB.
55. Alldridge to Colonial Secretary, n.d. (between February and April) 1897, SLPA/SHER LB.
56. Alldridge to Colonial Secretary, n.d. (between February and April) 1897, SLPA/SHER LB.
57. "Sherbro Affairs: The Human Alligator Society," *Sierra Leone Weekly News*, June 19, 1897.
58. "Sherbro Affairs: The Human Alligator Society" *Sierra Leone Weekly News*, June 19, 1897.
59. Minutes from the Executive Council Chamber. May 1, 1897. BNA/CO 270/34. Petition from the Chamber of Commerce re: prevention of trade by Chiefs of Sherbro. Sentiments like this were backed by the Sierra Leone Chamber of Commerce. In their petition to the Governor, they referred to the Poro as a "contagion" that needed a "speedy remedial measure" in order to prevent it from spreading to remaining Chiefs.
60. "Sherbro Affairs: The Human Alligator Society," *Sierra Leone Weekly News*, June 19, 1897.
61. The Acting DC wrote to inform Beh Sherbro that "His Excellency will be sorry to take such strong measures against you but that if you do not withdraw the Poro on trade and do all you can in the interest of trade, it will be His Excellency's duty in the interest of the Colony to take such measures, and in that case, you will doubtless be the Chief sufferer." DC Wilbraham to Banna Lewis. August 5, 1897. Quoted in Kalous. Unable to locate original in SLPA.
62. Minutes from the Executive Council Chamber. June 19, 1897. BNA/CO 270/34.
63. Legislative Council Chamber. November, 1897. BNA/CO 270/36.
64. J. C. E. Parkes, deposition. *Chalmers' Commission*, Volume II, 35.
65. Governor Cardew to the Colonial Office. December 28, 1897. BNA/CO 267/434/1478.
66. Cardew's Response. *Chalmers' Commission*, Volume II, 549.
67. Governor Cardew to the Colonial Office. December 28, 1897. BNA/CO 267/434/1478.
68. Mr. Mudge, deposition. *Chalmers' Commission*, Volume II, 118. Most of the men arrested were released, but at some point Gberri was arrested again and sent to Freetown. He died in prison before deportation.
69. Beh Sherbro of Yoni, deposition. *Chalmers' Commission*, Volume II, 120.
70. Sandy Mannah, deposition. *Chalmers' Commission*, Volume II, 359–360.
71. "Origin of the Sherbro Massacre," *Sierra Leone Weekly News*, May 21, 1898.
72. E. D. Fairtlough, DC of Ronietta. Kwalu August 4, 1898. Appendix L. 146. Moses Zacchaeus Macaulay, deposition. *Chalmers' Commission*, Volume II, 170. One trader, Mr. Macaulay, stated that he believed there were other meetings held at Bumpe, Yonni, Moryowah, and Jama.
73. J. C. E. Parkes, deposition. *Chalmers' Commission*, Volume II, 34; Parkes Report. Confidential No. 18. June 9, 1898. SLPA/NA LB.

74. Parkes Report. Confidential No. 18. June 9, 1898. SLPA/NA LB.
75. Mr. Mudge, deposition. *Chalmers' Commission*, Volume II, 118; Rev C. H. Goodman, deposition. *Chalmers' Commission*, Volume II, 72.
76. Samuel Lewis, deposition. *Chalmers' Commission*, Volume II, 145. "Piccan" is the Krio word for child.
77. Mrs. Martin, deposition. *Chalmers' Commission*, Volume II, 316.
78. Madam Yoko, deposition. *Chalmers' Commission*, Volume II, 237.
79. 1899 Record of Chiefs. SLPA.
80. Parkes to Governor Cardew. Confidential Native Affairs. No. 19. May 1898. SLPA/ Department of Native Affairs Letterbook.
81. "The Crisis in Sierra Leone," *Sierra Leone Weekly News*, May 14, 1898.
82. "Secret Societies," *Sierra Leone Times*, July 16, 1898.
83. For a detailed accounts of the Insurrection, see Michelle Gordon, Extreme Violence and the 'British Way (Sage, 2020) Chapter 3; Michael Lobban, *Imperial Incarceration: Detention Without Trial in the Making of British Colonial Africa* (Cambridge University Press, 2021), 260–277. Neither account situates the violence of the Insurrection within a deeper historical context. Lobben's account focuses primarily on Bai Bureh and the Insurrection, not the "Mende Rising."
84. For a detailed primary account on the military strategy during the Insurrection, see Wallis, *The Advance of Our West African Empire*.
85. Martial law was declared in March 1898 when the Insurrection began in the North. Cardew to Chamberlain (telegram). April 21, 1898. CO 879/55/1. 60. In a previous confidential memo, Cardew explained that a "Commission" would include a President and one or more additional persons who would have "practically the same powers as those possessed by the Supreme Court in a trial by judge and jury." Cardew to Chamberlain April 13, 1898. CO 879/55/1. 69.
86. Chamberlain to Cardew. April 23, 1898. CO 879/55/1. 66.
87. Cardew to Chamberlain April 13, 1898. CO 879/55/1. 69.
88. D. F. Wilbraham and E. T. Packard, *A Revised Edition of the Ordinances of the Colony of Sierra Leone, Vol. IV 1904–09* (Waterlow and Sons, 1909), 30.
89. Jurisdiction over the Imperri, August 26, 1890. BNA/CO 267/384/18004; Governor to Queen's Advocate, August 16, 1890. SLPA/ABOR LB. 217.
90. "Sherbro Affairs," *Sierra Leone Weekly News*, November 12, 1898.
91. David Patrick Chalmers Official Report. *Chalmers' Commission*, Volume I, 73.
92. David Patrick Chalmers Official Report. *Chalmers' Commission*, Volume I, 69.
93. David Patrick Chalmers Official Report. *Chalmers' Commission*, Volume I, 45.

94. David Patrick Chalmers Official Report. *Chalmers' Commission*, Volume I, 66.
95. David Patrick Chalmers Official Report. *Chalmers' Commission*, Volume I, 49.
96. David Patrick Chalmers Official Report. *Chalmers' Commission*, Volume I, 77.
97. Bonny Ibhawoh, *Imperial Justice: Africans in Empire's Court* (Oxford University Press, 2013), 11.
98. David Patrick Chalmers Official Report. *Chalmers' Commission*, Volume I, 77.
99. Some men, like Soru Bai Forki and Alimai Lahai from the north remained in British custody until 1901 in a state of legal limbo. January 5, 1901. CO 267/457/3752. The fate of other leaders are often single mentions in the archives and it is unclear what their fate was.
100. Frederick Cardew, rebuttal. *Chalmers' Commission*, Volume II, 545.
101. Martin Wiener, *An Empire on Trial: Race, Murder, and Justice under British Rule, 1870–1935* (Cambridge University Press, 2009).

CHAPTER FIVE. MAKING PARAMOUNT CHIEFS AND CHIEFDOMS: CONFLICTS OVER LAND AND LEADERSHIP IN THE PROTECTORATE, 1899–1915

1. "Governor King-Harman's Visit to Moyamba," *Sierra Leone Weekly News*, March 2, 1901.
2. Appendix 1. Speech to the Chiefs of Bandajuma. GOV to CO. Visit to Bandajuma and Ronietta. February 26, 1901. CO 267/457/10021.
3. Some of these coastal areas were incorporated into the Protectorate in 1905.
4. Jane Burbank and Frederick Cooper, *Empires in World History: Power and the Politics of Difference* (Princeton University Press, 2011), 4.
5. Moses Ochonu, "Protection by Proxy: The Hausa-Fulani as Agents of British Colonial Rule in Northern Nigeria," in *Protection and Empire: A Global History* ed. Lauren Benton, Adam Clulow, and Bain Attwood (Cambridge University Press, 2018), 228.
6. This debate was especially brought to the forefront after the publication of Mahmood Mamdani's *Citizen and Subject* (Princeton University Press, 1996).
7. For example, two leaders that went from being titular leaders to Paramount Chiefs were the So /Se Lokko (Mano Bagru), Beh Kelleh (Lower Banta).
8. See Lynda Day, *Gender and Power in Sierra Leone: Women Chiefs of the Last Two Centuries* (Palgrave Macmillan, 2012), Chapter 4.
9. Day, *Gender and Power*. Also see Carol P. Hoffer, "Mende and Sherbro Women in High Office," *Canadian Journal of African Studies/La Revue canadienne des études africaines* 6, no. 2 (1972): 151–164.
10. Day, *Gender and Power*, 108–109.

11. Jutta Bolt et al., "African Political Institutions and the Impact of Colonialism" (National Bureau of Economic Research, 2022).
12. For examples of this position of change over continuity see, see Arthur Abraham, *Mende Government and Politics Under Colonial Rule: A Historical Study of Political Change in Sierra Leone, 1890–1937* (Oxford University Press, 1979); William Reno, *Corruption and State Politics in Sierra Leone* (Cambridge University Press, 1995), 83; Matthew Lange, *Lineages of Despotism and Development: British Colonialism and State Power* (University of Chicago Press, 2009).
13. Abraham, *Mende Government and Politics*, 241.
14. Abraham, *Mende Government and Politics*, 245.
15. Abraham, *Mende Government and Politics*, 249–268.
16. Frederick Cardew, deposition. David Patrick Chalmers, *Report by Her Majesty's Commissioner and Correspondence on the Subject of the Insurrection in the Sierra Leone Protectorate, 1898*, Volume II (1899), 81.
17. Frederick Cardew, deposition. *Chalmers' Commission*, Volume II, 133.
18. Leslie Probyn, "Sierra Leone and the Natives of West Africa," *Journal of the Royal African Society* 6, no. 23 (1907): 255.
19. For Cardew in 1896, the framework of indirect rule was a seen as a pathway towards the eventual abolition of Chiefs themselves, rejecting, for example, the notion of calling the "hut tax" a "Tribute for the Chiefs," which he assumed would be "abolished sooner or later, in view of the advancing civilization, and the diminishing authority of the chiefs." Cardew to Colonial Office, May 1, 1899. Published in *Chalmers' Commission*, Volume I, 133.
20. Probyn, "Sierra Leone and the Natives of West Africa," 255.
21. Eric Hobsbawm and Terence Ranger, eds., *The Invention of Tradition* (Cambridge University Press, 1983); Thomas Spear, "Neo-Traditionalism and the Limits of Invention in British Colonial Africa," in *The Rise and Fall of Modern Empires*, vol. 3, ed. Sarah Stockwell (Routledge, 2013), 419–444; Carolyn Hamilton, Terrific Majesty: The Powers of Shaka Zulu and the Limits of Historical Invention (Harvard University Press, 1998).
22. "The Protectorate Ordinance, 1896," *Sierra Leone Weekly News*, September 12, 1896.
23. Laura Channing, "Taxing Chiefs: The Design and Introduction of Direct Taxation in the Sierra Leone Protectorate, 1896–1914," *The Journal of Imperial and Commonwealth History* 48, no. 3 (2020): 409–410.
24. For an interesting analysis of the introduction and collection of tax by Chiefs in the Sierra Leone Protectorate, see Channing, "Taxing Chiefs."
25. "Protectorate Native Law, No. 16 1905," in *Revised Edition of the Ordinances of Sierra Leone.*

26. Abraham, *Mende Government and Politics*, 265.
27. One exception is the election of Nancy Tucker as "Paramount Chief" of Bagru in 1897.
28. List of Chiefs and Districts, *Chalmers' Commission*, 556.
29. List of Chiefs and Districts, *Chalmers' Commission*, 558.
30. List of Chiefs and Districts, *Chalmers' Commission*, 559. Imperri chiefdom and its leader Humpa Karwonjoe are not listed anywhere in this appendix. It could have been because Imperri was technically part of the Colony in 1898, but so was Sherbro Island and Beh Sherbro of Yoni is listed.
31. Betsy Gaye is listed a Paramount Chief in Bandajuma District. Unlike today, the Jong River was the dividing line between the Jong chiefdom and the Imperri chiefdom.
32. Many histories written on the transition from informal to formal rule in Sierra Leone characterize the "Hut Tax War," (rather than the declaration of the Protectorate itself) as the moment when the "arc of history in Sierra Leone bent sharply." Day, *Gender and Power*, 96. The Insurrection of 1898, however, did not significantly challenge the proposed structure of indirect rule in the Protectorate as Lange asserts in his chapter "Sierra Leone: Indirect Rule and Despotism," 95. His argument, borrowed from Mahmood Mamdani's 1999 book *Citizen and Subject: Contemporary Africa and the legacy of late colonialism* that poor development in Sierra Leone was set in motion by the "despotism" of leaders as a result of the imposition of indirect rule is based on quite a number of incorrect "facts" in order to get Sierra Leone to fit his model.
33. David Patrick Chalmers. *Chalmers' Commission*, Volume I, 82.
34. This would be Parkes' last act of service to the colonial government. He died at age thirty-one on August 11, 1899.
35. Stipends and Annual Presents for Chiefs. August 2, 1895. BNA/CO 267/418/14432.
36. David Patrick Chalmers. *Chalmers' Commission*, Volume I, 44; Ernest Parkes, deposition. *Chalmers' Commission*, Volume II, 60.
37. Appendix H, letter from John Augustus Aboyomi Cole. *Chalmers' Commission*, Volume I, 141; Allen Edward Caulker, deposition. *Chalmers' Commission*, Volume II, 173–175.
38. Governor Probyn to Colonial Office. January 5, 1909. Enclosure 2—Notes of proceedings on Saturday Meeting at Shenghe. December 19, 1908. BNA/CO 267/511/2471.
39. Madam Neighbo had also been married to Thomas Neale, though it was said they had separated at some point in the 1880s after he "gave up her uncle to the British Government." It is possible this was William Caulker (but could have been Richard Canreba Caulker.) Probyn to Colonial Office. January 5, 1909. Enclosure 2: Notes of proceedings on Saturday Meeting at Shenghe. December 19, 1908. BNA/CO 267/511/2471.
40. Record of Paramount Chiefs 1899 SLPA. Governor Nathan to Colonial Office. June 21,

1899. BNA/CO 267/447/17842.

41. George Domingo was accused of being part of the Human Leopard Society and stood trial in 1901.
42. Probyn to Colonial Office. January 5, 1909. Enclosure 1—Attachment B: Subchieves [*sic*] and Elders of the Cargboraw [*sic*] Settlement to District Commissioner. April 27, 1908. BNA/CO 267/511/2471.
43. Probyn to Colonial Office. January 5, 1909. Enclosure 1—Attachment D: Sophia Caulker to Bear Bokar and Seye Lebbee. November 5, 1908. BNA/CO 267/511/2471.
44. V. R. Dorjahn and Christopher Fyfe, "Landlord and Stranger: Change in Tenancy Relations in Sierra Leone," *The Journal of African History* 3, no. 3 (1962): 392.
45. Fyfe and Dorjahn, "Landlord and Stranger," 392. Domingo was also tried as a human leopard in 1901, yet another accusation of the misappropriation or unlawful hoarding of community resources.
46. Probyn to Colonial Office. January 5, 1909. Enclosure 1—Attachment C: Subchiefs of Cockboror [*sic*] to District Commissioner. June 5, 1908. BNA/CO 267/511/2471. It is possible that Madam Neighbo was educated at the Shenge mission and met Thomas Neale there. My emphasis.
47. Probyn to Colonial Office. January 5, 1909. Enclosure 1—Attachment E: Beah Bokah and Seye Lebby, Mocob Town to District Commissioner. August 11, 1908. BNA/CO 267/511/2471.
48. The "first" Caulker people are referred to as ram Ba Kaki or ram Ba Mulath (mulatto).
49. Hoffer, "Mende and Sherbro Women in High Office," 105–106.
50. As late as 1960s, some members of the Ya Cumba and Sosant family still claimed that the "Caulkers began to call themselves the 'owners' of parts of the Ya Kumba ancestral land, disregarding their client status. They began to call themselves chiefs without acknowledging the rights they acquired through their mothers." Hoffer, 'Mende and Sherbro Women in High Office," 107. The author also recounts the Caulker side of the story in the 1960s, stating that the Ya Cumba were strangers from the interior and had invited the Caulkers to leave the Plantain islands to help them drive away some Mende warriors. In exchange, the Caulker leader received land in the Shenge area and began to bury their dead at Tasso.
51. Governor Probyn to Colonial Office. January 5, 1909. Enclosure 2: Notes of proceedings on Saturday Meeting at Shenghe. December 19, 1908. BNA/CO 267/511/2471.
52. Probyn to Colonial Office. January 5, 1909. Enclosure 3: The Governor's Decision. December 22, 1908. BNA/CO 267/511/2471.
53. Probyn to Colonial Office. July 19, 1909. BNA/CO 267/515/26268.

54. Governor Probyn to Colonial Office. Attachment 1: Attorney General to Governor. October 25, 1910. BNA/CO 267/526/35355.
55. Frederick Lugard, "The Speech at Sokoto," in *The Principles of Native Administration in Nigeria*, ed. Anthony Hamilton Millard Kirk-Greene (Oxford University Press, 1965), 43.
56. These claims were first made in 1895 by Richard Canreba Caulker. They were then reinvigorated by his cousin Thomas Caulker in 1908 when he became Paramount Chief. Petition from Chiefs and Headman of Bompeh. June 26, 1908. BNA/CO 267/510/34446.
57. Probyn to Colonial Office. November 18, 1909. BNA/CO 267/513/16064.
58. Imodale Caulker-Burnett, *The Caulkers of Sierra Leone: The Story of a Ruling Family and Their Times* (Xlibris Corporation, 2010), 151.
59. While the process of initially drawing chiefdom boundaries in 1896 is unclear, the colonial administration likely utilized the same treaties, stipendiary information, maps, and information from leaders they used to select Paramount Chiefs.
60. In the "personal amorphous" states that had previously been ruled by prominent warriors, colonial administrations engaged in a "divide and conquer" technique that ensured that no single leader could challenge British hegemony. Arguably, the historically flexible nature of these borders, which expanded and contracted within an individual leaders' lifetime, made the resulting chiefdom borders more susceptible to "invention" when creating chiefdoms in the Protectorate. For example, in 1898, Mende chiefdoms (north of the Sherbro state) totaled 27, whereas by 1922 there were 115 chiefdoms. Abraham, *Mende Government and Politics*, 172–175. In contrast, the area that encompassed the precolonial Sherbro state only added two additional chiefdoms by dividing Lower and Upper Banta and dividing Bagru to create Mano-Bagru in 1899.
61. Governor King-Harman's Tour of Ronietta and Bandajuma. February 26, 1901. BNA/CO 267/457/10021.
62. Governor King-Harman's Tour of the Protectorate. February 23, 1903. BNA/CO 267/467/8954.
63. Sherbro District Annual Report, 1908. George Page. April 22, 1909. BNA/CO 267/513/15278.
64. Laws and Customs of the Protectorate. (Ronietta) by E. C. D. H. Fairtlough. February 15, 1907. BNA/CO 267/501/8463.
65. Thomas Joshua Alldridge, *A Transformed Colony, Sierra Leone, as It Was, and as It Is: Its Progress, Peoples, Native Customs and Undeveloped Wealth* (J. B. Lippincott, 1910), 274. Although it appears he was elected in the traditional manner, the imposition of Protectorate rule hampered anyone in the position's ability to project power in the same way they had in the pre-Protectorate period.

66. Governor King-Harman to CO. Visit to Bandajuma and Ronietta. February 26, 1901. BNA/CO 267/457/10021.
67. Governor King-Harman to CO. February 23, 1903. BNA/CO 267/467/8954.
68. Governor King-Harman to Colonial Office. April 8, 1904. Attachment: Report of Mr. Wallis, Acting D. C. for the Sherbro District. BNA/CO 267/472/14840; Governor to Colonial Office. November 13, 1907. BNA/CO 267/497/41741.
69. Governor to Colonial Office. November 13, 1907. BNA/CO 267/497/41741.
70. See Ordinances regulating movement: Protectorate Courts Jurisdiction No. 6 of 1903 and Fangay Ordinance No. 5 of 1905. Also see the regulation of the Snake Society in Bandajuma. April 21, 1906. BNA/CO 267/484/16752 and Snake Society. July 5, 1906. BNA/CO 267/485/27366 and Report from Dr. Hunter. September 14, 1906. BNA/CO 267/488/35794.
71. James A. Robinson and Tristan Reed, *The Chiefdoms of Sierra Leone*, 53.
72. Laws and Customs of the Protectorate. (Ronietta) by E. C. D. H. Fairtlough. February 15, 1907. BNA/CO 267/501/8463.
73. Complaints emerged in 1886 that the MaKelleh people were frequently attacking the Mongray people. Historically, the Banta, Imperri, and Small Boom were aligned. Mongray was aligned with the Kpaa-Mende. Historically, Gaye worked with Lahai Serifoo and Cleveland's son when she became leader in 1888. Governor Rowe to CO. April 19, 1886. BNA/CO 267/362/8235.
74. This map was utilized for a number of purposes, including for use in Sierra Leone schools, to label treaties, to create plans for the frontier road and where to place Frontier Force stations. In 1895, the map was modified with more towns and rivers but again did not include Jong. "CO 700/SierraLeone24: I. D. W. O. 592: Map of Sierra Leone and Neighbouring Territories. Compiled in the Intelligence Division, War Office, 1886. 1 Inch to 8 Miles. With 1888 Edition." In *The National Archives: Selected Maps Representing the Long 19th Century*. Primary Source Media, 1886–1888. *Nineteenth Century Collections Online* (accessed January 30, 2025). https://link.gale.com/apps/doc/CLLTHY223078787/NCCO?u=ubcolumbia&sid=bookmark-NCCO&xid=ef54a1f0&pg=1. Great Britain. War Office General Staff Geographical Section, and Great Britain. War Office Intelligence Division. "Map of Sierra Leone, IDWO 1118." *British Library: Ministry of Defense Maps*, Primary Source Media, 1895. *Nineteenth Century Collections Online*, link.gale.com/apps/doc/CHCILI237591355/NCCO?u=ubcolumbia&sid=bookmark-NCCO&xid=84448b20&pg=1. Accessed 30 Jan. 2025.
75. In February 1897, Gaye sent her representative to protest with several other leaders from the Boom River who were closely aligned with the colonial Government. *Chalmers'*

Commission, Volume II, 28, 548. In 1903, King-Harman reversed this position and named her as one of the "chief fomenters of the '98 rising."

76. Boundary Dispute between Imperri and Jong. February 26, 1896. SLPA/SHER LB. 23.
77. District Commissioner Alldridge to J. C. E. Parkes. Attachment: Betsy Gaye, Queen of the Jong, to Alldridge, April 12, 1895. SLPA/NA MP 1894. 184. Bundle 2. It is unclear why she didn't mention the other towns.
78. District Commissioner Alldridge to J. C. E. Parkes. Attachment: Betsy Gaye, Queen of the Jong, to Alldridge, April 12, 1895. SLPA/NA MP 1894. 184. Bundle 2.
79. Mocharch is also the name of a town that was founded by a group of Mane hunters from Banta who settled near Tasso in the Shenge district. They are founders of the Sosant Dick house, one of the Founding Families in Shenge/Kagbor. Caulker-Burnett, *The Caulkers of Sierra Leone*, 49.
80. Boundary Dispute between Imperri and Jong. February 26, 1896. SLPA/SHER LB. 23.
81. It is unclear if Sessi Temmi is the son of Sessi Gama. Boundary Dispute between Imperri and Jong. February 26, 1896. SLPA/SHER LB. 23.
82. Robinson and Reed, *Chiefdoms of Sierra Leone*, 39. The Solundo house remains today as a "Ruling Family" that can put forth candidates for Paramount Chief. It is said that Kpanaboam's settlement, under a great M'bellie tree, gave the region the name "Imperri."
83. Boundary Dispute between Imperri and Jong. February 26, 1896. SLPA/SHER LB. 23.
84. Governor Probyn to Colonial Office. May 3, 1906. BNA/CO 267/484/17410. I have been unable to locate a copy of the original 1901 petition in the archives.
85. May 3, 1906. Attachment: Leaders of Mongray to Governor King-Harman. May 30, 1903. BNA/CO 267/484/17410.
86. In 1898, "Mongray" was not listed as a recognized Native District or town of any importance. *Chalmers' Commission*, Volume II, 558. King-Harman to Colonial Office. May 3, 1906. Attachment: Leaders of Mongray to Governor King-Harman. May 30, 1903. BNA/CO 267/484/17410.
87. Governor Probyn to Colonial Office. May 16, 1906. Attachment: Petition from Mongray Chiefs. 1903. BNA/CO 267/484/17437. A Chief named Lucenne is named as the leader of Mongray in 1886 and his brother was named Sahrehmoo. In this dispatch, they were at war with Beh Kelleh, the historic allies of the Imperri. Also see Governor Rowe to CO. April 19, 1886. BNA/CO 267/362/8235. This is confirmed Rowe to Colonial Office. December 28, 1876. BNA/CO 267/380/15310.
88. Governor Probyn to Colonial Office. May 16, 1906. Attachment: Petition from Mongray Chiefs (1903). BNA/CO 267/484/17437.
89. Governor to Colonial Office. July 4, 1906. BNA/CO 267/485/27394.

90. Governor to Colonial Office. Attachment: Captain Bond's Report on Imperri. June 4, 1906. BNA/CO 267/485/27394.
91. Robinson and Reed, *Chiefdoms of Sierra Leone*, 39.
92. Governor Haden Smith to Colonial Office. Enclosure: George Page's Report on the Deposing of Madam Alice Gaye. January 15, 1910. CO 267/521/3098.
93. Governor to Colonial Office. Attachment: 1913 Beatty Manuscript. November 11, 1913. BNA/CO 267/552/40437. Reed and Robinson collected an oral history that Bunting Williams was a Muslim and the descendent of Habib Sheriff, Lahai Serifoo's father. Thus, while I have not found any archival reference from the period to support this, it seems reasonable to assume that Queen Betsy Gaye's daughter Priscilla Gaye was married to one of Lahai Serifoo's sons to try and strengthen their (at times) tenuous alliance. Two children of that union were likely Alice Gaye and Bunting Williams. Robinson and Reed, *Chiefdoms of Sierra Leone*, 38.
94. Governor to Colonial Office. Attachment: 1913 Beatty Manuscript. November 11, 1913. BNA/CO 267/552/40437.
95. Governor Probyn to Colonial Office. May 16, 1906. BNA/CO 267/484/17437. This may have been the year of Priscilla's death. The 1903 Petition is an attachment in this dispatch.
96. Governor Probyn to Colonial Office. July 30, 1910. BNA/CO 267/524/25659.
97. Governor Probyn to Colonial Office. July 30, 1910. BNA/CO 267/524/25659. It is possible this occurred because a new type of "revenue" of £53 was promised to him with the collection of the hut tax (but with it he had to relinquish the right to demand agricultural labor from the people for a year). He would still also receive the customary fees for his court.
98. Governor to Colonial Office. Attachment: 1913 Beatty Manuscript. November 11, 1913. BNA/CO 267/552/40437. Also see Katrina Keefer, *Cannibalism Myths, Empire, and Identity in Colonial Sierra Leone* (Lexington Books, 2024).
99. Also see Day, *Gender and Power*, 114–116.
100. Charles William Tucker was elected after the deposing of Ta Bompey (1905–1911). Tucker, *The Tuckers of Sierra Leone*, 116. Charles William Tucker was the son of Ba Tucker and a woman from the Gallinas royal family. He was a wealthy trader and was married to a Krio woman named Lydia Rose Anthony and converted to Catholicism. If Peter Tucker is correct in his genealogy that means that Nancy Tucker—the Paramount Chief of Bagru—was Charles Williams's sister. This fact differs in standard interpretation of her being a leader whose position was not based on ancestral lineage.
101. District Commissioner of Sherbro to Governor. July 11, 1911. SLPA/SHER LB. 15.
102. Tucker, *The Tuckers of Sierra Leone 1665–1914*, 119.

CHAPTER SIX. LITIGANTS AND LEOPARDS: THE HUMAN LEOPARD SOCIETY IN PROTECTORATE LAWS AND COURTS, 1901–1914

1. *R. v. Lamina and Others*, December 9, 1908, SLPA/Circuit Court Record Book 1908–1909.
2. *R. v. Lamina and Others*, December 9, 1908, SLPA/Circuit Court Record Book 1908–1909.
3. The request for a permanent ordinance began in 1903. In 1903, upon travelling in the Imperri and Banta chiefdom, the Governor expressed his concerns that "the operations of the cannibalistic Societies were still being carried on to the terror of the population" and requested that the ordinance be permanent after a series of murders were reported in Shenge, Imperri, Timdale, and Bargru. King-Harman to Colonial Office. May 26, 1903. BNA/CO 267/468/21842. This ordinance was renewed every year until 1906 when it was made permanent.
4. Martin Chanock, *Law, Custom, and Social Order: The Colonial Experience in Malawi and Zambia* (Heinemann, 1985); Richard Roberts and Kristin Mann, "Law in Colonial Africa" (Heinemann 1991), 3–58; Kristin Mann, Toyin Falola, and Christian Jennings, "Interpreting Cases, Disentangling Disputes: Court Cases as a Source of Understanding Patron-Client Relationships in Early Colonial Lagos," in *Sources and Methods in African History: Spoken, Written, Unearthed*, vol. 15 (University Rochester Press, 2003), 195; Richard Roberts, *Litigants and Households: African Disputes and Colonial Courts in the French Soudan, 1895–1912* (Heinemann, 2005); Brett Lindsay Shadle, *'Girl Cases': Runaway Wives, Eloped Daughters and Abducted Women in Gusiiland, Kenya, c. 1900–c. 1965* (Northwestern University, 2000); Emily S. Burrill, *States of Marriage: Gender, Justice, and Rights in Colonial Mali* (Ohio University Press, 2015); Jessica Reuther, "Street Hawking or Street Walking in Dahomey?: Debates about Girls' Sexual Assaults in Colonial Tribunals, 1924–41," *The Journal of African History* 63, no. 3 (2022): 368–383.
5. Among the most prevalent are Rosalind Shaw, Paul Richards, and Mariane Ferme.
6. For example, in her article on Daniel Wilberforce, Christine Whyte states that the Special Commissions court constituted an "information panic," a panic induced by "the feeling of the fledgling colonial administration that it knew nothing of the local society and that the locals were combining to deny it information." On the contrary, by 1912, the Government had already witnessed many cases in Protectorate courts and had knowledge of the society before indirect rule.
7. I have largely refrained from using published materials from the period written by amateur or "armchair" anthropologists on the "human leopards" who did not have a deep understanding of Sierra Leone. For examples of this work see: R. G. Berry, "The Sierra Leone cannibals, with notes on their history, religion, and customs." *Proceedings of the Royal Irish Academy. Section C: Archaeology, Celtic Studies, History, Linguistics, Literature*

30 (1912): 15–70; Donald Burrows, "The Human Leopard Society of Sierra Leone." *Journal of the Royal African Society* 13, no. 50 (1914): 143–151.

8. This runs in contrast to Paul Richards who asserts it was an act of "political masquerade" to frame land-holding chiefs who worked with the colonial administration. Richards," Public Authority and its Demons," 232.
9. Richards, "Chimpanzees as Political Animals."
10. District Commissioner Fairtlough, deposition. *Chalmers' Commission*, Volume II, 281. See also Response of Cardew to Chalmers. *Chalmers' Commission*, Volume I, 93.
11. Captain Sharpe, deposition. *Chalmers' Commission*, Volume II, 192. Captain Fairtlough, deposition, *Chalmers' Commission*, Volume II, 281.
12. Captain Hood, deposition. *Chalmers' Commission*, Volume II, 3. Captain Sharpe, deposition, *Chalmers' Commission*, Volume I, 192.
13. Alldridge, *Sherbro and Hinterland*, 62.
14. The amount given may or may not represent the "damages" that the plaintiff felt owed to them. It appears to have been situational.
15. The amount given may or may not represent the "damages" that the plaintiff felt owed to them. It appears to have been situational. If an accused refused to acknowledge the summons, he would be brough by force to the courts and given "kassi," a fine that indicated he was in contempt of court. Wallis, "In the Courts," 406.
16. Bandajuma District Report. George Page. March 13, 1903. BNA/CO 267/476/10417. Also see Little, *The Mende*, 41.
17. Bandajuma District Report. George Page. March 13, 1903. BNA/CO 267/476/10417.
18. In his 2021 article, Paul Richards states that the "sasswood trials" were banned by the colonial state, but I have not found any evidence to confirm its criminalization in either the British or Sierra Leonean archives. Richards, "Public Authority and its Demons," 237.
19. "Ordinance to Facilitate the Detection and Punishment of Crime" (No. 15, 1895). The ordinance was prompted by the trial and the execution of three "human leopards" in Gbangbaia in Imperri that year. Governor to Colonial Office. August 28, 1895. BNA/CO 267/418/16169.
20. A. Gray, "Legislation of the Empire 1895, West Africa VII: Sierra Leone," *Journal of Comparative Legislation and International Law* 1897, 101. Also see Governor to Colonial Office. November 8, 1895. BNA/CO 267/419/21411. Also see Governor to Colonial Office. September 14, 1896. CO 267/459/32424.
21. Cardrew's response to Chalmers. *Chalmers' Commission,* Volume I, 93.
22. For more on African Assessors throughout the Empire, see Bonny Ibhawoh, "Historical Globalization and Colonial Legal Culture: African Assessors, Customary Law, and

Criminal Justice in British Africa," *Journal of Global History* 4, no. 3 (2009): 429–451; Ruth Ginio, "Negotiating Legal Authority in French West Africa: The Colonial Administration and the African Assessors, 1903–1918," in *Intermediaries, Interpreters, and Clerks: African Employees in the Making of Colonial Africa* (University of Wisconsin Press, 2006), 115–135.

23. Thomas George Lawson, deposition. *Chalmers' Commission*, Volume II, 95.
24. *R. v. Gbanna Lacka.* July 24, 1901. SLPA/Moyamba Mixed Courts, 1901–1903.
25. Several witnesses in the court pointed out some of the inconsistencies in the trial and why they did not believe that it was a "human leopard murder" including that it had occurred inside a house and not "in the bush." Furthermore, after it was discovered that the boy had died, Lacka had paid fines to the family.
26. *R. v. Gbanna Lacka.* SLPA/Moyamba Mixed Courts, 1901–1903.
27. *R. v. Seisei Talliah and Woojoo.* August 5, 1901. SLPA/Moyamba Mixed Courts, 1901–1903.
28. *R. v. Seisei Talliah and Woojoo.* SLPA/Moyamba Mixed Courts, 1901–1903.
29. *R. v. George Domingo.* August 9, 1901. SLPA/Moyamba Mixed Courts, 1901–1903.
30. *R. v. George Domingo.* SLPA/Moyamba Mixed Courts, 1901–1903.
31. *R. v. George Domingo.* SLPA/Moyamba Mixed Courts, 1901–1903.
32. Human Leopard Ordinance of 1901. September 14, 1901. BNA/CO 267/459/32424.
33. Minutes of the Bar Association of Sierra Leone. July 12, 1898. *Chalmers' Commission*, Volume II, 653.
34. These members of the Legislative Council included Krio barristers A. G. Shronkeh-Sawyerr, C. H. Wright, and A. B. Hebron.
35. "Legislative Council Proceedings," November 28, 1901. *Sierra Leone Weekly News.*
36. In another petition submitted by the Bar Association that same month, the Bar argued the "machinery for administering justice in the Protectorate . . . is defective, in that it gives excessive powers to the District Commissioner over the life and liberty of the subject." To counter this power, the Bar's final recommendation was that lawyer or itinerant judge be appointed to travel throughout the Protectorate and hear cases in every district. "Memorial of the Bar Association," November 28, 1901. *Sierra Leone Weekly News.*
37. Governor to Colonial Office. December 6, 1901. BNA/CO 267/459/44590.
38. Governor to Colonial Office. December 6, 1901. BNA/CO 267/459/44590.
39. See Draft for the Ordinance for the Change in the Court System of the Protectorate. May 8, 1902. BNA/CO 267/463/19990; Minutes of the Legislative Council, May 18, 1903. BNA/CO 270/40.
40. Edward Turner Packard and Donald Fortescue Wilbraham, "Protectorate Courts Jurisdiction Ordinance No. 6 of 1903," *The Revised Edition of the Ordinances of the Colony*

of Sierra Leone Vol II, 676–692. On the introduction of Circuit Courts in South Africa see H. J. Erasmus, "Circuit Courts in the Cape Colony during the Nineteenth Century: Hazards and Achievements," *Fundamina: A Journal of Legal History* 19, no. 2 (2013): 266–299.

41. Draft copy of Protectorate Ordinance. September 16, 1896. BNA/CO 267/426/74304.
42. "The Sierra Leone Bar," October 16, 1904. *Sierra Leone Weekly News.*
43. Report of the Attorney General on Circuit Courts. December 14, 1904. BNA/CO 267/473/43719.
44. William Hart, "The 'Lawyer' of Poro?: A Sixteenth-Century West African Masquerade." *RES: Anthropology and Aesthetics* 23, no. 1 (1993): 83–95.
45. Report of the Attorney General on Circuit Courts. December 14, 1904. BNA/CO 267/473/43719.
46. We have clear statistics on these cases from 1904 to 1908. The number of cases between 1908 and 1913 have been estimated from Governor dispatches to the Colony. Amazingly, within the first two years of its creation, the Circuit Court heard upwards of sixteen cases of human leopard murder.
47. This analysis is based on five full transcripts of human leopard cases in the Circuit Court. Other entries for cases in the Moyamba Circuit Court books are either incomplete, written in summary form, or illegible due to lack of preservation in the archives.
48. *R. v. Peah Yumbo and Others,* SLPA/Circuit Court Record Book, 1909.
49. *R. v. Lamina and Others,* December 9, 1908, SLPA/Circuit Court Record Book, 1909.
50. *R. v. Beah Kindo,* SLPA/Circuit Court Record Book, 1904. Also attached to BNA/CO 267/475/3640. This feature can also be seen in *R. v. Peah Yumbo and Others,* SLPA/Circuit Court Record Book, 1908.
51. *R. v. Humpha Saloo and Others,* SLPA/Circuit Court Record Book, 1904. Also attached to Human Leopard Trials. January 17, 1905. BNA/CO 267/475/3640. This exact language is used in *R. v. Peah Yumbo and Others.* SLPA/Circuit Court Record Book, 1908.
52. *R. v. Beah Kindo,* SLPA/Circuit Court Record Book, 1904.
53. *R. v. Beah Kindo,* SLPA/Circuit Court Record Book, 1904.
54. *R. v. Humpha Saloo and Others,* SLPA/Circuit Court Record Book, 1904.
55. *R. v. Humpha Saloo and Others,* SLPA/Circuit Court Record Book, 1904.
56. *R. v. Lamina and Others,* December 9, 1908, SLPA/Circuit Court Record Book, 1909.
57. *R. v. Beah Kindo,* SLPA/Circuit Court Record Book, 1904. Also attached to BNA/CO 267/475/3640; *R. v. Humpha Saloo and Others,* SLPA/Circuit Court Record Book, 1904; *R. v. Peah Yumbo and Others,* SLPA/Circuit Court Record Book, 1908; *R. v. Lamina and Others.* SLPA/Circuit Court Record Book, 1909.

58. *R. v. Lamina and Others*, December 9, 1908, SLPA/Circuit Court Record Book, 1909.
59. *R. v. Beah Kindo*, SLPA/Circuit Court Record Book, 1904. In this case, yet another murder (death of Ya Woo) where the parents were also fined. *R. v. Humpha Saloo and Others*, SLPA/Circuit Court Record Book, 1904. Also attached to BNA/CO 267/475/3640. The father was fined two heads of money.
60. Lauren Benton, *Law and Colonial Cultures: Legal Regimes in World History, 1400–1900* (Cambridge University Press, 2002), 28.
61. As one witness stated, "We have a custom in the country that if we complain against the chief and then return to the country we shall be tied and perhaps killed." *R. v. Beah Kindo*, SLPA/Circuit Court Record Book, 1904.
62. It is unclear if Saloo was under Nancy Tucker (Bagru) or Beah Kindo (Timdale) as witnesses give conflicting testimony.
63. *R. v. Lavarri and Others*, October 15, 1907. SLPA/Circuit Court Record Book, 1907.
64. There is no full transcript of this trial in the archives, just a short summary of each day in the Moyamba Record Books.
65. *R. v. Peah Yumbo and Others*. SLPA/Circuit Court Record Book, 1908.
66. *R. v. Humpha Saloo and Others*, SLPA/Circuit Court Record Book, 1904.
67. Report of the Circuit Court, Judge Arthur Hudson. June 5, 1905. BNA/CO 267/478/21669.
68. Governor Probyn to Colonial Office. Enclosure: Report of the Attorney General. October 2, 1907. BNA/CO 267/496/36920.
69. Governor to Colonial Office. January 18, 1905. CO 267/475/3640; Governor Probyn to Colonial Office. Enclosure: Report of the Attorney General. October 2, 1907. BNA/CO 267/496/36920.
70. Governor Probyn to Colonial Office. February 2, 1909. BNA/CO 267/512/5982.
71. Governor Probyn to Colonial Office. April 11, 1908. BNA/CO 267/503/14786; Governor Probyn to Colonial Office. February 2, 1909. BNA/CO 267/512/5982.
72. Governor Probyn to Colonial Office. Attachment: George Page's Report on Recommendations for Human Leopard Society. December 5, 1908 and February 2, 1909. BNA/CO 267/512/5982.
73. Stacey Hynd, "Killing the Condemned: The Practice and Process of Capital Punishment in British Africa, 1900–1950s," *The Journal of African History* 49, no. 3 (2008): 403–418.
74. Between 1904 and 1911, eighty-seven people were executed for human leopard murder. Kenneth James Beatty, *Human Leopards: An Account of the Trials of Human Leopards before the Special Commission Court* (H. Rees, 1915), 251.
75. In the case of *R. v. Peah Yumbo and 28 others*, colonial administrators debated the case and what to do with the wide range of prisoners, including the second Paramount Chief

of Timdale, to be convicted of human leopard murder. Due to a lack of what he saw as "hard evidence," the Acting Governor wanted to commute all of the sentences of capital punishment to deportation. The other members of the Executive Council disagreed. In the end, the primary high-status defendants, including the Paramount Chief, were executed. *R. v. Peah Yumbo and Others.* SLPA/Circuit Court Record Book, 1908.

76. An Ordinance to Amend the Human Leopard Society Ordinance of 1909, No. 17 of 1912," *The Revised Edition of the Ordinances of the Colony of Sierra Leone Vol II.* My emphasis.
77. Debate in the Legislative Council regarding the Human Leopard Ordinance. December 10, 1912. BNA/CO 267/544/39904.
78. An Ordinance to Amend the Human Leopard Society Ordinance of 1909, No. 17 of 1912, *The Revised Edition of the Ordinances of the Colony of Sierra Leone Vol II.*
79. Debate in the Legislative Council regarding the Human Leopard Ordinance. December 10, 1912. BNA/CO 267/544/39904.
80. Governor to Colonial Office. Attachment: 1913 Beatty Manuscript. November 11, 1913. BNA/CO 267/552/40437.
81. I have only been able to locate one full transcript of these four cases. However, several detailed summaries of the cases written by both Judge Griffith and Kenneth Beatty exist, including Beatty's unpublished manuscript of his book which contains more detail than the published book, including names of people and places. Governor to Colonial Office. Attachment: 1913 Beatty Manuscript. November 11, 1913. BNA/CO 267/552/40437. For a detailed analysis of the Special Commission Court and its cases, see Katrina Keefer, *Cannibalism Myths, Empire, and Identity in Colonial Sierra Leone* (Lexington Books, 2024).
82. For more on the "Kale Case," see Katrina Keefer, "Poro on Trial: The 1913 Special Commission Court Case of *Rex v. Fino, Bofio and Kalfalla,*" *African Studies Review* 61, no. 3 (2018): 56–78 and Keefer, *Cannibalism Myths*, 122–128.
83. Sir Branforth William Griffiths' Report on the Human Leopard Society. June 5, 1913. BNA/CO 267/555/19114.
84. This object was likely the royal insignia of the Sei Kama. It is described in 1875 when Tom Cabbie Smith (likely Bunting William's great-grandfather) took control of the Jong province. Nicholas Darnell Davis, *Chiefs and their Wars in West Africa*, 6.
85. Paul Richards asserts that the Special Commission's Court was a series of "political masquerades" where people framed these Chiefs for the purposes of preventing more land acquisition by the colonial state. His theory is interesting but limited to only the highly edited documents in Kalous, so he doesn't have enough evidence to prove it. He explains the disappearance of these accusations and trials to a firmer entrenchment of land acquisition after WWI. Richards, "Public Authority and its Demons."

86. Governor to Colonial Office. Attachment: 1913 Beatty Manuscript. November 11, 1913. BNA/CO 267/552/40437.
87. *Rex v. Bunting Williams*. Deportation Case. April 11, 1913. SLPA/CJ MP. 30; Warrant for the Trial of Farma Yanni. Deposed. May 10, 1913. CJ MP 31; *Rex v. Daniel Flickinger Wilberforce*. Report on Deposition. April 18, 1913. CJ MP 33.
88. Beatty, *Human Leopards*, 73–74.
89. Unlawful Societies Banishment. October 2, 1913. BNA/CO 267/552/36051.
90. Governor Merewether to Colonial Office. July 9, 1913. BNA/CO 267/550/25053.
91. Arlette Farge, *The Allure of the Archives* (Yale University Press, 2013), 27–28.

CONCLUSION

1. Emily Lynn Osborn, *Our New Husbands Are Here: Households, Gender, and Politics in a West African State from the Slave Trade to Colonial Rule* (Ohio University Press, 2011); Elizabeth Thornberry, *Colonizing Consent: Rape and Governance in South Africa's Eastern Cape* (Cambridge University Press, 2019); Karen Elizabeth Flint, *Healing Traditions: African Medicine, Cultural Exchange, and Competition in South Africa, 1820–1948* (Ohio University Press, 2008).
2. Elizabeth Kolsky, "The Colonial Rule of Law and the Legal Regime of Exception: Frontier 'Fanaticism' and State Violence in British India," *American Historical Review* 120, no. 4 (2015): 1221.
3. Lauren Benton, *They Called It Peace: Worlds of Imperial Violence* (Princeton University Press, 2024).
4. In some ways, this mirrored other global spaces that were deemed "quasi-sovereign," though Africans' supposed lack of "civilization" doubly barred them from having a place within international relations. Lauren Benton, "From International Law to Imperial Constitutions: The Problem of Quasi-Sovereignty, 1870–1900," *Law and History Review* 26, no. 3 (Fall 2008): 595–619.

Bibliography

Archives

British National Archives (BNA)

CO 267—Correspondence

CO 879—Parliamentary Papers

CO 270—Minutes of the Sierra Leone Executive and Legislative Council

Sierra Leone Public Archives (SLPA)

Governor Interpreter (GI)

Department of Aborigines/Department of Native Affairs (ABOR/NA)

Commandant of Sherbro (SHER)

Circuit Judge (CJ)

Northern Sherbro (NSHER)

District Commissioner Courts

Protectorate Mixed Courts

Circuit Court Record Books

Types of Sources:

Letterbooks (LB)

Minute Papers (MP)

Newspapers

The Independent

The Early Dawn

Sierra Leone Times

Sierra Leone Weekly News

The Watchman

Published Sources

Abraham, Arthur. *An Introduction to the Precolonial History of the Mende*. Edwin Mellon Press, 2003.

———. "Bai Bureh, The British, and the Hut Tax War." *The International Journal of African Historical Studies* 7, no. 1 (1974): 99–106.

———. "Cannibalism and African Historiography." *Présence Africaine*, no. 1 (1978): 216–229.

———. *Mende Government and Politics Under Colonial Rule: A Historical Study of Political Change in Sierra Leone, 1890–1937*. Oxford University Press, 1979.

———. "Nyagua, the British, and the Hut Tax War." *The International Journal of African Historical Studies* 5, no. 1 (1972): 94–98.

Acemoglu, Daron, Isaías N. Chaves, Philip Osafo-Kwaako, and James A. Robinson. "Indirect Rule and State Weakness in Africa: Sierra Leone in Comparative Perspective." In *African Successes, Volume IV: Sustainable Growth*, 343–370. University of Chicago Press, 2014.

Acemoglu, Daron, Tristan Reed, and James A. Robinson. "Chiefs: Economic Development and Elite Control of Civil Society in Sierra Leone." *Journal of Political Economy* 122, no. 2 (2014): 319–368.

Addison, William. "The Wunde Society: Protectorate of Sierra Leone, British West Africa." *Man*, 1936, 207–209.

Albrecht, Peter. "Secrets, Strangers, and Order-Making in Rural Sierra Leone." *Journal of Contemporary African Studies* 34, no. 4 (2016): 519–537.

Alldridge, Thomas Joshua. *A Transformed Colony, Sierra Leone, as It Was, and as It Is: Its Progress, Peoples, Native Customs and Undeveloped Wealth*. J. B. Lippincott, 1910.

———. *The Sherbro and Its Hinterland*. Macmillan and Company, 1901.

———. "Wanderings in the Sierra Leone Hinterland." 1894, 131.

Allin, Leslie. "Bodily Disintegrations: Forensic Exposure and the Human Leopard Society in Sierra Leone," in *Penetrating Critiques*. University of Toronto Press, 2020.

Alusine Jalloh and David E. Skinner, ed. *Islam and Trade in Sierra Leone*. Africa World Press, 1997.

Anderson, Richard Peter. *Abolition in Sierra Leone: Re-Building Lives and Identities in*

Nineteenth-Century West Africa. Cambridge University Press, 2020.

Anghie, Antony. "Finding the Peripheries: Sovereignty and Colonialism in Nineteenth-Century International Law." *Harvard International Law Journal* 40, no. 1 (Winter 1999): 1–71.

Arewa, E. Ojo, and Everett E. Hale. "Poro Communications (West Africa). A Spiritual Channel Where Men Are the Means of Transmission." *Anthropos*, 1975, 78–96.

Basu, Paul. "Reanimating Cultural Heritage: Digital Curatorship, Knowledge Networks, and Social Transformation in Sierra Leone." In *Museum Transformations*. Edited by Annie E. Coombes and Ruth B. Phillips. Vol. 4 of *The International Handbooks of Museum Studies*, edited by Sharon MacDonald and Helen Rees Leahy. John Wiley and Sons, 2013.

Beatty, Kenneth James. *Human Leopards: An Account of the Trials of Human Leopards before the Special Commission Court*. H. Rees, 1915.

Bellman, Beryl L. *The Language of Secrecy: Symbols & Metaphors in Poro Ritual*. Rutgers University Press, 1984.

Belmessous, Saliha. *Empire by Treaty: Negotiating European Expansion, 1600–1900*. Oxford University Press, 2014.

———. *Native Claims: Indigenous Law against Empire, 1500–1920*. OUP USA, 2012.

Benton, Lauren. *A Search for Sovereignty: Law and Geography in European Empires, 1400–1900*. Cambridge University Press, 2009.

———. "From International Law to Imperial Constitutions: The Problem of Quasi-Sovereignty, 1870–1900." *Law and History Review* 26, no. 3 (Fall 2008): 595–619.

———. *Law and Colonial Cultures: Legal Regimes in World History, 1400–1900*. Cambridge University Press, 2002.

———. *They Called It Peace: Worlds of Imperial Violence*. Princeton University Press, 2024.

Benton Lauren, and Adam Clulow. "Protection Shopping Among Empires: Suspended Sovereignty in the Cocos-Keeling Islands." *Past & Present*, 2021.

Benton, Lauren, Adam Clucow, and Bain Attwood. *Protection and Empire: A Global History*. Cambridge University Press, 2018.

Benton, Lauren, and Lisa Ford. *Rage for Order: The British Empire and the Origins of International Law, 1800–1850*. Harvard University Press, 2016.

Berry, R. G. "The Sierra Leone Cannibals, with Notes on Their History, Religion, and Customs." *Proceedings of the Royal Irish Academy. Section C: Archaeology, Celtic Studies, History, Linguistics, Literature* 30 (1912): 15–70.

Blyden, Nemata Amelia. *West Indians in West Africa, 1808–1880: The African Diaspora in Reverse*. University of Rochester Press, 2000.

Bolt, Jutta, Leigh Gardner, Jennifer Kohler, Jack Paine, and James A. Robinson. "African Political Institutions and the Impact of Colonialism." National Bureau of Economic Research, 2022.

Booth, Alan R. "'European Courts Protect Women and Witches': Colonial Law Courts as Redistributors of Power in Swaziland 1920–1950." *Journal of Southern African Studies* 18, no. 2 (1992): 253–275.

Burbank, Jane, and Frederick Cooper. *Empires in World History: Power and the Politics of Difference*. Princeton University Press, 2011.

Burrill, Emily S. *States of Marriage: Gender, Justice, and Rights in Colonial Mali*. Ohio University Press, 2015.

Burrows, Donald. "The Human Leopard Society of Sierra Leone." *Journal of the Royal African Society* 13, no. 50 (1914): 143–151.

Campbell, Mavis Christine, and George Ross. *Back to Africa: George Ross and the Maroons: From Nova Scotia to Sierra Leone*. Africa World Press, 1993.

Carpenter, Nathan. "Ransom as Political Strategy: Captivity beyond Commercial Transaction on the Upper Guinea Coast in the Late Nineteenth and Early Twentieth Centuries." *Journal of West African History* 4, no. 2 (2018): 1–18.

Caulker-Burnett, Imodale. *The Caulkers of Sierra Leone: The Story of a Ruling Family and Their Times*. Xlibris Corporation, 2010.

Chalmers, David Patrick. *Report by Her Majesty's Commissioner and Correspondence on the Subject of the Insurrection in the Sierra Leone Protectorate, 1898*. 2 vols. Darling & Son, 1899.

Channing, Laura. "Taxing Chiefs: The Design and Introduction of Direct Taxation in the Sierra Leone Protectorate, 1896–1914." *The Journal of Imperial and Commonwealth History* 48, no. 3 (2020): 395–424.

Chanock, Martin. *Law, Custom, and Social Order: The Colonial Experience in Malawi and Zambia*. Heinemann, 1985.

Chopra, Ruma. *Almost Home: Maroons between Slavery and Freedom in Jamaica, Nova Scotia, and Sierra Leone*. Yale University Press, 2018.

Clarke, Robert. *Sierra Leone: A Description of the Manners and Customs of the Liberated Africans; With Observations upon the Natural History of the Colony, and a Notice of the Native Tribes*, vol. 1. J. Ridgway, 1843.

Cole, Festus. "Anglo-Krio Relations: A Study of a Disadvantaged Community in a Colonial Setting, 1895–1922." *The Journal of Imperial and Commonwealth History* 50, no. 4 (2022): 607–638.

Cole, Gibril R. *The Krio of West Africa: Islam, Culture, Creolization, and Colonialism in the Nineteenth Century*. Ohio University Press, 2013.

Craven, Matthew. "What Happened to Unequal Treaties? The Continuities of Informal Empire," *Nordic Journal of International Law* 74 (2005): 335–382.

Davidson, John. *Trade and Politics in the Sherbro Hinterland, 1849–1890*. University of

Wisconsin–Madison dissertation, 1969.

Davies, Sarah Louise. "The Sasswood Ordeal of the West Atlantic Tribes of Sierra Leone and Liberia: An Ethnohistoriographic Survey." Master's thesis, Portland State University, 1973.

Davis, Nicholas Darnell. *Chiefs, and Their Wars, in West Africa*. For private circulation, 1876.

Day, Lynda. *Gender and Power in Sierra Leone: Women Chiefs of the Last Two Centuries*. Palgrave Macmillan, 2012.

DeCorse, Christopher R. "Fortified Towns of the Koinadugu Plateau: Northern Sierra Leone in the Pre-Atlantic and Atlantic Worlds." In *Power and Landscape in Atlantic West Africa: Archaeological Perspectives*, edited by J. Cameron Monroe and Akinwumi Ogundiran, 278–308. Cambridge University Press, 2012.

Delius, Sarah. "The Same in All but Name? The Intersections of Marriage and Slavery in Sierra Leone, 1890–1930." *Slavery & Abolition* 43, no. 2 (2022): 320–345.

Dixon-Fyle, Mac, and Gibril Raschid Cole. *New Perspectives on the Sierra Leone Krio*. Peter Lang, 2006.

Dorjahn, V.R., and Christopher Fyfe. "Landlord and Stranger: Change in Tenancy Relations in Sierra Leone." *The Journal of African History* 3, no. 3 (1962): 391–397.

Dorsett, Shaunnagh. "Metropolitan Theorising: Legal Frameworks, Protectorates and Models for Māori Governance 1837–1838." *Law & History* 3, no. 3 (2016): 1–18.

Ellis, Stephen. *The Mask of Anarchy: The Destruction of Liberia and the Religious Dimension of an African Civil War*. New York University Press, 1999.

———. "Mystical Weapons: Some Evidence From the Liberian War." *Journal of Religion in Africa* 31, no. 2 (2001): 222–236.

Erasmus, H. J. "Circuit Courts in the Cape Colony during the Nineteenth Century: Hazards and Achievements." *Fundamina: A Journal of Legal History* 19, no. 2 (2013): 266–299.

Everill, Bronwen. *Abolition and Empire in Sierra Leone and Liberia*. Springer, 2012.

Fahey, Richard P. "The Poro as a System of Judicial Administration in Northwestern Liberia: Its Intraclan and Interclan Functions," *Journal of Legal Pluralism and Unofficial Law* 3, no. 4 (1971): 1–25.

Farge, Arlette. *The Allure of the Archives*. Yale University Press, 2013.

Ferme, Mariane C. *The Underneath of Things: Violence, History, and the Everyday in Sierra Leone*. University of California Press, 2001.

Flint, Karen Elizabeth. *Healing Traditions: African Medicine, Cultural Exchange, and Competition in South Africa, 1820–1948*. Ohio University Press, 2008.

Fulton, Richard M. "The Political Structures and Functions of Poro in Kpelle Society," *American Anthropologist* 74, no. 5 (1972): 1218–1233.

Fyfe, Christopher. *A History of Sierra Leone*. Oxford University Press, 1962.

———. "European and Creole Influence in the Hinterland of Sierra Leone before 1896." *Sierra Leone Studies* 6 (1956): 113–123.

Gibbs, James L. Jr., "Poro Values and Courtroom Procedures in a Kpelle Chiefdom," *Southwestern Journal of Anthropology* 18, no. 4 (1962): 341–350.

Ginio, Ruth. "Negotiating Legal Authority in French West Africa: The Colonial Administration and the African Assessors, 1903–1918." In *Intermediaries, Interpreters, and Clerks: African Employees in the Making of Colonial Africa*, 115–135. University of Wisconsin Press, 2006.

Gordon, Michelle. *Extreme Violence and the 'British Way': Colonial Warfare in Perak, Sierra Leone and Sudan*. Bloomsbury Academic, 2020.

Grace, John. *Domestic Slavery in West Africa: With Particular Reference to the Sierra Leone Protectorate, 1896–1927*. Barnes & Noble, 1975.

Gray A. "Legislation of the Empire 1895, West Africa VII: Sierra Leone," *Journal of Comparative Legislation and International Law*, 1897, 101.

Griffiths, Gareth. "The Other Mr Wilberforce: Role Conflict and Colonial Governance in Sierra Leone 1878–1913." *African Identities* 7, no. 4 (2009): 435–449.

Guyer, Jane I., and Samuel M. Eno Belinga. "Wealth in People as Wealth in Knowledge: Accumulation and Composition in Equatorial Africa." *The Journal of African History* 36, no. 1 (1995): 91–120.

Hamilton, Caroline. *Terrific Majesty: The Power of Shaka Zulu and the Limits of Historical Invention*. Harvard Press, 1998.

Harris, Steven M. "Manufacturing International Law: Pre-Printed Treaties in the 'Scramble for Africa,'" *Journal of the History of International Law* 23, no. 3 (May 2020): 439–465.

Hart, William. "The 'Lawyer' of Poro?: A Sixteenth-Century West African Masquerade." *RES: Anthropology and Aesthetics* 23, no. 1 (1993): 83–95.

Hawthorne, Walter. "States and Statelessness." In *The Oxford Handbook of Modern African History*, 77–78. Oxford University Press, 2013.

Hill, Matthew H. "Where to Begin? The Place of the Hunter Founder in Mende Histories." *Anthropos*, 1984, 653–656.

Hobsbawm, Eric, and Terence Ranger, eds. *The Invention of Tradition*. Cambridge University Press, 1983.

Hoffer, Carol Pulley. *Acquisition and Exercise of Political Power by a Woman Paramount Chief of the Sherbro People*. Bryn Mawr College, 1971.

———."Mende and Sherbro Women in High Office," *Canadian Journal of African Studies/La Revue canadienne des études africaines* 6, no. 2 (1972): 151–164.

———. *See also* MacCormack, Carol.

Hogg, Trina Leah. "From Bandits to Political Prisoners: Detention and Deportation on the

Sierra Leone Frontier." In *Africans in Exile: Mobility, Law, and Identity*, 54–68, 2018.

Howard, Allen M. "Nineteenth-Century Coastal Slave Trading and the British Abolition Campaign in Sierra Leone." *Slavery and Abolition* 27, no. 1 (April 2006): 23–49.

———. "Nodes, Networks, Landscapes, and Regions: Reading the Social History of Tropical Africa 1700s–1920." In *The Spatial Factor in African History*, edited by Allen Marvin Howard and Richard Matthew Shain, 21–140. Brill, 2005.

———. "Re-Marking on the Past: Spatial Structures and Dynamics in the Sierra Leone-Guinea Plain, 1860–1920s." In *The Spatial Factor in African History*, edited by Allen Marvin Howard and Richard Matthew Shain, 291–348. Brill, 2005.

Hussain, Nasser. *The Jurisprudence of Emergency: Colonialism and the Rule of Law*. University of Michigan Press, 2019.

Hynd, Stacey. "Killing the Condemned: The Practice and Process of Capital Punishment in British Africa, 1900–1950s." *The Journal of African History* 49, no. 3 (2008): 403–418.

Ibhawoh, Bonny. "Historical Globalization and Colonial Legal Culture: African Assessors, Customary Law, and Criminal Justice in British Africa." *Journal of Global History* 4, no. 3 (2009): 429–451.

———. *Imperial Justice: Africans in Empire's Court*. Oxford University Press, 2013.

Inyang, Anietie A., and Manasseh Edidem Bassey, "Imperial Treaties and the Origins of British Colonial Rule in Southern Nigeria, 1860–1890," *Mediterranean Journal of Social Sciences* 5, no. 20 (September 2014): 1946–1953.

Jalloh, Alusine. *African Entrepreneurship*. Ohio University Press, 1999.

Jalloh, Alusine, and David E. Skinner, *Islam and Trade in Sierra Leone*. Africa World Press, 1997.

Kalous, Milan. *Cannibals and Tongo Players of Sierra Leone*. Published by the author, 1974.

Kasaba, Reşat. "Treaties and Friendships: British Imperialism, the Ottoman Empire, and China in the Nineteenth Century," *Journal of World History* 4, no. 2 (Fall 1993): 215–241.

Keefer, Katrina. "Poro on Trial: The 1913 Special Commission Court Case of *Rex v. Fino, Bofio and Kalfalla*." *African Studies Review* 61, no. 3 (2018): 56–78.

———. "Poro, Witchcraft and Red Water in Early Colonial Sierra Leone: G. R. Nylander's Ethnography and Systems of Authority on the Bullom Shore." *Canadian Journal of African Studies/Revue Canadienne Des Études Africaines*, 2020, 1–17.

———. *Cannibalism Myths, Empire, and Identity in Colonial Sierra Leone*. Lexington Books, 2024.

Keene, Edward. "The Treaty-Making Revolution of the Nineteenth Century." *The International History Review* 34, no. 3 (September 2012): 475–500.

Kelley, Sean. "The Dirty Business of Panyarring and Palaver: Slave Trading on the Upper Guinea Coast in the Eighteenth Century." In *Slavery, Abolition and the Transition to Colonialism in Sierra Leone*, edited by Paul Lovejoy and Suzanne Schwarz, 89–108. Africa World Press, 2014.

Kolsky, Elizabeth. "The Colonial Rule of Law and the Legal Regime of Exception: Frontier 'Fanaticism' and State Violence in British India." *American Historical Review* 120, no. 4 (2015): 1218–1246.

Kopytoff, J. H. *A Preface to Modern Nigeria: The Sierra Leonians in Yoruba, 1830–1890*. University of Wisconsin Press, 1965.

Korf, Benedikt, Tobias Hagmann, and Martin Doevenspeck. "Geographies of Violence and Sovereignty: The African Frontier Revisited." In *Violence on the Margins: States, Conflict, and Borderlands*, 29–54. Springer, 2013.

Lange, Matthew. *Lineages of Despotism and Development: British Colonialism and State Power*. University of Chicago Press, 2009.

Law, Robin. *From Slave Trade to "Legitimate" Commerce: The Commercial Transition in Nineteenth-Century West Africa*. Cambridge University Press, 2002.

Lebbie, Aiah R., and Raymond P. Guries. "Ethnobotanical Value and Conservation of Sacred Groves of the Kpaa Mende in Sierra Leone." *Economic Botany*, 1995, 297–308.

Lester, Alan, and Fae Dussart, "Trajectories of Protection: Protectorates of Aborigines in Early 19th Century Australia and Aotearoa New Zealand," *New Zealand Geographer* 64, no. 3 (2008): 205–220.

Lobban, Michael. *Imperial Incarceration: Detention Without Trial in the Making of British Colonial Africa*. Cambridge University Press, 2021.

Little, Kenneth. "The Political Function of the Poro, Part I." *Africa* 35, no. 4 (October 1965): 349–365.

———. "The Political Function of the Poro, Part II." *Africa* 36, no. 1 (January 1966): 62–72.

———. The *Mende of Sierra Leone*. Routledge, 1967, reprinted 2013.

Lugard, Frederick. "The Speech at Sokoto." In *The Principles of Native Administration in Nigeria*, edited by Anthony Hamilton Millard Kirk-Greene. Oxford University Press, 1965, 43.

Luongo, Katherine. *Witchcraft and Colonial Rule in Kenya, 1900–1955*. Cambridge University Press, 2011.

Lynn, Martin. *Commerce and Economic Change in West Africa: The Palm Oil Trade in the Nineteenth Century*. Cambridge University Press, 2002.

———. "Technology, Trade, and 'A Race of Native Capitalists': The Krio Diaspora of West Africa and the Steamship. 1852–95." *The Journal of African History* 33, no. 3 (1992): 421–440.

MacCormack, Carol. "Human Leopards and Crocodiles: Political Meanings of Categorical Ambiguities." In *The Ethnography of Cannibalism*, 51–60. Society for Psychological Anthropology, 1983.

———. "Wono: Institutionalized Dependency in Sherbro Descent Groups (Sierra Leone)." In *Slavery in Africa: Historical and Anthropological Perspectives*, edited by S. Miers and I. Kopytoff, 181–203, 1977.

———. "Slaves, Slave Owners and Slave Holders: Sherbro Coast and Hinterland." In *Women and Slavery in Africa*, edited by C. Robertson and M. Klein, 271–295, 1983.

———. "Control of Land, Labor, and Capital in Rural Southern Sierra Leone." In *Women and Work in Africa*, 35–53. Westview Press Boulder, 1982.

———. "Dying as Transformation to Ancestorhood: The Sherbro Coast of Sierra Leone." *Sterben Und Tod Eine Kulturvergleichende Analyse*, 1986, 117–126.

———. *See also* Hoffer, Carol Pulley.

Major, Andrea. *Sovereignty and Social Reform in India: British Colonialism and the Campaign against Sati, 1830–1860*. Routledge, 2010.

Mamdani, Mahmood. *Citizen and Subject: Contemporary Africa and the Legacy of Late Colonialism*. Princeton University Press, 1996.

Mann, Kristin, Toyin Falola, and Christian Jennings. "Interpreting Cases, Disentangling Disputes: Court Cases as a Source of Understanding Patron-Client Relationships in Early Colonial Lagos." In *Sources and Methods in African History: Spoken, Written, Unearthed*. University Rochester Press, 2003.

Marriott, HP Fitzgerald. "The Secret Societies of West Africa." *Journal of the Anthropological Institute of Great Britain and Ireland* (1899): 21–27.

McGowan, Winston. "The Establishment of Long-Distance Trade between Sierra Leone and Its Hinterland." *The Journal of African History* 1, no. 31 (1990): 25–41.

Ménard, Anaïs. *Integrating Strangers: Sherbro Identity and The Politics of Reciprocity along the Sierra Leonean Coast*. Berghahn Books, 2023.

Misevich, Philip. *Abolition and the Transformation of Atlantic Commerce in Southern Sierra Leone, 1790s to 1860s*. Africa World Press, 2019.

———. "The Mende and Sherbro Diaspora in Nineteenth-Century Southern Sierra Leone." *The Rise and Demise of Slavery and the Slave Trade in the Atlantic World*, 2016, 247–265.

Mouser, Bruce L. "Accommodation and Assimilation in the Landlord-Stranger Relationship." In *West African Culture Dynamics: Archaeological and Historical Perspectives*, 495–514. De Gruyter, 1980.

———. "Trade, Coasters, and Conflict in the Rio Pongo from 1790 to 1808." *The Journal of African History* 14, no. 1 (1973): 45–64.

Mugambwa, John. "Treaties or Scraps of Paper? A Second Look at the Legal Character of the Nineteenth Century British/African Colonial Agreements," *Comparative and International Law Journal of Southern Africa* 20, no. 1 (1987): 79–93.

Newbury, Colin W. "Credit in Early Nineteenth Century West African Trade." *Journal of African*

History 13, no. 1 (1972).

Newton, John. *Thoughts upon the African Slave Trade.* Printed for J. Buckland, in Pater-Noster-Row; and J. Johnson, in St. Paul's Church-yard, 1788.

Nooter, Mary H. "Secrecy: African Art That Conceals and Reveals." *African Arts* 26, no. 1 (1993): 55–102.

Ochiai, Takehiko. "In a Grove? Sierra Leone's 1898 Hut Tax War Reconsidered." *Asian Journal of African Studies* 41 (2017): 53–86.

Ochonu, Moses. "Protection by Proxy: The Hausa-Fulani as Agents of British Colonial Rule in Northern Nigeria." In *Protection and Empire: A Global History*, edited by Lauren Benton Adam Clucow, and Bain Attwood, 228–244. Cambridge University Press, 2018.

Ojo, Olatunji, and Jennifer Lofkrantz. "West African Responses to Illegal Enslavement and Failed Ransom Negotiations." *Journal of African History* 52 (2012).

Osborn, Emily Lynn. *Our New Husbands Are Here: Households, Gender, and Politics in a West African State from the Slave Trade to Colonial Rule.* Ohio University Press, 2011.

Owusu-Ansah, David. "Islamic Influence in a Forest Kingdom: The Role of Protective Amulets in Early 19th Century Asante." *Transafrican Journal of History* 12 (1983): 100–133.

Pieterse, Jan Nederveen. *White on Black: Images of Africa and Blacks in Western Popular Culture.* Yale University Press, 1992.

Pratten, David. *Man-Leopard Murders: History and Society in Colonial Nigeria.* Edinburgh University Press, 2007.

Price, Richard N. "The Psychology of Colonial Violence." In *Violence, Colonialism and Empire in the Modern World*, edited by Philip Dwyer and Amanda Nettlebeck, 25–52. Palgrave Macmillan, 2018.

Probyn, Leslie. "Sierra Leone and the Natives of West Africa." *Journal of the Royal African Society* 6, no. 23 (1907): 250–258.

Ranger, Terence. "The Invention of Tradition in Colonial Africa." *Perspectives on Africa: A Reader in Culture, History, and Representation*, 1997, 597–612.

Rarey, Matthew Francis. *Insignificant Things: Amulets and the Art of Survival in the Early Black Atlantic.* Duke University Press, 2023.

Reed, Tristan, and James Robinson. "The Chiefdoms of Sierra Leone." Unpublished manuscript, Harvard University, July 15, 2013. https://scholar.harvard.edu/files/jrobinson/files/history.pdf.

Reno, William. *Corruption and State Politics in Sierra Leone.* Cambridge University Press, 1995.

Reuther, Jessica. "Street Hawking or Street Walking in Dahomey?: Debates about Girls' Sexual Assaults in Colonial Tribunals, 1924–41." *The Journal of African History* 63, no. 3 (2022): 368–383.

Richards, Paul. "Chimpanzees as Political." *Natural Enemies: People-Wildlife Conflicts in*

Anthropological Perspective, 2000, 78–103.

———. *Fighting for the Rainforest: War, Youth, and Resources in Sierra Leone*. International African Institute/Currey, 1996.

———. "Public Authority and Its Demons: The Sherbro Leopard Murders in Sierra Leone." *Africa* 91, no. 2 (2021): 226–248.

Roberts, Richard L. *Litigants and Households: African Disputes and Colonial Courts in the French Soudan, 1895–1912*. Heinemann, 2005.

———. *Conflicts of Colonialism: The Rule of Law, French Soudan, and Faama Mademba Seye*. Cambridge University Press, 2022.

Roberts, Richard, and Kristin Mann. *Law in Colonial Africa*. Heinemann, 1991.

Rodney, Walter. *History of the Upper Guinea Coast: 1545–1800*. New York University Press, 1982.

Ryan, Lyndall. "Martial Law in the British Empire." *Violence, Colonialism and Empire in the Modern World*, edited by Philip Dwyer and Amanda Nettlebeck, 93–109. Palgrave Macmillan 2018.

Scanlan, Padraic X. *Freedom's Debtors: British Antislavery in Sierra Leone in the Age of Revolution*. Yale University Press, 2017.

Schwarz, Suzanne. "Land and Settlement: Temne Responses to British Abolitionist Intervention in Sierra Leone in the Late Eighteenth and Early Nineteenth Centuries." *African Economic History* 49, no. 1 (2021): 222–248.

Senior, M. M. "Some Mende Proverbs." *Africa* 17, no. 3 (1947): 202–205.

Shadle, Brett Lindsay. *"Girl Cases": Marriage and Colonialism in Gusiiland, Kenya, 1890–1970*. Social History of Africa. Heinemann, 2006.

Shadle, Brett Lindsay. *"Girl Cases": Runaway Wives, Eloped Daughters and Abducted Women in Gusiiland, Kenya, c. 1900–c. 1965*. Northwestern University, 2000.

Shaw, Rosalind. "Cannibal Transformations: Colonialism and Commodification in the Sierra Leone Hinterland." In *Magical Interpretations, Material Realities*, edited by Henrietta L. Moore and Todd Sanders, 50–70. Routledge, 2003.

———. *Memories of the Slave Trade: Ritual and the Historical Imagination in Sierra Leone*. University of Chicago Press, 2020.

———. "The Production of Witchcraft/Witchcraft as Production: Memory, Modernity, and the Slave Trade in Sierra Leone." *American Ethnologist* 24, no. 4 (1997): 856–876.

———. "The Politician and the Diviner: Divination and the Consumption of Power in Sierra Leone." *Journal of Religion in Africa* 26, no. 1 (1996): 30–55.

Shumway, Rebecca, "Palavers and Treaty Making in the British Acquisition of the Gold Coast Colony (West Africa)." *Empire by Treaty: Negotiating European Expansion, 1600–1900*, 2014, 161–185.

Siddle, David J. "War-Towns in Sierra Leone: A Study in Social Change." *Africa* 38, no. 1 (1968):

47–56.

Skinner, David E. “Mande Settlement and the Development of Islamic Institutions in Sierra Leone.” *The International Journal of African Historical Studies* 11, no. 1 (1978): 32–62.

———. “Thomas George Lawson: Colonial Servant in Sierra Leone, 1846–1889,” *West African Colonial Civil Servants in the Nineteenth Century: African Participation in British Colonial Expansion in West Africa*. University of Leiden, 1985.

Skinner, David, and Barbara E. Harrell-Bond. “Misunderstandings Arising from the Use of the Term ‘Creole’ in the Literature on Sierra Leone.” *Africa: Journal of the International African Institute* 47, no. 3 (1977): 305–320. https://doi.org/10.2307/1158865.

Spear, Thomas. “Neo-Traditionalism and the Limits of Invention in British Colonial Africa.” In *The Rise and Fall of Modern Empires*, vol. 3, edited by Sarah Stockwell, 419–444. Routledge, 2013, 419–444.

Spitzer, Leo. *Sierra Leone Creole Reactions to Westernization, 1870–1925*. University of Wisconsin–Madison, 1969.

Stern, Philip J. “‘A Politie of Civill & Military Power’: Political Thought and the Late Seventeenth-Century Foundations of the East India Company-State.” *Journal of British Studies* 47, no. 2 (2008): 253–283.

Szabla, Christopher. “Civilising Violence: International Law and Colonial War in the British Empire, 1850–1900.” *Journal of the History of International Law/Revue d'histoire Du Droit International* 25, no. 1 (2023): 70–104.

Thompson, George. *Thompson in Africa: Or, An Account of the Missionary Labors, Sufferings, Travels, and Observations, of George Thompson, in Western Africa, at the Mendi Mission*. Published by the author, 1854.

Thornberry, Elizabeth. *Colonizing Consent: Rape and Governance in South Africa's Eastern Cape*. Cambridge University Press, 2019.

Touval, Saadia. “Treaties, Borders, and the Partition of Africa.” *The Journal of African History* 7, no. 2 (1966): 279–293.

Tucker, Peter L. *The Tuckers of Sierra Leone: 1665–1914*. Self-Published, 1997.

Twomey, Christina. “Protecting Slaves and Aborigines.” *Pacific Historical Review* 87, no. 1 (2018): 10–29.

Twomey, Christina, and Katherine Ellinghaus. “Protection: Global Genealogies, Local Practices.” *Pacific Historical Review* 87, no. 1 (2018): 2–9.

Van Hulle, Inge. *Britain and International Law in West Africa: The Practice of Empire*. Oxford University Press, 2020.

———. “British Humanitarianism, International Law and Human Sacrifice in West Africa.” In *International Law in the Long Nineteenth Century (1776–1914)*, 105–125. Brill, 2019.

Waller, Richard D. "Witchcraft and Colonial Law in Kenya." *Past & Present*, no. 180 (2003): 241–275.

Wallis, Charles Braithwaite. *The Advance of Our West African Empire*. T. Fisher Unwin, 1903.

White, E. Francis. *Sierra Leone's Settler Women Traders: Women on the Afro-European Frontier.* University of Michigan Press, 1987.

White, Luise. *Speaking with Vampires: Rumor and History in Colonial Africa.* University of California Press, 2000.

Whyte, Christine. "'The Strangest Problem': Daniel Wilberforce, the Human Leopards Panic and the Special Court in Sierra Leone." In *Anxieties, Fear and Panic in Colonial Settings*, 345–368. Springer, 2016.

Wiener, Martin J. *An Empire on Trial: Race, Murder, and Justice under British Rule, 1870–1935.* Cambridge University Press, 2009.

Wilberforce, Daniel Flickinger, *Sherbro and the Sherbros: Or, a Native African's Account of His Country and People.* United Brethren Publishing House, 1886.

———. "The True Verdict," 11. UB Foreign Missions 2280–3-3.

Wilbraham, D.F., and E. T. Packard. *A Revised Edition of the Ordinances of the Colony of Sierra Leone, Vol. IV 1904–09*. Waterlow and Sons, 1909.

Winterbottom, Thomas. *Account of the Native Africans in the Neighbourhood of Sierra Leone: To Which Is Added, an Account of the Present State of Medicine among Them.* Vol. 1. Cambridge University Press, 1803.

Wlodarczyk, Nathalie. *Magic and Warfare: Appearance and Reality in Contemporary African Conflict and Beyond.* Palgrave Macmillan, 2009.

Wyse, Akintola J. G. "On Misunderstandings Arising from the Use of the Term 'Creole' in the Literature on Sierra Leone: A Rejoinder," *Africa* 49, no. 4 (1979): 408–417.

———. *The Krio of Sierra Leone: An Interpretive History*. C. Hurst & Co., 1989.

Zehnle, Stephanie. "Liminal Youth between Town and Bush: Humans, Leopards and Initiation in West African History." *Animal History in the Modern City*, Bloomsbury Academic, 2019.

Index

Page numbers in *italics* indicate illustrations.

A

B

C

Q

R

Q

R

T